The Complete DUKW

Historical Reference

Written by David Doyle

Squadron Signal Publications

About the Historical Reference Series

Volumes in the *Historical Reference* series bring you the results of in-depth research into primary documents, providing extensive information, direct from original sources, much of just now entering the published historical record. The wartime history of a particular type of aircraft, vehicle, or vessel is recounted systematically.

Hard cover ISBN 978-0-89747-720-8

Proudly printed in the U.S.A.
Copyright 2013 Squadron/Signal Publications
1115 Crowley Drive, Carrollton, TX 75006-1312 U.S.A.

Military/Combat Photographs and Snapshots

If you have any photos of aircraft, armor, soldiers, or ships of any nation, particularly wartime snapshots, why not share them with us and help make Squadron/Signal's books all the more interesting and complete in the future? Any photograph sent to us will be copied and returned. Electronic images are preferred. The donor will be fully credited for any photos used. Please send them to:

Squadron/Signal Publications
1115 Crowley Drive
Carrollton, TX 75006-1312 U.S.A.
www.SquadronSignalPublications.com

Front cover: The DUKW, seen here on a beach in southern France in August 1944, was military vehicle developed almost entirely outside of the military – in fact, the Army initially opposed its production. Its origins lay with the National Defense Research Committee, headed by Dr. Vannevar Bush, who reported directly to the President. Other projects led by this team of scientific elite included proximity fuses and the early work on the atomic bomb. With this pedigree, it is little surprise that the DUKW was an unqualified success. (Naval History and Heritage Command)

Rear cover: From its initial combat use in Sicily, where these DUKWs are shown, U.S. forces came to use the DUKW in every theater. Additional, thousands were furnished to Allied nations, chiefly Commonwealth forces. The Royal Marines continue to use DUKWs into the 21st century. (National Archives)

Title page: The DUKW was built by General Motors. Production initially was carried out at the Yellow Truck and Coach (later GMC) plant in Pontiac, Michigan, although GMC soon contracted Chevrolet to build additional examples in their St. Louis, Missouri, plant. This DUKW is undergoing marine propulsion testing near the end of the Michigan assembly line. (General Motors)

Dedication

To the unique pool of talented and dedicated men and women who conceived, designed, built, and employed the DUKW in combat and continue to use the finest amphibian today.

Contents

Introduction

The GMC DUKW is unquestionably the most successful amphibious vehicle used by the U.S. – or any other military – to date. Even 70+ years after the first DUKW took to the road and water, they are still found on the roadways and waterways around the world, now hauling tourists, who continue to be amazed by the seagoing truck.

It is a shame that to date so little factual information has been published about such an impressive vehicle. That heretofore books, magazine and internet resources have been riddled with error is probably in part due to first wartime secrecy, and later wartime propaganda clouding the information provided to journalists during WWII, and then later writers relying heavily on such tainted material as their primary sources.

The book that you are now holding in your hands was a decade in the making, and tells the story of the DUKW primarily through the eyes, and words, of three men: P. C. Putnam, Technical Advisor for the National Defense Research Committee which conceptualized the

DUKW; R. A. Crist, Production Control Manager for Yellow Truck and Coach Division, General Motors Corp. who built the DUKW; and Roderick Stephens II, with Sparkman & Stephens, marine architects, who designed the DUKW. Not only did Stephens design the DUKW, he was instrumental in developing the training program and tactics for the vehicle – Stephens, in his unpublished autobiographical manuscript, writes "I know more about these vehicles than any one in the world" – and he was no doubt correct in this statement.

As you will see, these three men played key roles in the development, production and use of the DUKW, and this author has been fortunate to be able to consult thousands of pages of wartime documents written by these men, as well as thousands of additional pages of wartime documentation, in preparing this manuscript.

Not surprisingly, many of the facts presented in this volume fly in the face of 70 years of partial, or in many cases, full mis-information concerning the DUKW. I believe you will find that the truth is actually a much better story than the half-truths that have circulated for years.

Acknowledgments

In the seven decades since its conception, many pages, both paper and electronic, have been devoted to the DUKW. Regrettably, many, if not most, of these pages are rife with error. Unlike most of what has been previously written, this book draws almost entirely upon primary source documents. Many of these documents are held by General Motors, whose staff, including Keith Nattress, Larry Kinsel, and Christo Dantini, provided immeasurable help in bringing this project to life.

The thousands of additional pages of documentation found at the National Archives and provided by Jim Gilmore were added to the materials that my wife Denise and I had located during our many trips to this institution. The staff at the Mystic Seaport Archives helped us sift through their collection's files on brothers Roderick and Olin Stephens and photographer Stanley Rosenfeld. Further, the staff of Sparkman & Stephens graciously provided considerable material from that firm's files.

Elizabeth Brown with Cleaver-Brooks provided scarce photos of the WTCT-6 trailer. Larry Roberts with the U.S. Army Engineer School History Office opened his files for research, as did Kip Lindberg with the Chemical Corps Museum. The staffs of the Army Transportation Museum, Quartermaster Museum, and Ordnance Museum were inordinately helpful.

David Welch, who upon our first meeting urged me to write this book, since has become a good friend and, drawing upon his first-hand experiences with the DUKW, has answered many questions. My friends Tom Kailbourn, Manny Rogers, Tom Wolboldt, Steve Preston, Steve Greenberg, Reg Hodgson, Lloyd White, David E. Harper, Steve Zaloga, and Scott Taylor all made major contributions to this volume.

DUKW expert Manny Rogers provided considerable insight as this volume was created, and also connected me with DUKW professional Bob McDowell. Bob, in addition to being helpful himself, connected me to Julius Grigore, who was Project Manager for the Flying DUKW and Super DUKW.

Special thanks are due to my long-suffering wife Denise, who carefully scanned thousands of pages of documents and photos used in this volume. The entire staff at Squadron Signal Publications not only went the extra mile – they went metaphorically around the world to present this material in the clearest manner possible.

Bibliography

Adkins, Douglas D. *Dorade: the History of an Ocean Racing Yacht,* Jaffrey, New Hampshire: David R. Godine, publisher, 2012.

Bush, Vannevar. *Pieces of the Action,* New York: William Morrow and Company, 1970.

Daugherty, Sam. *On Hostile Shores.* Miami: 1st Books Library, 2001.

Eisenhower, Dwight D. *Crusade in Europe,* New York: Doubleday and Company, 1948.

Kinney, Francis S. *"You Are First": the Story of Olin and Rod Stephens of Sparkman & Stephens, Inc.* New York: Dodd, Mead and Company, 1978.

Office of Scientific Research and Development. *Summary Technical Report of Division 12, NDRC, Volume 1, Transportation Equipment and Related Problems,* Washington, D.C.: U.S. Government Printing Office, 1946.

Puleston, Dennis, *Blue Water Vagabond, Six Years' Adventure at Sea,* New York: Doubleday, Doran and Company, 1939.

Puleston, Dennis. *The Gull's Way – A Sailor/Naturalist's Yarn,* New York: Vantage Press, 1995.

Rifkind, Herbert R. *The Jeep – Its Development and Procurement Under the Quartermaster Corps, 1940-1942,* Washington, D.C.: Office of the Quartermaster General, 1943.

Stephens, Olin J., II. *All This and Sailing Too,* Mystic, Connecticut: Mystic Seaport Museum, 1999.

Stewart, Irvin. *Organizing Scientific Research for War,* New York: Little, Brown and Company, 1948.

Wells, Arthur W. *The Quack Corps,* Chico, California: DolArt, 1992.

Zuehlke, Mark. *Operation Husky,* Vancouver, British Columbia: Douglas & McIntyre, 2009.

Chapter 1

The NDRC

"….the quantity production of the "duck" an amphibious vehicle that proved to be one of the most valuable pieces of equipment produced by the United States during the war."

No less an authority than Dwight D. Eisenhower wrote these words in his 1948 memoir *Crusade in Europe.*

The power of these words is compounded when it is considered that initially, the military had almost no interest in the vehicle. That the vehicle was widely considered to be an unqualified success is in no small part due to the caliber of people involved in its design and production.

The amphibious truck was the result of work of a government agency outside of the War Department, the National Defense Research Committee, or NDRC. The NDRC was the brainchild of Vannevar Bush. Bush, born 11 March 1890 in Everett, Massachusetts, received his Ph.D. in engineering from the Massachusetts Institute of Technology (MIT) in 1916. While Bush was an accomplished engineer and inventor, perhaps more importantly, he was a notably competent science administrator. In 1932 he became Vice President of MIT and Dean of the MIT School of Engineering, and in 1938, President of the Carnegie Institution of Washington. Also in 1938 he was appointed to the National Committee of Aeronautics (NACA), forerunner of today's NASA, and following the retirement of Joseph Ames in October 1939, Bush became NACA chairman.

Seeing the signs that the United States would soon be mobilizing for war, and concerned about a disconnect between the nation's military and rapidly advancing science, Bush formulated a plan to create a committee remedy this condition. When Hitler invaded Poland, the matter became somewhat more urgent, and Bush managed to arrange for a 12 June 1940 meeting with President Roosevelt. The brief meeting was positive, with the President approving his proposal.

This approval was formalized a on 27 June, with the newly formed National Defense Research Committee being placed under the auspices of the Council of National Defense, which had been created in 1916 "for the co-ordination of industries and resources for the national security and welfare."

The eight people to make up the committee included two who were appointed by virtue of their positions as President of the National Academy of Sciences and Commissioner of Patents respectively, four who were appointed without reference to other offices, and two who were selected by the Secretary of War and the Secretary of the Navy respectively. All served without compensation.

As specified in a 15 June letter, Bush chaired the committee. The other seven original members were:

Rear Admiral Harold G. Bowen, Director of the Naval Research Laboratory; Conway Peyton Coe, Commissioner of Patents, attorney; Karl Taylor Compton, President of MIT, physicist; James Bryant Conant, President of Harvard University, chemist; Frank Baldwin Jewett, President of the National Academy of Sciences and President of the Bell Telephone Laboratories, electrical engineer; Brigadier General George V. Strong, attorney; Richard Chace Tolman, Professor of Physical Chemistry and Mathematical Physics, California Institute of Technology, physicist.

The committee members all served without compensation, and in addition to their committee work, continued their normal employment. It was believed that extremely high-caliber people could be recruited to do committee work one or two days per week, but that few leading scientists would be willing to abandon their scientific or research careers to devote their full energies to government work.

Because of their stature within their fields, most of these men knew

Dr. Vannevar Bush, father of the National Defense Research Committee and Office of Scientific Research and Development, was arguably one of the greatest minds in engineering and scientific communities of the United States for over 60 years. He was one of the co-founders of American Appliance Company – known more widely by the name it adopted in 1925 – Raytheon. He also was chairman of the NASA predecessor NACA, was Dean of MIT School of Engineering and President of the Carnegie Institution of Washington. In a 1945 paper he predicted a data retrieval system similar in size and scope to the World Wide Web – inspiring future engineers.

Although taken at the War Department in 1947 to show The General Advisory Committee to the United States Atomic Energy Commission, this photograph none the less includes two key members of the NDRC/OSRD. The men shown are left to right, (seated): Professor Enrico Fermi, University of Chicago; Professor Glenn T. Seabors, University of California; Hartley Rowe, Vice President, United Fruit Company and head of Division 12, which created the DUKW; James B. Conant, Chairman of the NDRC and President, Harvard University; (standing in back): Hood Worthington, chemical engineer, E. I. Dupont and Company; Cyril Stanley Smith, University of Chicago; and Professor I. I. Rabi, Columbia University. (Corbis)

Palmer C. Putnam was the driving force behind the DUKW, but years prior he had led an equally innovative initiative. He is shown here at left in the offices of the S. Morgan Smith Company in Boston, being briefed by Stanton Dornbirer concerning the progress of the production of the Smith-Putnam Wind Turbine, a model of which stands in the background. This wind-driven powerplant, successfully installed in Vermont, was comparable in size to the largest such structures being built today. The Boston offices of S. Morgan Smith were only half a mile from that of Hartley Rowe's offices in United Fruit Company. (Carl Wilcox in the possession of Paul Gipe)

each other prior to their appointment to this committee, and in fact two informal meetings were held prior to the 27 June formal creation of the NDRC.

At the first formal meeting, on 2 July, the Committee selected as its Secretary Irvin Stewart, a political scientist and Director of the Committee on Scientific Aids to Learning of the National Research Council. Brigadier General R. C. Moore succeeded General Strong as Army member of the Committee on 17 January 1941.

With a broad task ahead of them, it was apparent that the work of this committee had to be broken into various subgroups, and as it was the intent of the NDRC to coordinate the nation's entire scientific community in regard to defense, five divisions were created. The five divisions were:

Division A, Armor and Ordnance; R. C. Tolman, chairman.

Division B, Bombs, Fuels, Gases, Chemical Problems; J. B. Conant, chairman.

Division C, Communications and Transportation; F. B. Jewett, chairman.

Division D, Detection, Controls and Instruments; K.T. Compton, chairman.

Division E, Patents and Invention; C. P. Coe, chairman.

Each of these various Divisions were further divided into sections.

NDRC had one other operating unit, the Committee on Uranium, with L. J. Briggs, Director of the National Bureau of Standards, as Chairman. Briggs reported directly to Bush, and Bush reported directly to Roosevelt.

Office of Scientific Research and Development

A year and a day after the establishment of the NDRC, the structure of the organization changed. Executive Order 8807 signed on 28 June 1941, established the Office of Scientific Research and Development (OSRD). Notable was the addition of "and Development" in this organization's name.

While the NDRC was originally placed under the Council for National Defense, the OSRD was put within the purview of the Office of Emergency Management of the Executive Office of the President. The Director of the OSRD would be appointed by, and report directly to, the President of the United States. Executive Order 8807 specifically moved the NDRC to the auspices of OSRD.

President Roosevelt named Vannevar Bush as Director of Office of Scientific Research and Development. Bush, feeling he could not direct both OSRD and NDRC, appointed J. B. Conant as Chairman of NDRC, with Roger Adams, previously Vice-Chairman of Division B, becoming chair of that Division. Bush also appointed Irvin Stewart as Executive Secretary of OSRD.

The transformation of the NDRC into a unit of the OSRD meant that the NDRC lost the authority to act on its own, beyond making recommendations for action by the OSRD. The reorganized NDRC first met on 18 July 1941. One interesting aspect of both the NDRC and OSRD operations was the premise that research itself should be non-profit, whether conducted by an institution or university, or by a commercial enterprise. The contracts used by NDRC/OSRD were therefore structured so that those contracted would neither gain nor lose financially for the work contracted.

At this point, the Divisional structure of the NDRC remained largely unchanged, but for the addition of a new division, Division F, which worked on radar countermeasures, and for the shifting of the Committee on Uranium directly to OSRD.

The increasing workload experienced in the first year of U.S. involvement in the war led to a reorganization of the NDRC's internal structure in November 1942. The original division structure of the initial five, and later six, divisions with their letter designations gave way to the establishment of 19 numbered divisions and four panels.

Within the original Division C, Communications and Transportation, there had previously been established Section C-2, Transportation. Under the 1942 reorganization Division C was redesignated Division 12.

Amphibian request

It was to Division C that the Quartermaster Corps turned for help in designing an amphibious vehicle on 7 May 1941. This request would have come to the attention of 58-year-old Hartley Rowe, Chairman of the Transportation section. Rowe maintained his office at 1 Federal Street, Boston, in the headquarters of United Fruit Company. Rowe had become the company's chief engineer 15 years earlier. With an Electrical Engineering degree from Purdue University, Rowe had served as Resident Engineer, Building Division, of the Panama Canal until August 1919. Equipped with theoretical expertise and years of on-the-job experience, Rowe not only had a clear grasp of engineering in general, but also a feel for administering large-scale and complex engineering projects. Fortuitously, Rowe's experiences also provided insightful knowledge into the difficulties of moving cargo, be it bananas or munitions, from ship to shore, as well as the hurdles of operating in a tropical environment.

Under Rowe's leadership, the Division would be central to the development of the ¼-ton wheeled amphibian, the original and amphibious forms of the Weasel, as well as the 2½-ton DUKW that is the subject of this volume.

The first of these projects was the ¼-ton 4x4 amphibian. The genesis for this vehicle can be traced to June 1940, when the Chief of Infantry

After handily winning the 1931 Transatlantic race, *Dorade*'s crew, including owner Roderick Stephens, Sr., designer Olin J. Stephens II, and construction superintendent Roderick Stephens, Jr., were honored by a welcome home ticker tape parade in New York. Here the parade, with touring cars leading the way, leaves the Battery, heading up Broadway to City Hall. *Dorade* and the Stephens family had returned to the U.S. aboard the liner *Homeric*. (Sparkman & Stephens)

Dorade's designer, Olin J. Stephens II, shakes hands with New York's deputy mayor as his father, and *Dorade*'s owner, Roderick Stephens, Sr., stands to his left, beaming at the camera. At the far left, in the second row, is Olin's brother and later DUKW virtuoso Rod Stephens, Jr.

drew up the requirements for a vehicle that would ultimately become the jeep. The original requirements stipulated that, if feasible, the frame and body should be designed to provide amphibious characteristics. If work on such characteristics would delay the production of the basic vehicle, the statement said, future "experimentation and development along this line [should] be continued until successfully concluded."

While development of the jeep progressed, the amphibian concept languished until a meeting of the Quartermaster Corps Technical Committee on 10 March 1941 took up a recommendation of the Motor Transport subcommittee to proceed with a project to create an amphibious version of the jeep. The following month it was decided that a War Department liaison unit should ask the NRDC to conduct the necessary research work for this project, dubbed QMC-4.

Rowe passed the task to his 40-year-old Executive Officer, Palmer Cosslett Putnam. A holder of a degree in geology from the prestigious MIT, Putnam was the son of George H. Putnam, president of G. P. Putnam's Sons Publishing Company. Palmer Putnam took over as president of the publishing company upon his father's death in 1924, but then retired from that post in 1932.

Intrigued by the high winds – and the high cost of electricity – on Cape Cod in 1934, Putnam envisioned a large-scale wind generator system as a cost-effective alternative. He crafted a preliminary design with cost estimates, and in 1937 sought the advice of the Dean of Engineering at MIT. The Dean, who was impressed by Putnam's work, was Vannevar Bush, who would soon head the NDRC. Bush introduced Putnam to General Electric's vice-president, and this began a snowballing effect of connections within the scientific and industrial communities. Ultimately Putnam did erect a large experimental wind generation plant in 1941, and until the 1980s, Putnam's 1.25-megawatt wind turbine was the largest in the world. Technically successful – if not economically profitable – the turbine led NASA in 1974 to recognize Palmer, saying "Whatever has been accomplished in the U.S. in an effort to develop the wind as an important source of power can be credited largely to the imagination and talents of one man – Palmer C. Putnam." Dennis Puleston, in his book *The Gull's Way – A Sailor/Naturalist's Yarn,* described Putnam as "… an eccentric but brilliant thinker, a man who believed in his own importance, and feared no

Dennis Puleston, seen here in the mid 1980s, was a British-born sailor, artist, and adventurer, who upon becoming a U.S. citizen, was employed by Sparkman & Stephens. Dennis was instrumental in establishing DUKW training schools around the world, and after the war served as the editor of the official historical record of the NDRC. Interestingly, he is best known as one of the founders of the Environmental Defense Fund, and championed the banning of DDT.

man, no matter how many stars he carried on his lapels."

Putnam, like many of his family and contemporaries along the seaboard, made a hobby of sailing. Palmer C. Putnam was a founding member of the Stone Horse Yacht Club, Harwichport, Massachusetts, in 1933.

He was undoubtedly familiar then with two brothers who were the sensation of the international sailing scene, Olin and Roderick Stephens, Jr.

Rod and Olin Stephens

The Stephens family was in the anthracite coal business, operating the Stephens Fuel Company with four locations in New York City. Founded by James Stephens, the business was in the hands of Olin James Stephens by the end of the 19th century, and he was later joined by his son, Roderick Stephens. In time, Roderick married Marguerite Dulon and started his own family, which included two sons, Olin J. Stephens, II, and Roderick, Jr. and a daughter, Marguerite, known as Marite. During summer vacations in the Adirondacks, the Stephens boys always enjoyed Lake George. With the children so enamored of the water, the family gave the Adirondacks a miss in 1920 and summered in a rented cottage on Sandy Neck, Cape Cod, instead. When Olin was 12, Mr. Stephens bought a 16-foot sloop. The following year a 26-foot vessel replaced

Rod Stephens peers into the engine compartment of a DUKW, a vehicle whose hull design was largely the result of his work, along with that of fellow Sparkman & Stephens designer Gil Wyland. Such was his association with the vehicle that when he passed away on 10 January 1995, Rod left behind 100 pages of book manuscript in which he wrote concerning the DUKW: "I know more about these vehicles than anyone in the world."

it. Olin and Rod, just over a year younger, along with their father, mother, and sister, enjoyed many quiet days learning the art of sailing aboard these vessels.

As years passed, Mr. Stephens bought successively larger or more advanced boats, and his boys became accomplished yachtsmen and racers. Olin, as far back as his school days, had longed to design yachts, even enrolling in MIT's marine architecture program upon graduation from high school in 1926. However, he soon left the program, having quickly developed a distaste for its emphasis on large ships.

With the then-youngest generation of Stephens interests firmly planted in sea, rather than coal, and faced with mounting pressure from the home heating oil industry, during the winter of 1929-1930 the decision was made to sell the Stephen's Coal Company. Olin was working as a draftsman for Philip Rhodes and Henry J. Gielow, a specialist in large power boats, when he met yacht broker Drake Sparkman. On 11 November 1929 with financial backing from Roderick Stephens, Sr., the two formed Sparkman & Stephens.

As Olin entered into this business venture, his brother Rod was enjoying Christmas break from Cornell, where in addition to pursuing a degree in Mechanical Engineering, he was also a promising athlete. During the break, Rod helped Henry Nevins at his shipyard and Nevins was so impressed with Stephens that he called his father, saying he would like to offer Rod a position with his firm, rather than see him go back to Cornell in spring, and asking if the elder would object. The senior Stephens' left the choice up to Rod, who, after consideration, accepted the offer. This was a decision that he would not regret.

It would have seemed logical Nevins Yard would undertake the work on the new yacht, commissioned by the elder Roderick and designed by Olin, II. But in 1929 business at the Nevins Yard was booming and no new construction could have been undertaken until the following year. Hence, the neighboring Minneford Yacht Yard was contracted to build the new Stephens' yacht, the *Dorade*, under the supervision of Roderick Stephens, Jr.

Dorade would catapult the Stephens brothers from notable local yachting talent in the New York area to world celebrities in 1931. At 5:45 a.m., Tuesday, 21 July 1931 *Dorade* passed the Lizard Point Light, Cornwall, England. She had left Newport, Rhode Island, at noon, on 4 July, crewed by the Stephens brothers, their father, and four friends. When she passed the Lizard Point and arrived in Plymouth, England, 16 days and 55 minutes out, *Dorade* and her crew won the Transatlantic Race – besting the competition by two days (almost four days on corrected time).

Back in the U.S., *Dorade*'s crew received a ticker-tape parade up Broadway in New York City. *Dorade*'s decisive victory brought Olin acclaim as a designer, and both brothers a well-founded reputation as skillful seamen. Roderick joined Sparkman & Stephens as a designer in 1933. *Dorade*'s 1931 race victory would not be the brothers' only brush with transatlantic racing. Rod won the 1935 race with another of Olin's designs, *Stormy Weather*. Olin would go on to be the original designer of six successful 12-meter defenders of America's Cup from 1958 through 1980. For his part, in 1937 Rod was part of the crew of successful America's Cup defender *Ranger,* and later aided in the design of and crewed America's Cup defenders *Columbia* and *Constellation*.

More importantly for this narrative, the celebrity the brothers attained in the 1930s brought them into contact with an expanding circle of members of the sailing community.

Dennis Puleston

One of these sailors was British-born adventurer Dennis Puleston, whom the Stephens brothers had met at Cruising Club of America meetings.

Puleston too had acquired quite a reputation in the sailing community prior to the U.S. involvement in WWII. Upon Puleston's 2001 death, his obituary in *The Daily Telegraph* recorded "On his travels, he ate human flesh with cannibals in New Guinea, flirted with virgins in Samoa, managed a derelict coconut plantation in the Virgin islands, adopted a pet boa constrictor, tattooed his arm with sharks' teeth, searched for sunken treasure off Santo Domingo, was shipwrecked on Cape Hatteras and gave his pet cockatoo to the Emperor of Japan. Eventually he was captured in China by Japanese soldiers fighting the Sino-Japanese war. When Puleston received a handwritten letter from the Emperor thanking him for the cockatoo, his captors were so impressed that they packed him back to Europe on the Trans-Siberian railway."

Puleston's 1995 memoirs, *The Gull's Way – A Sailor/Naturalist's Yarn,* confirms all of this, except the last incident which is told a bit differently. Puleston did in 1937 provide three cockatoos for the Emperor's private zoo, and was presented with a scroll from the Emperor thanking him for the gift. When Puleston, a British subject, was stranded in Japanese-held Beiping (now Beijing), he showed this scroll to an English-fluent Japanese officer, and suddenly found himself revered. When asked by the Japanese if there was anything that could be done for him, Puleston requested safe passage to the Siberian border, where he could board the Trans-Siberian Railway. He was accorded this passage, often traveling on Japanese troop trains, until reaching a border town, Manzhouli, on the Manchurian side, and Chita on the Soviet side. There he began a 22- day rail journey to the Hook of Holland, and from there, passage back to England.

Word of Puleston's remarkable exploits reached the U.S., and an offer from Doubleday, Doran and Company was tendered to publish an account of these adventures.

In December 1937 Puleston arrived in New York to write such a book. Puleston's sole prior trip to the U.S. had been as a crew member of the yacht *Pinta* a few years earlier, and during that visit he had met Betty Wellington, whose acquaintance was renewed upon his 1937 return. For Puleston, 1939 would be a remarkable year. His book *Blue Water Vagabond* appeared, further raising his notoriety in yachting circles, and he and Betty were married, further cementing the U.S. as his home, and immigration proceedings were begun. Settling in Brookhaven, Long Island, Puleston took up a successful career in painting, with sailing and bird watching being passionate hobbies.

Following the Japanese attack on Pearl Harbor, Puleston sought to combine his new national loyalty with his passion for sailing by joining the Coast Guard Auxiliary, which at that time was using civilian sailing vessels for picket duty. But with his U.S. citizenship not yet confirmed, he could not enlist. Thus, Dennis was available when brothers Roderick and Olin Stephens offered him a designer position at Sparkman & Stephens. Until his U.S. citizenship was conferred, Dennis was unable to work on classified projects, a restriction that was lifted when he became a citizen early in 1942. Once this status was attained, he immersed himself in work that included a project of the OSRD concerning amphibian vehicles. Puleston was so deeply involved with this project that after WWII he was tasked first with writing the detailed technical report of all the wartime activities of Division 12, and later became director of the group that compiled all 72 volumes that chronicle the wartime work of the OSRD, occupying an entire floor of the Empire State Building to do this.

Chapter 2
QMC-4 Project

On 19 April 1941, Experimental, Development and Test Program (EDT) Project No. 33-41 was set up at the Quartermaster Corps Holabird Quartermaster Depot to study the general problem of converting various sizes of military vehicles to amphibians. The first of these was to be an amphibious variant of the new ¼-ton 4x4 reconnaissance car, then in the early stages of production. The amphibian vehicle project, dubbed QMC-4, was tasked to the newly formed Division 12 of the NDRC, becoming the first major project undertaken by the Division.

In July 1941, Palmer C. Putnam with the NDRC called on Olin and Rod Stephens at their offices at 11 East 44th Street, New York. In his biography, *All this and Sailing Too,* Olin recalls that in this meeting Putnam first suggested a triphibian, able to operate on land, in water, and in the air – the last attribute being quickly discarded by Olin and his brother Rod as being beyond the talent of Sparkman & Stephens. Quickly the concept became a matter of creating an amphibious conversion of the ¼-ton 4x4. Rod Stephens was designated the project engineer, and he along with Sparkman & Stephens' chief engineer Gilbert Wyland (called Gil by his associates) began work on the project immediately, although a formal contract was not issued until 19 November 1941.

One reason for the delay in formalizing the contract was the desire to have the Stevens Institute of Hoboken, New Jersey, do hydrodynamic testing in their Experimental Towing Tank. Then there were difficulties reconciling the Institute's flat-sum contracting practices with the cost-plus practices of the NDRC. Ultimately it was decided that the Stevens Institute should work as a subcontractor to Sparkman & Stephens, and the result was the issuance of the 19 November contract, for a maximum of $25,000. This contract, numbered OWMsr-154, would cover work on the ¼-ton amphibian project for the period from 1 July 1941 until 30 June 1942. Later supplements would broaden its scope, extend its length, and increase the total amount expended.

Brief consideration was given to the possibility of using add-on accessories to float the jeep – the Willys MA (the first mass-produced variant manufactured by Willys). But it was quickly decided that a better route would be to permanently convert the vehicle to an amphibian variant. Stephens and Wyland laid down hull designs, which were then tested at the Stevens Institute. A number of different lengths forward and aft of the wheel wells, as well as various shapes for the wheel wells, were tried, all in an effort to obtain water speeds of 7 to 8 m.p.h. Interestingly, Stevens suggested that "Hydrofoils may provide the most reasonable means of getting really good speed" – a concept that would resurface a decade later with the Flying DUKW. At the same time it was suggested that special shock absorbers be installed

The first amphibian developed under the auspices of the NDRC was this vehicle built by Marmon-Herrington. This amphibian, which came to be referred to by the Quartermaster Corps project name, QMC-4, featured a hull designed by Sparkman & Stephens. (Ordnance Museum)

that would allow the wheels to be retracted in order to increase water speed – another concept that would be revisited in the 1950s, through the Drake.

With the hull form roughly established, in the first week of October, three Willys MA jeeps were delivered to Marmon-Herrington in Indianapolis for conversion to amphibian vehicles, utilizing the Sparkman & Stephens hull design. Rod Stephens visited the Indianapolis plant on 14-15 October to aid in the adaptation of the ground vehicle components to their new use. One of the jeeps was dismantled so that these parts could be measured and weighed, with weight being of considerable concern from the outset of the project.

The following week Rod Stephens paid a visit to the chief engineer at Willys-Overland in Toledo, Barney Roos, who showed Rod the forthcoming new jeep model, the MB, so he could see how its more evolved components could be incorporated into the amphibians. Returning to Indianapolis, Rod was dismayed to learn that Marmon-Herrington had only one engineer, a Mr. Meyer, working on the project. Responding to this situation, he directed that Ernest Strothenk, one of Sparkman & Stephens' engineers, go to Indianapolis to assist from 28 October.

It had been suggested that a wooden mockup be produced, but that plan was abandoned when Col. Arthur Herrington (ret) opted to build the pilot out of steel, hoping to produce an operating vehicle more quickly. By 12 December actual construction of the Marmon-Herrington pilot was underway and the Indianapolis operation had progressed to the point that Mr. Strothenk could return to New York. Nevertheless, it was the second week of March 1942 before the vehicle was finally completed, well behind the original forecast completion date of the end of January.

Marmon-Herrington, however, was not alone in the ¼-ton amphibian program. On 19 December 1941, Palmer C. Putnam and Roderick Stephens had approached Ford, asking it to become involved in the amphibian program. Ford was a logical choice, for not only did it boast vast engineering and production facilities, it also had considerable experience in the ¼-ton reconnaissance car program.

At that program's outset, then, three ¼-ton vehicle models had

Sparkman & Stephens designed a hull form that could envelope the Army's ¼-ton scout car, popularly known as the jeep. The standard wheel base, width, and height of the vehicle were maintained. A scow-type body was used, since this form could provide maximum floatation with minimum overall dimensions. Wooden models of several variations on this form were then created, and they in turn underwent study in the test tank at the Stevens Institute in Hoboken, New Jersey. Model 376-4, seen here, was near the final design. (Stevens Institute)

The test tank data were used to refine the design for optimum efficiency in terms of speed as well as buoyancy and minimal wake. This photo, taken during the testing of model 376-3e on 13 August 1941, which was being towed at 7.7 MPH, is indicative of the detailed studies made and illustrates the bow wave action, which was improved in subsequent models. Many of these comparative tests led to minor changes in the shape of the wheel cutouts as well as the corners of the bow. (Stevens Institute)

In December 1941, Palmer C. Putnam of the NDRC and Rod Stephens met with representatives of Ford, presenting them with the S&S hull design. Ford constructed three pilot vehicles which met the QMC-4 requirements and utilized the S&S hull form. This is the first of the three pilots which were hand-built in Ford's engineering laboratory.

been placed in production: the Bantam BRC, the Willys MA, and Ford's GP. After the initial production runs, the Army opted to go with a "standard" second-generation ¼-ton vehicle, which would be the Willys MB that Barney Roos had shown to Rod Stephens in October. The Army was unsure whether Willys had the capability to meet the demand for these vehicles, however, and accordingly contracted with Ford to build duplicates of the Willys design – the Ford designation being GPW.

While general details were reviewed with Laurence Sheldrick, who was effectively Ford's chief engineer, Ford engineer Clarence Kramer went over the Sparkman & Stephens hull design, making minor modifications in order to incorporate Ford's production techniques. He also offered improvements that he believed would enhance on-road performance. Rod Stephens reported that by 28 December detailed drawings were well underway at Ford. Naturally Ford was incorporating the mechanical attributes of the GPW in its prototypes. Three pilot models of the new amphibian, designated GPA, were intended to be ready for testing by the end of January 1942. These three vehicles were hand-built in Ford's Engineering Laboratory.

Clarence Kramer and his staff worked out the crucially important details of creating waterproof junctions between an automobile drive train and the hull of a boat. These details were openly shared with General Motors engineers at the outset of the DUKW project, saving many man-hours of duplicated labor in a project that was rushed for time.

Production of the three pilots of the GPA lagged slightly behind schedule, with the first pilot being completed during the first week of February. Ford began testing the vehicle, under the observation of Roderick Stephens and Army representatives, on 9 February 1942. Incorporating lessons learned from these tests, Ford's second pilot was completed during the third week of February. The third pilot incorporated further improvements, and it was finished in the last week of the month.

Trials of the Ford and Marmon-Herrington pilot vehicles were conducted at Fort Holabird and Fort Belvoir, Fort Knox, Fort Bragg, and Fort Benning. The Ford GPA consistently bested the Marmon-Herrington offering in these trials, and accordingly the Dearborn firm was awarded a production contract.

At this time the NDRC exited the GPA picture – and this itself proved a valuable lesson when it came to the DUKW program. The GPA was not deemed a resounding success, and later analysis lay most of the blame not on design or engineering problems in the vehicle itself, but rather on a lack of follow-through support from the engineers and project managers at the NDRC. NDRC, in essence, told the Army: "Ok, here it is, use it." A far different scenario would prevail with the DUKW.

The second Ford prototype, completed only days after the first one, incorporated design improvements based on the initial testing of the first prototype.

Left: U.S. Army registration number 702328 is an early-production GPA, as distinguished by the absence of raised, horizontal stiffening ribs on the coaming. This was the 225th production Ford GPA, the first having been U.S.A. number 702104.

Below: Ultimately Ford was contracted to mass-produce its design. Ford assigned the vehicle their model designation GPA to the vehicle. Included were many refinements to the S&S design initiated by Ford Design Engineer Clarence Kramer in order to ease mass production by an automotive firm rather than boat builders. (TACOM LCMC History Office)

Chapter 3
A Larger Amphibian

Part of the problem with developing amphibious vehicle designs in 1941 was that this was a new science. As Palmer C. Putnam wrote in a memo regarding the outset of the QMC-4 project "…whereas there are several dozen people in the country who could whittle out a passable battleship, there was nobody who could whittle out a passable amphibian."

The creation of the GPA had resolved many of the unknowns. The Sparkman & Stephens hull design had proven viable, Clarence Kramer of Ford had refined the hull form so that it could be produced in an automobile assembly plant, and effective water seals for the powertrain had been developed.

There remained, however, the problem of transporting large quantities of men and equipment to shore. The GPA was never intended to address this – it was an amphibious scout car. A large amphibian would be required to quickly move tons of supplies and thousands of men ashore without the use of proper dock facilities, which no doubt would be savaged by both defending and attacking forces during a war. Hartley Rowe had broached this subject with Vannevar Bush prior to Pearl Harbor but the Army initially exhibited a notable lack of interest in such a vehicle.

This situation changed, however, on 24 March 1942, following the successful first tests of the ¼-ton amphibian. General Jacob Devers of the Armored Force wrote to Dr. Bush asking that the NDRC look into the problem of transporting tanks from ship to shore, through surf and over beach.

The British Commandos, who were keenly interested in the ¼-ton amphibian, were on 14 April advised that a larger amphibian was under consideration and were asked for suggestions. A conference was held the next evening in Mr. Rowe's room at the Mayflower Hotel, with General Dillon, Mr. Rowe and Palmer C. Putnam attending, to discuss further amphibian development. The next day General Dillon suggested that two larger amphibians be designed, one each around two of the army's standard trucks at that time, the 2½-ton 6x6 and the 6-ton 6x6.

On the evening of April 16th Palmer C. Putnam, Rod Stephens, Jr., and Ford's Clarence Kramer met in Detroit to discuss mass production techniques in general, and specifically to see whether Ford would be interested in participating in the larger amphibian program, based on the firm's experience with the smaller amphibian. The next day Ford's Laurence Sheldrick stated that Ford would not be able to participate in the larger amphibian program. Ford corporate historian Charles C. LaCroix recorded that Ford declined the NDRC request, citing Ford's lack of suitable components, most notably axles and engines, for vehicles in this size range.

Later the same day, Putnam, along with Rod Stephens, brought the problem to General Motors Yellow Truck and Coach. Yellow Truck and Coach was also a very logical choice. While Ford had experience building amphibians, Yellow Truck and Coach was then producing

When serious work began on developing a larger amphibian, the base vehicle chosen was the GMC AFKWX-353 2½-ton 6x6 truck. This vehicle was selected in part because it was thought that its cab-over design would offer a higher position for the driver's seat than the CCKW 6x6 chassis. (General Motors)

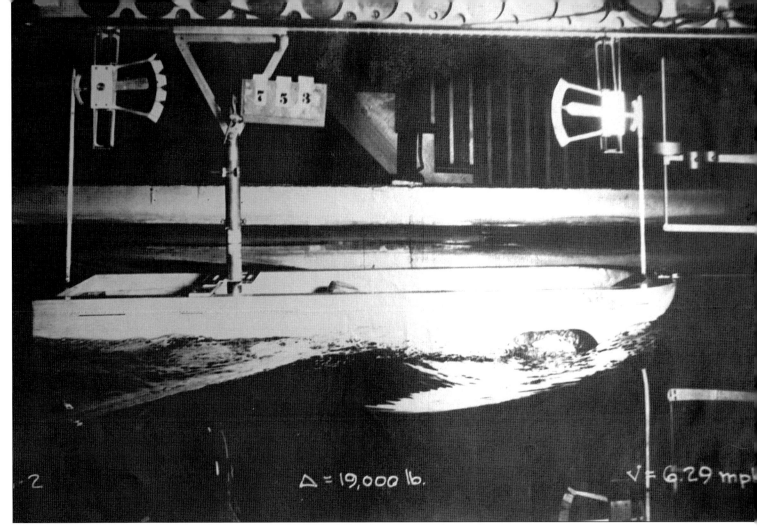

A scale model of a DUKW undergoes hydrodynamic tests in a water tank at a speed of 6.29 miles per hour. These tests were conducted to determine the wave forms generated by the craft, with a view to minimizing waves and wakes, and to assess and the craft's buoyancy and performance in water before committing the design to a full-scale vehicle. (Stevens Institute)

Yellow Truck & Coach produced drawings of an amphibian 6x6 2½-ton truck for Rod Stephens. This plan was developed for the first scale model of the vehicle, designated No. 413-1. To the left are sectional profiles of three points in the tandem suspension area.

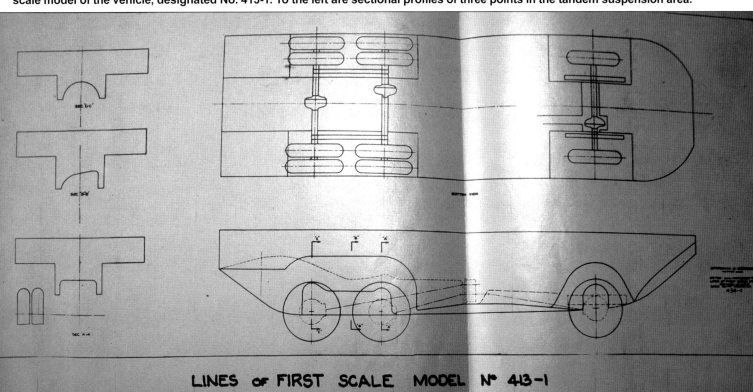

LINES of FIRST SCALE MODEL N° 413-1

The DUKW construction program formally began at Plant No. 2 of Yellow Truck & Coach Manufacturing Co. on 24 April, when work began on a mockup fabricated from plywood, cardboard, and steel. The mockup was finished within three days. (General Motors)

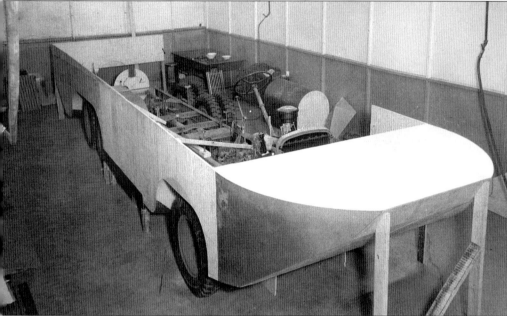

The DUKW mockup is viewed from the forward starboard quarter. Visible behind the bow section are the radiator, engine, and steering wheel. Parts of the chassis frame and dual tandem tires can be seen inside the wooden hull parts of the mockup. (General Motors)

in large quantities the U.S. Army's standard 2½-ton 6x6 trucks, the GMC conventional-cab model CCKW and the cab-over-engine variant, the AFKWX. Putnam and Stephens studied a 2½ truck and Yellow Truck and Coach's Pontiac plant, and Yellow Truck provided Rod Stephens with layout drawings of the vehicle for Stephens to use to begin the hull layout. Yellow Truck's Chief Engineer Charles O. Ball then accompanied Palmer Putnam and Rod Stephens to Dearborn to look over Ford's ¼-ton amphibian.

At 7 p.m. on the evening of the 17th Putnam and Stephens boarded a plane to fly back to D.C. *En route* they discussed the amphibian situation in general, and determined that the task of transporting tanks to shore as General Devers requested was something that a ferry made of two of 2½-ton amphibians could do. Rod Stephens also felt this size amphibian was also viable as pontoon for pontoon bridge construction. At 10 p.m. that night they briefed General Dillon on all these matters, and Dillon approved their proposal.

At 10 the next morning the proposal was presented to Dr. Bush, who approved. The proposal was further discussed with General Dillon that day at lunch, which was followed by a brief meeting with Dr. Bush and Dr. Lewis. It was explained that General Brehon B.

Summerville of Service of Supply could not give a letter of intent to Yellow Truck and Coach without an expression of interest by General McNair. Yellow Truck would likely be unable to come up with the materials for the program, given wartime priorities and rationing, without this documentation, and General McNair would be looking to General Devers for advice on this matter. Thus, Palmer C. Putnam was instructed to fly to Fort Knox that evening in order to meet with General Devers.

At 4 p.m. on 19 April General Devers and his staff were shown a movie of the ¼-ton amphibian successfully operating in the surf, and the proposed 2½-ton amphibian-based tank ferry was explained. The General and his staff felt this was the best option that they had yet been presented, and the General stated he would call General McNair at 7 a.m. the next morning to express his opinion.

Putnam then boarded a Detroit-bound train, along with Major Heath of the Armored Force and Captain Cushman of the Tank Destroyer Force. At 8:30 on the morning of 20 April 1942 Palmer Putnam, along with Rod and Olin Stephens, a Dr. Bowman of Drexel Institutes, and numerous representatives of Cadillac, manufacturer of the M5 light tank, met at Cadillac to discuss the amphibian-based

After the mockup was completed, construction began on a first pilot vehicle at Yellow Truck & Coach. Here, the bottom of the hull of the prototype is taking shape. Incorporated into the bottom were drive-shaft tunnels, wheel houses, and, in the background, the tunnel for the marine propeller. (General Motors)

Seen from the front of the body of the first pilot DUKW are the tunnels for the forward drive shaft and, farther aft, the two tunnels, one over the other, for the drive shafts for the tandem axles. The tunnel for the aft tandem axle is the upper one. (General Motors)

The underside of the hull of the first pilot is seen from the rear. The two holes mark where the drive shafts for the tandem axles exit from the hull. These points were fitted with watertight water seals when the drive shafts were installed. (General Motors)

The forward part of the first DUKW pilot's body is observed from the side of the port forward wheel house. Hat-section stiffeners are attached to the tops of the wheel houses, and lumber braces are temporarily fastened with C-clamps to the bow and wheel houses. (General Motors)

The bow section of the first DUKW pilot is viewed from the port side. The shape of the bow even at this early stage was quite similar to the bow on production DUKWs. The vertical stiffeners on the front of the bow were fashioned from hat-section channels. (General Motors)

ferry project. By 11 that morning many of the same men were meeting with executives and engineers at Yellow Truck and Coach's Pontiac, Michigan plant, where they dropped off drawings and photographs of the ¼-ton amphibian. Putnam, Bowen and Stephens then traveled to Cleveland to visit the offices of the White Motor Company, builders of the 6-ton 6x6, and meet with their engineers.

At 8:10 that evening the trio of Putnam, Bowen, and Stephens boarded a Washington-bound train, and *en route* conferred to summarize the status of the program to date.

At 9:30 the next morning Putnam went over the progress on the amphibian program with Dr. Bush, who then suggested that Putnam review the program with General Williams. At 1:30 that afternoon Putnam and Williams had lunch and reviewed the program, and Williams offered to take Putnam to see General Lucius Clay, one of General Summervelle's assistants. By 2:30 Putnam, conferred with General Williams and General Clay, along with his assistant, Col. Anthony McAuliffe (who would later gain fame as General McAuliffe

at besieged Bastogne with his famous "Nuts!" response to German surrender demands). During this meeting General Clay stated that he personally felt that the 2½-ton amphibian would be just another vehicle that would complicate the Army's logistics. He went on to state that as of 18 April General Devers was on record as not sufficiently in favor of the 2½-ton amphibian to warrant immediate action. Clay did admit, however, that the Army would not object to the NDRC pursuing this project on its own.

At 3:15 the same day, 21 April, Putnam saw Col. Van Deusen, of the Tank-Automotive Command, who stated he had an oral directive from General Frink, which Frink had received from General Summervelle via General Dillon on 16 April to proceed with the development of a 2½ ton amphibian "with all possible urgency." Van Deusen, when told of General Clay's position, stated his previous instructions had not been rescinded, and the project should proceed.

This position was reaffirmed 15 minutes later during a meeting between Van Deusen, Putnam, Yellow Truck and Coach President

Workmen construct the bottom of the hull of the first DUKW pilot. In the foreground is the starboard side of the hull. The longitudinal hat sections on the side of the hull were called rub rails; they acted as reinforcers and protected the sides when the craft was maneuvering next to docks and ships. (General Motors)

A welder crouches in the front starboard wheel house of the upended hull of the first pilot vehicle. The hull was constructed of welded sheet metal. The hat-section rub rails and stiffeners were tack-welded to the sheet-metal skin of the hull. (General Motors)

The shell of the first pilot DUKW's hull has been turned upright. It formed a watertight assembly into which the chassis would be installed. Over the fronts and the rears of the aft wheel houses are transverse frame members or partial bulkheads; these appear to have been temporary and were not found on production DUKWs. (General Motors)

Workers and engineers confer over details of the first pilot DUKW, here turned upside down, with the stern in the foreground. A plywood spacer or form is attached to the propeller tunnel. (General Motors)

Irving Babcock, and Yellow Vice-President Mr. Little. At 4:45 the group of Babcock, Little, and Putnam met with Dr. Bush, and after a briefing, the group was instructed to go see NDRC Executive Secretary Irvin Stewart to formalize the agreement in principle to produce pilot models of the 2½-ton amphibian.

Under the agreement, Yellow Truck and Coach would go ahead with the project, with GM assuming the risk of the expense of the tooling drawings. Sparkman & Stephens would handle the marine design, and Drexel Institute would provide additional engineering expertise. A contract was drafted for Yellow Truck and Coach to fabricate and test three or more pilot models of a 2½-ton amphibious truck for the Army; development of portable structures to be carried by these trucks to permit the floating ashore of the Armored Force light tanks; and – supplementary to work already undertaken for the Engineer Corps through Drexel Institute under the supervision of H.L. Bowman – the development of means whereby these amphibious trucks could serve as pontoon units in bridges and ferries."

The NDRC's Palmer C. Putnam contacted Sparkman & Stephens on the evening of 23 April to give the firm the official "go ahead" on the 2½-ton amphibian design. Eleven days earlier, Sparkman & Stephens had delivered to the Stevens Institute model lines for the 2½-ton amphibian hull. The model was built and tested, with the test data being reported to Rod Stephens by telephone. At that time Rod was *en route* from Pontiac, where for that week he had been working with Yellow Truck, to New Orleans. Rod had interrupted his work in Pontiac to join his brother Olin and Palmer Putnam on a visit to Higgins Industries in New Orleans. Higgins at the time was building successful landing craft, and Stevens hoped that a visit to the company's plant would yield a more complete understanding of amphibious landings.

Back in the Pontiac-Detroit area on the 29th, Stephens and the Yellow truck personnel most closely involved in the amphibian engineering, visited the Ford plant again and made a detailed inspection of the Ford GPA (¼-ton amphibian). Ford Motor Company, principally chief engineer Clarence Kramer, provided the Yellow Truck team with the engineering data gleaned from their ¼-ton truck program.

Now that the Yellow Truck and Coach Division of General Motors was formally and actively involved, it was necessary that the 2½-ton amphibian be given a General Motors model designation. During the time period in question, the model designations were established by an informal committee consisting of C.J. Bock, Truck Division Engineer; George Oliver, Truck Sales Engineering; and R.A. Crist, production control manager. The model designation convention used by Yellow Truck and Coach consisted of groups of letters and numbers. The first letter in the group represents the year of the vehicle introduction, A being 1939, B being 1940, etc. The second letter is indicative of the type of vehicle – C being conventional, F being Cab over engine, etc. The letter "U" represents "utility," as it had been previously used to indicate "public utility." The third and fourth letters represent various special chassis. "K" represents front-wheel drive, while "W" is indicative of 6-wheel dual-driving axles (as with the standard army CCKW 6x6). The numbers following the letters are a coded indicator of the specific wheelbase of the vehicle.

Thus in the company dining room over lunch in late April, this informal committee christened the new vehicle the DUKW-353.

Between 1 and 5 May, the team at Pontiac constructed a mockup of the proposed amphibian, and the basic arrangement was agreed upon. On 6 May the final hull drawings were sent to the Stevens Institute, where the model was altered to mimic the refined drawings, and additional test-tank data were compiled. In Pontiac, pilot model construction began on 11 May, utilizing as its basis AFKWX-353 from contract W-398-QM-11425, originally built on Yellow Truck and Coach Sales Order TC-200254. On 13 May the government paperwork began to catch up with the earnest efforts of the GM team, and the amphibian pilot construction was designated OSRD Project PDRC-413. General Motors issued sales order TC-200405 which served as the work order for the build, which the War Production Board gave a rating of A-1a, Code 13, which was a high priority.

By 23 May, the vehicle frame was secured in the hull. Five days later the vehicle was standing on its own wheels, and every indication was that the vehicle would be operational in a week to 10 days.

On the afternoon of Tuesday, 2 June 1942, the pilot model was run in the shop, and by 8 a.m. the next morning the vehicle was ready for water testing. In a mere 43 days – albeit very long days – the DUKW had gone from an agreement in principle to an operational prototype, a remarkable tribute the determination and ingenuity of all involved.

The inside of the hull of the first pilot vehicle is observed from the front. The chassis frame had been installed by this time and is visible between the forward and aft wheel houses. To the rear is the bulbous shape of the marine propeller tunnel. (General Motors)

The bow of the first pilot DUKW is viewed from underneath, with the front of the bow toward the top. Toward the bottom of the photograph, the scooped-out contours intended to provide clearance for the front axle and drive shaft are visible. (General Motors)

The cab-over design of the first pilot DUKW is apparent in this forward-facing view from the center of the hull. The box-shaped structures will hold the driver's and passenger's seats. The transmission, brake, and shift levers are between the boxes. (General Motors)

A worker adjusts the shift levers between the bases of the driver's and assistant driver's seats, highlighting the hand-built construction of the first DUKW pilot. In the foreground is the radiator, separated from the workman by the GMC engine. (General Motors)

The forward deck, with lateral stiffeners, is installed on the pilot vehicle, and the front edge of the deck is secured with C-clamps. Through the open hatch on the deck, the radiator is visible. Production DUKWs would have two hatches on this deck. (General Motors)

More of the driver's compartment of the first pilot DUKW has been completed, and the driver's seat and steering wheel are present. The windshield has been installed, and a bow to support a canvas top over the driver's compartment is in place. In the foreground is a drive shaft. (General Motors)

Army personnel look on as Yellow Truck & Coach technicians put the final touches on the first pilot DUKW in preparation for its trial runs. This vehicle was finished on 2 June 1942, just 38 days after Yellow received orders to commence work on it. (General Motors)

Chapter 4
The Duck Leaves The Nest

The initial pilot of the DUKW, which was completed in remarkable time, was prepared for water testing, slated to begin on Wednesday, 3 June 1942. The day prior – the same day it was finished – the DUKW was driven around the field outside the Experimental Shop where it had been built. The bottom of the hull was filled with water, testing its water-tight integrity, and then the truck's bilge pumps were called on to empty the hull, thereby testing them. The completed vehicle tipped the scales at 13,500 pounds, 500 pounds less than the estimates used for the Stevens Institute tests, and very close to Yellow Truck and Coach's engineering estimate.

On-road testing indicated that the DUKW's performance while *en route* to Crystal Lake near Pontiac, Michigan, was a bit sluggish. Some of this was ascribed to the general tightness of the new vehicle, while the updraft carburetor, brought over from the AFKWX parent vehicle, was also believed to hamper performance.

Water testing on 3 June indicated that the propeller was too heavy, dampening water speed. Although no measured course had yet been set up, it was estimated that the DUKW could only attain a water speed of about 5 MPH.

It was also noted that while in the water the vehicle had a much broader left turn radius than had been hoped for. Traction while entering and leaving water was excellent, and this attribute would be of great importance during later tests. Reverse performance was fair, but the rudder was sheared off during a full-power reverse test. Subsequently it was learned that the front wheels provided a reasonable amount steering force while in the water. After the day's tests were complete, the DUKW returned to Yellow Truck's "Secret Room" for not only repair, but also modifications based on the lessons learned in the day's trials. This test and modify pattern was adhered to for the remainder of the week. Among these modifications were several changes in propeller size and location, as well as numerous alterations to the propeller tunnel.

On Thursday, 4 June, a water course was set up, smaller props made available, and a strengthened rudder installed. Speed was measured on the prepared course, revealing that the DUKW could attain 5.25 m.p.h., and it was expected that changing the ratio of the propeller

During the days after its completion, the first pilot DUKW was subjected to a series of land and water trials at General Motors' Milford Proving Ground in Michigan. Here, the bulged front panels of the coamings on each side of the front of the driver's compartment, visible in the preceding photograph, had been removed. Draft marks have been painted to the front of the forward wheel house and the rear of the aft wheel house to help gauge the vehicle's trim and performance in water. The man leading the group to the DUKW appears to have been Rod Stephens. (General Motors)

drive would improve this figure.

Further tests on the fifth showed the DUKW to be very stable, and Rod Stephens noted in his interim report that the DUKW "should be a very useful unit." During the day, 65 employees of Yellow Truck and Coach and Sparkman & Stephens boarded the DUKW, which then took to the water and operated normally, despite its 10,000-pound human payload. At the end of the day Colonel Van Deusen was informed that the vehicle was ready for a local demonstration to the Army.

That demonstration was scheduled for the following Friday, 12 June, at GM's Milford, Michigan, Proving Ground. There, the DUKW ran up to 37 m.p.h. on level track, negotiated a 60% grade while burdened with a 5,000-pound load, and was tested off-road. During the off-road portion of the tests it was learned that the DUKW had a "remarkable ability to push over trees." During the water portion of the testing the DUKW transported an 8,000-pound cargo in and out of water, and demonstrated its rear-mounted winch by pulling itself and a 3,000-pound load up a rocky causeway.

During a lunch break Rod Stephens spoke with Colonel R.R. Robins, to urge that the Army to act quickly to procure the truck, a sentiment not surprisingly echoed by the Yellow Truck personnel present. Additional testing was planned, to be carried out a Fort Belvoir and at Virginia Beach's Fort Story, at a date to be determined in the future.

On the front of the forward deck of the first pilot is a collapsible surf deflector. This rather flimsy fixture would soon be replaced by a rigid surf board. The lowered windshield rests on two posts attached to the deck. The hatch cover on the deck is partially open. Sandbags for loaded weight testing are in the cargo compartment. (General Motors)

The first pilot DUKW was fitted with a port and a starboard array of service headlight, blackout headlight, and blackout marker lamp. Bow-shaped headlight guards with front braces were included. A small spotlight was to the front of the driver's compartment on the port side; above it is the top of the steering wheel. (General Motors)

Nine civilians, probably Yellow or GMC employees, take the first pilot DUKW for a test drive. The coaming around the cargo compartment, intended to keep out waves, was of a uniform height; later, the height of the rear of the coaming would be increased. (General Motors)

Left: The rear of the first pilot DUKW is situated in a roadside ditch, and the starboard tandem wheels are articulated to conform to the rough ground. The man at the rear of the vehicle is sitting on sand bags, probably included for load or trim testing. (General Motors)

Below: The first pilot vehicle enters the water at a steep angle during initial tests at the Milford proving ground. DUKW doctrine instructed that it was best to enter the water on a moderately sloping beach. The marine propeller was not to be started until the vehicle was fully afloat. (General Motors)

The civilian test crew takes a ride on the first pilot DUKW at the Milford Proving Ground. Judging from the forward and aft draft marks and the attitude of the rub rails along the side of the hull, the craft was riding low in the stern. (General Motors)

Left: The first pilot DUKW is down at the stern as it makes a test run at the Milford proving ground. The raised object on the forward deck was the engine compartment hatch door. The collapsible surfboard, which helped cope with waves, is not present on the front of the forward deck. (General Motors)

Below: The first pilot vehicle heads toward shore at Milford. In this photo, the windshield, partially lowered in the preceding photograph, is fully raised. The hatch door on the forward deck is also raised; on production DUKWs, it was required that all hatches be secured during operations on water. (General Motors)

Rod Stephens is at the wheel as the first pilot DUKW comes ashore with a handful of passengers at the Milford proving ground. Stephens took a passionate and genuinely hands-on role in the design and development of the DUKW. (General Motors)

Right: The first pilot DUKW uses its winch, mounted in the rear of the hull, to pull itself out of the water, in a test conducted at the Milford Proving Ground. One such winch test was conducted during the vehicle's first official demonstration, at Milford on 12 June 1942. (General Motors)

Below: Sixty-five GMC builders and designers embark on the vehicle and go for a water ride during the preliminary trials of the first pilot DUKW. The men constituted a heavy load, and the water came up to the top rub rail, but they enjoyed a safe and successful ride. (General Motors)

The propeller tunnel of the first pilot DUKW is observed from the rear with the propeller removed. The propeller tunnel was designed to be as high as possible without raising its outlet above the waterline when the vehicle was unloaded, since air could then reach the propeller when operating in reverse, severely diminishing thrust. (General Motors)

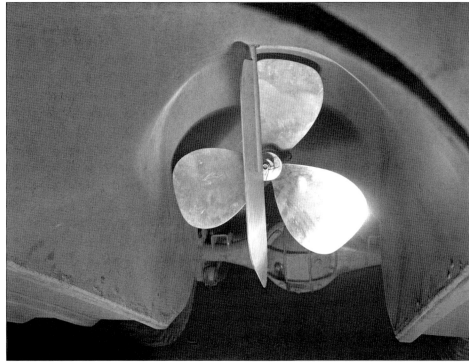

Nestled within the propeller tunnel, as viewed from the rear of the first pilot DUKW, are the rudder and the marine propeller. In the background is the rear tandem axle. The propeller tunnel underwent several design changes to improve performance; this version featured flat, vertical sides. (General Motors)

After initial tests of the DUKW, the propeller tunnel was redesigned. Now, the middle section of the tunnel flares out at the bottom, for increased speed, and the rear of the tunnel has been opened up somewhat, for better maneuverability. As a downside, the propeller now is more vulnerable to damage. The final design of the tunnel is shown here. (General Motors)

Chapter 5
Journey To The Coast

In this instance, the "future" proved to be the next day, Saturday the 13th, when the Army called and advised that the tests in Virginia were scheduled to begin on Tuesday the 16th. To meet this schedule the team set out for Washington, leaving Pontiac at noon on Sunday, stopping in Pittsburgh for the evening at 10 p.m. The journey was resumed at 10 a.m. Monday morning, and the team arreived without incident in Washington at 6 p.m.

The demonstrations began the next day at nearby Fort Belvoir, just as scheduled, with the DUKW carrying 6,000-pounds in and out of the water, up steep embankments and over moderate land courses. The successful demonstration served to fuel the desire for a surf test. Until such tests could be scheduled, the DUKW would continue testing at Fort Belvoir. From the 17th through the 20th, the DUKW was trialed with fast, loaded entries into the water, and was also fitted with two 10-horsepower outboard motors to be tested at Virginia Beach.

Rod Stephens returned to Fort Belvoir on Sunday the 21st and tested the outboard setup in the lake there. The outboards seemed to have the effect of raising the speed from 5.3 m.p.h. to 6.1 m.p.h., although accurate measurement was impossible due to weeds choking the pond. At 3 p.m. Rod and the DUKW left for Virginia Beach with the temperature near 100° in the shade.

Despite the searing heat, road performance during the ride south was satisfactory and no engine overheating was observed, even though most of the trip was made at full throttle. The DUKW, with Rod at the wheel, arrived at Virginia Beach at 11 p.m.

Testing began at Fort Story the next morning. Choppy water conditions proved to be no obstacle at all for the DUKW, although on the beach the DUKW's movement was very slow in soft sand, and it even became mired in gravel along the edge of the beach while carrying an 8,000-pound cargo. These events pointed to the need for improved tires, an additional shovel in the on-vehicle equipment, and some form of a sand anchor, which would permit the DUKW to recover itself absent trees, other vehicles or large rocks to winch against. Further testing indicated that airing the tires down to about 15 pounds (vs. their 45-pound norm) made a dramatic improvement on the performance in sand. However this process, like the reinflation, was slow, in part because of the dual wheels. The DUKW had carried these wheels over from the 2½-ton AFKWX 6x6 truck on which they were standard. The observers of the tests were very impressed when the DUKW took to the sea with 75 troops aboard.

Tuesday morning, the 23rd, found the waters off Fort Story to be dead calm, disappointing everyone who wanted to subject the DUKW to a more rigorous test. For the day a second tire and wheel was mounted on each end of the front axle of the DUKW, resulting in dual 7.50-20 8-ply tires in each of the six positions on the vehicle. This modification, combined with reducing the tire pressure to 25

Seen here at its third official demonstration at Fort Story, Virginia, on 23 June 1942, the first pilot DUKW had already given its first official demonstration and then, a week before this photo was shot, it had given its second official demonstration at Fort Belvoir, Virginia, on 16 June.

Twenty civilians and officers of the various branches witnessed the demonstration at Fort Story, and all of them apparently are aboard the vehicle for a ride. Next to the DUKW is a prototype Ford GPA, the amphibious version of the Jeep, which, like the DUKW, was a design of Rod Stephens.

Left: During the third official demonstration of the DUKW, at Fort Story, the vehicle underwent its first troop-landing exercise. Here, as a GPA leads the way, most of the troops have already disembarked, while the last few are going over the side. Lacking a ramp, disembarking troops had to expose themselves to enemy fire in this manner.

Below: As the pilot DUKW comes ashore at Fort Story, Virginia, G.I.s leap overboard while others sweep inland. During this demonstration, the DUKW achieved a speed on the water of a paltry 5.3 miles per hour, causing concern in officials who witnessed the event.

Above: Embarked on the pilot DUKW is a complement of soldiers, participating in a landing demonstration. Attached to the cowl along the front of the driver's compartment is the driver's rear-view mirror. To the front of the cowl are a small spotlight and a siren.

Left: During trials of the first pilot DUKW at Fort Belvoir in June 1942, experiments were conducted with two Evinrude 10-horsepower outboard motors attached to the transom. They increased the speed of the vehicle by a little under one mile per hour Between the motors is the winch. Faintly visible above the tow pintle is the U.S. Army registration number, 4209658. This is the registration number of the AFKWX-353 upon which chassis this DUKW was built, incidentally the final registration number on its particular contract for 2172 of the cab-over-engine trucks.

pounds resulted in improved performance in the sand. The 25-pound air pressure was seen as a compromise between the optimum highway pressure of 45 pounds and the ideal pressure for sand, a lower 15 pounds.

Faced with the disappointing surf at Fort Story, the DUKW team then drove the vehicle, laden with a 3,000-pound cargo, with dual front wheels still inflated to 25 pounds, the 150 miles south to Kitty Hawk, North Carolina, in hopes of finding more challenging seas. The team found the seas there no more challenging than those in Virginia, but drove to the Bodie Island Coast Guard Station where they lowered the tire pressure further to 15 pounds and demonstrated the DUKW for the Coast Guard personnel present.

On 24 June 1942 the test team got a chance to gauge the first pilot DUKW's performance in heavy surf, at Kitty Hawk, North Carolina. The vehicle prepares to enter the water. Conditions included a brisk breeze out of the northeast and a three-mile-per-hour current running south along the beach.

A handful of men, including Rod Stephens and some photographers, opted to keep the DUKW at Kitty Hawk overnight, and the next morning awoke to a hard breeze and very rough surf. The hasty decision to go south from Fort Story the day prior had resulted in the DUKW's custom fitted cargo and cab covers having been left at the Virginia installation. An expedient cover for the cargo area was rigged, and the DUKW was taken into the boiling sea.

Entering the ocean, the pilot DUKW's poor left turn ability resurfaced, causing the bow to swing to the right until the truck/boat was broadside to the crashing waves. The sea entered the cab and engine compartment, wetting the engine's ignition system, causing the engine, which not only drove the vehicle but also the bilge pumps, to stall – and resist efforts to restart. The pounding waves drove the hapless DUKW and her crew broadside onto the beach. All of this was dramatically and dutifully captured on film by the assigned photographers. While this failure dramatically demonstrated the need for a water-shielded ignition system and improved engine compartment sealing, it no less dramatically demonstrated the rough water ability and stability of the basic hull design – attributes that later would save the lives of thousands of men.

Once the vehicle came to rest, the crew dried the ignition and restarted the engine – only to find that the vehicle, still burdened with its 3,000 pounds of cargo, could not negotiate the sand crest without the use of the winch. Rod Stephens, in his report on this event, stated that this pointed to the need for:

(A) Sand Anchor
(B) Better Tires for Sand
(C) More power and speed on beach

All of these attributes would be found in time in the production vehicles.

The first pilot DUKW approaches the beach at Kitty Hawk on 24 June 1942 among high waves. Procedure for coming ashore called for the driver to engage all of the wheels while still outside of the surf and to approach the shore at right angles to the waves.

The pilot DUKW braves a heavy surf at Kitty Hawk on 24 June 1942. The vehicle was carrying a load of 3,000 pounds and was fitted with a makeshift canvas cover for its cargo compartment. The vehicle would soon encounter trouble.

Right: Heavy seas and current, wind, and poor left steering capability caused the DUKW to turn broadside to the waves, which swamped the driver's compartment and doused the distributor, causing the engine to stall. The vehicle came to rest on shore in this position.

Below: Despite the rather ignominious end of the demonstration at Kitty Hawk, the test run was considered a success, since it was felt that the DUKW handled the surf and current well enough. The report summarizing this demonstration called for modifications to the steering system and better shielding for the engine.

Chapter 6
A Move Toward Standardization

Following the experiences at Kitty Hawk, the Army immediately ordered the DUKW driven back to Pontiac for modification, and for use as a guide in the production of four additional pilot models.

Based on the tests conducted up to that point, Sparkman & Stephens revised the hull design (the base hull design of the DUKW was #434) and the Stevens Institute completed a new model in conformity with the revised lines. The revised hull, which was to be ready for tank testing on 1 July, incorporated a stern that was 18 inches longer, a flatter bow, altered front-wheel cutouts, and the addition of cover plates over the front wheel cutouts. Rod Stephens had estimated that these changes would raise the top water speed to 6½ miles per hour, thereby securing the Army's agreement to abandon ideas about adding outboard motors and other engine possibilities.

At the same time the engine from pilot #1 was removed and tested on a dynamometer. It was found to be low on power, in part due to incorrect valve settings. The settings were corrected, the updraft carburetor was replaced with the downdraft carburetor found on a CCKW, and the fan was replaced. Once reinstalled in the DUKW, the engine improvements resulted in a .38 m.p.h. increase in water speed.

On 31 July General Barnes inspected the original pilot, with its revised stern, at the GM Proving Ground, with Somervell doing the same the following day.

During the same time period, construction of pilots numbers 2, 3, and 4 were progressing rapidly, while assembly of the 5th pilot being held back. It was to serve as the production pilot, with components being production parts rather than the hand-crafted fabrication of the earlier models. Concurrently, the decision was made that the DUKW should be based upon the standard, conventional-cab CCKW rather than the cab-over-engine model AFKWX employed to build pilot number 1.

There were four major reasons for this change:

A – it offered better engine and steering gear accessibility,

B – it allowed use of a downdraft carburetor, with its improvement in power,

C – it facilitated making the engine compartment more watertight,

D – it allowed for far greater production, since the CCKW was the Army standard, while the AFKWX, which was also a standard, was a much more limited production model.

A method for shielding the ignition shielding was worked out, thereby not only solving the drowned ignition issue experienced at Kitty Hawk, but also providing radio suppression for the engine. Improved brake linings were located and employed, improving the DUKWs stopping ability after immersion. Important from a logistics standpoint, the cargo area of the DUKW was reconfigured into a single large space.

The GMC model CCKW was the U.S. Army's standard 2½ 6x6 truck during WWII. Versatile, agile, and reliable, the CCKW was used in every theater during the war, and was produced in large quantities. The decision to base the DUKW on the CCKW was a natural one, not only in terms of logistical support, but also the conventional, engine-ahead design was easier to maintain and provided a performance advantage over the AFKWX used as the basis for the first prototype. (General Motors)

After it was found that the first pilot DUKW's 7.50-20 tires (dual on the tandem axles and single on the front) gave very poor performance on sand, experiments were conducted, using CCKWs, to find better tires for DUKWs. One type tried was the General 38-inch Air Cat tire, as fitted to the CCKW in the foreground.

The DUKW underwent extensive water tests, with over 500 runs being conducted between 2 June and 31 August. The refinements that grew out of these tests resulted in a 25% increase in speed and a 75% reduction in turning radius. A part of these tests pointed to the use of a 3-blade 25-inch Federal Mogul weedless propeller, which provided a 6½ m.p.h. loaded speed with the engine turning 2,550 r.p.m., 200 r.p.m. below the governed maximum of a standard CCKW.

Consideration was given during to dividing the DUKW hull into 12 watertight compartments in order to provide some protection from flooding that might be caused by enemy gunfire. A design of this arrangement was prepared by Sparkman & Stephens, but was discarded after consideration was given to the additional weight that would be added, the difficulty that the compartments would present for routine maintenance, and the delays that such a change would entail in the production of the vehicle.

While considerable attention was given to the DUKW's water performance, equal attention was devoted to its land performance, particularly its performance in soft sand.

A test site with ample sand and dunes of various slopes was located

Above: The 38-inch Air Cats, seen on a test CCKW, were mounted on all axles as singles. In July 1942, four CCKWs were tested at Oxford, Michigan, using five types of tires. The Air Cats provided the best sand performance but were not chosen because of several faults.

Left: In tests at Oxford and later at Provincetown, Massachusetts, in November 1942, 11.00-18 8-ply desert-tread tires were selected as the best choice for the DUKW. Here, Goodrich Silvertown 11.00-18 8-ply desert-tread tires are mounted on the first pilot. For production, 11.00-18 10-ply desert-tread tires were the standard.

The tire tests at Oxford established that the pressure of the DUKW tires would have to be set at a minimum of 10 psi on sand and the standard 40 psi on roads. This doctrine proved to be sound, as later it was necessary to make small changes to these standards only as vehicle weights increased. (General Motors)

in Oxford, Michigan. To replicate the DUKW's ground performance, four CCKWs were used, their engines tuned to DUKW standards and the trucks loaded to equal the weight distribution of the DUKW.

Valuable guidance was provided by Dick Kerr, transportation specialist for California-Arabian Standard Oil Company. According to Rod Stephens, in his unpublished autobiographical manuscript held in the collection of Mystic Seaport, it was Kerr who suggested that larger single tires be used instead of the dual tires used on the first pilot DUKW and as standard on the CCKW.

Kerr, a geologist and pilot, had been hired by Standard Oil of California in the 1930s to make a survey of Saudi Arabia. Originally using large low-pressure tires on his plane when operating in the desert, Kerr continued to experiment with low-pressure tires, including ground use on ground vehicles. From 1934 the California-Arabian Standard Oil Company had been using 9.00-18 low-pressure tires on its sand-dune riding trucks.

At the Oxford tests dual 7.50-20 tires were further tested, as were 8.25-20 duals, 10.00-20 singles and 38-inch Air Cats, as well as 11.00-18 single tires. The 11.00-18 single tires were selected as offering the best off-and-on road performance. The larger single tires were only one part of the solution, lower tire pressure on sand being the other part. However, lightly inflated tires when operated on-road have a short life, with both tread wear and tire overheating being a problem. Off road, when lightly inflated, steel wheels tend to slip inside the tire proper, and with the optimal tire pressure of the 11.00-18 tires of the DUKW on sand being 12 psi, the Goodyear "L" series wheel was selected for use on the first 400 vehicles. This wheel was felt to provide a firm grip between the rim and the tire bead. Beyond those vehicles, the Firestone CV800 combat wheel would be available for use. Combat wheels feature an inner steel band that firmly clamps the tire bead to the rim.

Hartley Rowe, chief of NDRC's Division 12, requested that Rod Stephens and the #1 DUKW pilot be present at landing maneuvers at Solomons Island, Maryland, at the confluence of the Patuxent River and Chesapeake Bay, on 25 August. Once again the DUKW made the run from Michigan to the East Coast over a two-day period, leaving Michigan on the 23rd and arriving in Washington at 3:30 PM on the 24th. Despite the successful trip east, the Stephens noted in a report filed on 12 September 1942: "The demonstration was disappointing as

Crews of early DUKWs had to deflate the tires manually to get better flotation on sand, or refill the tires using air hoses preparatory to operating on hard surfaces. These time-consuming, tedious processes were often neglected, resulting in DUKWs mired in sand due to too high air pressure, or wearing out tires prematurely as a result of too low pressure for on-the-road operation. The drawings show a tire's profile (top) and its footprint (bottom) at 12 psi (right), for operation on sand, and at 40 psi (left), for operation on hard surfaces. (General Motors)

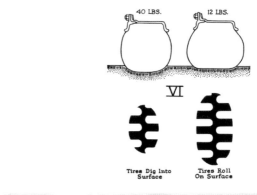

VI

Tires Dig Into Surface — Tires Roll On Surface

To speed up the original process of varying the tire pressure using the vehicle's onboard air compressor, hose, and tire gauge, experiments were conducted with a central tire-inflation system (CTIS). An early CTIS rig is shown in the photo to the left, while on the right is a proposed two-line CTIS, with separate air lines for inflation and deflation and a wire-actuated valve-in-stem. (General Motors)

The CTIS would become standard with DUKWs starting with serial number 2000. The driver operated the system using a control panel to the right of the steering wheel. This example appears to be a pre-production or early type with an air-pressure gauge and an inflation/deflation switch. (General Motors)

To inflate the tires, the CTIS included a Midland Steel Products tire pump, located forward of the engine. It was a two-cylinder, water-cooled, self-lubricating unit fitted with a governor. Also in view is the engine muffler and, behind the pump, the engine radiator. (General Motors)

we were given no definite assignment, and the observation group was too large to accomplish anything effectively. We did satisfy ourselves that we had made enormous strides from the late June demonstration in Virginia. The 11.00/18 (sic) tires and increased engine performance gave greatly improved sand performance while the water speed and maneuverability were fine."

As the other pilot vehicles were completed by Yellow Truck and Coach, they too began to be used in tests. The first of these was pilot number 3, which was delivered to Camp Edwards, on Cape Cod in Massachusetts on 11 September 1942. The Engineer Amphibian Command had activated at Camp Edwards on 10 June 1942, after Lt. General Somervell had assigned the amphibious training program to the Corps of Engineers.

Pilot number 3 stayed at Camp Edwards for three weeks, under the command of Colonel Walter D. Luplow of the Development Section, who placed Captain James Mueller in charge of the testing operation. On 28 September Palmer C. Putnam and Rod Stephens ventured to Camp Edwards intent on getting movies of the DUKW in operations in the surf. They were joined on this quest by Mueller and Lt. Bliss. While the calm sea prevented the capture of the desired motion pictures, the operation again pointed to the need for a tire pump. The need for a device to start the engine by hand from aboard a floating DUKW was also made apparent when the battery ran down (fortunately ashore) due to a loose connection.

General Devers' objective of landing tanks had not been forgotten; it was planned to test the ferry gear with pilots 1 and 4 on 1 September.

On 11 September 1942 the third pilot DUKW was delivered to Camp Edwards, Massachusetts. Five days later at that base, the camouflage-painted vehicle was demonstrated to some 100 officers at Beach K, near Waquoit.

The third pilot DUKW motors through a moderate chop during the demonstration of 16 September 1942. In the camouflage scheme, the light color that prevails was cut in around the draft marks near the bow and near the stern, so that the white draft marks contrast markedly with the dark original overall color of the vehicle. (General Motors)

Above: The third pilot DUKW cuts through light waves off Camp Edwards on 16 September 1942. This pilot was configured to the standards of the production DUKW and was the first pilot to include 8-ply, military desert-type 11.00-18 tires and a sand anchor, for securing the vehicle to a beach.

Right: The demonstration of the third pilot DUKW at Camp Edwards was considered highly successful, and the officers who witnessed the DUKW as it was put through its paces volunteered many positive and enthusiastic comments about this novel vehicle.

During the 16 September 1942 demonstration of pilot three at Camp Edwards, the DUKW was able to drive over the steep sand dunes along Beach K with relative ease, to the gratification of the test team. The third pilot conducted further operations at Camp Edwards through the remainder of September.

Chapter 7
The Cusp Of Mass Production

Even before pilots 2, 3, and 4 had been completed, production orders for DUKWs were being placed.

On 25 June 1942, Col. McAuliffe, on behalf of the the Quartermaster Corps, requested delivery of 600 DUKWs by 31 December, and a further 1,400 by March 1943, incorporating the changes dictated by the testing of the pilot.

At Yellow Truck and Coach, a meeting convened in the Conference Room on 29 June 1942 to determine just how the requested vehicles could be produced – especially given that the company was already overwhelmed with orders for CCKW cargo trucks – orders that were taxing its production capacity. Beyond the confines of GM, the war effort was consuming all available axles, radiators, and that most basic of all automobile components – steel.

The strategy set forth in this meeting would be that Engineering would build pilots 2 through 5 as Project 1042-28, and the remaining 1996 vehicles would be built from production, at a rate of 200 per month in October, November, and December, satisfying the immediate demand for 600 vehicles. A further 400 would be built in January, 500 in February, and the balance of the 2,000-vehicle order in March 1943. An additional four vehicles were added to the order on 7 August, making the total 2,004.

In order to supply the materials for these vehicles, it was decided to postpone production of a quantity of 6x6 trucks on contract W-398-QM-11595 to yield the needed driveline components, including the Chevrolet High Traction Axles. Construction of a number of buses was also set back so that some of the steel slated for their use could instead be turned into DUKWs, and so that labor and production line space might be freed up for the new vehicles. Additionally, the shortage of rolling capacity in the nation's steel mills would require GM to purchase stock sizes from warehouses and sheer the material itself, rather than following the customary, and more economical, procedure of buying the material rolled to the needed width.

Yellow Truck and Coach executives drafted Sales Order TC-200445 to cover the second pilot, TC-200446 to cover the third, TC-200447 to cover the fourth, and TC-200448 to cover the fifth pilot, which was to be the production pilot. The remaining 596 DUKWs of McAuliffe's 600-vehicle request were built on TC-200449, while TC-200450 would cover the rest of the initial order. The total value of these sales orders was $13,828,473.22.

Not quite a month later, on 24 July 1942, another meeting was held regarding this production program. At that time the DUKW assembly department was designated Number 29. Engineers set out to revise the layout of Plant 2 in Yellow's Pontiac, Michigan, complex to provide space for the DUKW line, yet still permit one assembly line to continue to build one model of bus, primarily for defense use. Particular emphasis was placed on clearing floor space by 1 September.

The decision was made to produce 10 sets of DUKW component parts from raw material that was in the Yellow plant, or easily obtainable,

A DUKW thought to have been the fourth pilot vehicle is fitted with a ring mount for a machine gun, as well as a tarpaulin and a driver's compartment cover. The standard machine-gun ring mount eventually adopted for the DUKW was considerably higher. (General Motors)

The same vehicle in the preceding photograph is viewed from the aft port quarter. A tail-light assembly and guard is on the rear deck to each side of the winch. Below the winch is a tow pintle. Round reflectors are on the rear corners of the hull. Draft marks are painted on the hull, indicating this DUKW's status as a test vehicle. (General Motors)

The same DUKW is viewed from in front of its bow. Now on the front deck, rearranged since the first pilot, are, front to rear, a rigid surfboard mounted on a piano hinge, replacing the early, flimsy one; the front deck hatch; and the engine access hatch. On the starboard side of the deck is a hand-operated bilge pump; this would become a standard fixture on all DUKWs. (General Motors)

The DUKW believed to have been the fourth pilot is observed from astern. On the rear deck is a spare tire and a Danforth anchor. Part of the marine propeller is visible in the propeller tunnel. Early DUKWs had propellers of malleable iron; after about chassis 2000, the propellers were bronze. (General Motors)

and to create one set of assembly jigs with which production could begin. These measures would be followed with additional tooling in order to increase production capacity.

By 6 August, work was advancing in earnest toward getting the DUKW into production. The Quartermaster Corps contract for the 2,000 vehicles had been issued (W-2425-QM-234) and assigned a preference rating of AA1. An AA1 rating was the normal top priority rating, exceeded only by AAA – which was the emergency priority rating. To put this in perspective, the Manhattan District's atom bomb development (also under the NDRC's Dr. Bush at this time) carried an AA3 rating, two steps below the DUKW, until 1 July 1944, when it was finally upgraded to AA1, at last on par with the DUKW.

The standard antiaircraft machine gun mount for the DUKW was this M36 ring mount, consisting of a M49 ring, D40721 pintle socket and carriage assembly, an M2 HB .50 caliber machine gun and either the square D40731 tray, used on early models, or the D90078 tray, shown here. The ring mount shown in the first photo in this chapter is an experimental lightweight mount that GM developed in part due to the shortages of this mount, and in part to reduce the weight of the DUKW. (Rock Island Arsenal Museum)

The vehicle thought to have been the fourth pilot DUKW is observed from the starboard side. It is rigged with a line and snatch block attached to a tree, most likely to test the winch's capacity to self-recover the vehicle in certain scenarios. (General Motors)

The fourth pilot DUKW is viewed from above with no deck panels installed in the cargo compartment, allowing a view of the chassis frame, tandem wheel-house tops, and drive shafts. The shaft powering the winch is on the inboard side of the port main frame member. (General Motors)

Chapter 8
DUKW-Based Ferries

The need to move tanks from ship to shore was one of the driving forces in the procurement of the DUKW, as outlined in Chapter 3. In fact, one of the first wartime projects contracted to Sparkman & Stephens had been the development of plywood floats that would permit tanks to be floated to shore. Early on, the potential for the DUKW to do a superior job of this had been seen, and work on the floats came to an early halt.

In time, two types of ferry system were developed for the DUKW. The original system, referred to as a wet-ferry system, took its name from its use of the displacement of the ferried load itself to help get the tank to the shore.

In this system, the tank – which initially was an M3 light tank – was suspended between two DUKWs, the lower portion of the tank submerged. Submersion of part of the tank, of course necessitated that the wetter portion of the tank hull be sealed watertight. Like a child's helium balloon that, when weighted down, sinks to the earth, despite its natural tendency to float, the sealed tank also tries, but fails, to float. If a little of the ballast weighting down the child's balloon is removed, it will float away, so too if enough of the load on the would-be floating tank is taken away, it too will float. The DUKWs on either side of the tank provided sufficient additional buoyancy to enable the tank to float. This example is a bit of oversimplification, for in reality, it is the DUKWs that are providing the bulk of the floatation, with the tank itself providing a little extra lift.

Compression members at the deck level of the DUKWs and tension cables near low points on the DUKW hull keep the DUKWs upright on either side of the tank. The tank's treads are the low point of the ungainly looking trio, meaning that as shore is approached, they make contact first, ultimately taking the load completely off the DUKW.

GM engineers led by Charles O. Ball devised the ferry apparatus, which was first demonstrated on GM's Proving Ground at Sloan Lake on 1 September 1942. DUKWs No. 1 and 4 were used in the test, which established a hook-up time of seven minutes for the tank and ferry apparatus, with an unhook time of about half that.

Initial tests indicated that the system would be improved if there were an additional free space of about six inches between the side of the tank and the side of the DUKWs. The tests also indicated that the standard rope bumpers were inadequate for this use.

The equipment was modified as indicated, and on 3 September was tested again. These tests, which reduced connect/disconnect time by about 30%, were witnessed by representatives of the British Purchasing Commission. Further modifications were made, and two days later the system was demonstrated for Olin J. Stephens II. At that time the hook up time was recorded as four minutes, with unhooking being accomplished in two minutes.

At last on 7 September the wet-ferry arrangement for the light tank was demonstrated for the NDRC's Palmer C. Putnam as well as various Army officers. By this time the hookup time had been cut to 1 minute 30 seconds, with the unhook time a remarkable 40 seconds. By the standards by which this project began, it was a success.

On 21 September 1942, DUKW pilots 1 and 4 conducted their first successful tests of the wet-ferrying process at Sloan Lake at the General Motors' Milford Proving Ground. The concept was to couple a DUKW on each side of a tank, in this case an M3 light tank, and ferry it across water. (General Motors)

Above: Rod Stephens tests a tension cable between the DUKWs during wet-ferrying tests. He is leaning over a compression strut, or spreader bar, that joins the bows of pilots 1, right, and 4, left. Between the vehicles is the M3 light tank. Sealing of the tank was a problem during the tests, and a hose from a bilge pump has been inserted in the turret hatch. (General Motors)

Left: Pilots 1 and 4 are coupled to the M3 light tank during wet-ferrying tests at Sloan Lake. The drivers of both vehicles are looking to the rear, probably an indication that they were in the process of backing the wet-ferrying rig into the water. (General Motors)

The pilot DUKWs are being coupled to the M3 light tank in Sloan Lake. The round pipes on each side of the vehicles are air intakes. The rectangular "box" on the stern of the M3 is for exhaust and exhaust air from the motor and cooling fan. During the first test on 1 September, hook-up time was seven minutes, and disconnecting time was about half of that. (General Motors)

45

The Army, however, seemed concerned about sealing the tank – in Rod Stephens's opinion, unduly concerned. Worse, by this time U.S. light tanks were being seen increasingly as inadequate on the world battlefield, and so the army in essence changed the rules, directing the team to develop a similar system with which to transport a medium tank – the M4 Sherman series of vehicles. Further, they also wanted a "dry ferry" system for moving tactical vehicles such as trucks to shore – and while they were at it, work out a system to utilize the DUKW as a pontoon for bridging operations. Coincidentally, it was Sparkman & Stephens that had designed the Army Engineers deck-balk pontoon bridge system.

The next day, 8 September, the light tank wet-ferry system gave one more demonstration, this time for Major Frank Besson of the Engineer Board. Besson, who gained fame as the father of Pierced Steel Planking (PSP) which was widely used to create expedient air fields, and after WWII commanded the U.S. Army Transportation Center and School at Fort Eustis and pioneered development of the later LARC and BARC amphibians.

As directed, the engineers at General Motors set out to adapt the wet-ferry apparatus for use with the medium tank. The first test was at Sloan Lake on 18 September, when an M4A4 Sherman was successfully ferried. This rapid and successful work was credited in Rod Stephen's report to the NDRC to "much good work by Todd and the General Motors Truck Company." Once again, the paperwork was slow to catch up to the reality of the work being done on this project, and on 2 October Yellow Truck and Coach was issued a supplemental appropriation to cover the work on the ferry and bridge pontoon apparatus.

However, floating a medium tank, which weighed almost twice as much as a light tank, meant that reserve buoyancy was dangerously low, and freeboard was at a minimum.

Once the wet-ferry problem had been addressed, attention was turned to fulfilling the dry ferry directive. The days 1 through 9

October were spent working on dry ferry gear. The first system tried was a continuous gutter with detachable ramp at the stern. This tested 2-4 October, then it was rebuilt into a teeter ramp. This ramp pivoted at the center of buoyancy of the DUKW, an arrangement that leant itself to increased carrying capacity since the load was applied to the DUKWs at an optimum point, rather than trying to force the stern underwater as had the original arrangement. With the teeter ramp, the cargo vehicle was driven up the ramp from a position ahead of the DUKWs, and as the vehicle crossed the pivot point, the ramp tilted to a level position, usually with a substantial and undesirable impact. This system was successfully tested on 9 October with 16,000-lb CCKW; 28,000-lb light tank; and 29,000-lb Staghound armored car.

It was this ramp/ferry arrangement that was demonstrated on 10 October to the Army and Hartley Rowe, chief of NDRC Division 12. Following that demonstration, on 13 October the Army requested that the final 1,400 of the 2,000 DUKWs then on order be reinforced for dry ferry – there was not enough time to secure the materials and make this addition to the initial urgent 600 vehicle order.

Charles Ball and the DUKW engineering team were not content to rest with the teeter ramp, and spent the 10 days following October 10 redesigning the dry ferry into something of a compromise between the initial fixed ferry and the later teeter ramp. In this, the ultimate dry ferry arrangement, the rear portion of the ferry treadways were fixed, while the portion from the center of buoyancy forward was hinged and dropped for loading. Wire rope was rigged from the DUKWs' rear-mounted winches forward to be used to raise and lower the forward treadways. This resolved the problem of the teeter ramp slamming down, and retained the near optimal loading forces on the DUKWs as the cargo vehicles were driven aboard.

With the system developed with pilots 1 and 4, pilots 2 and 3 were also modified to utilize the ferry gear, and a second set of such gear was fabricated. All that remained was to test the wet and dry ferry gear in the ocean surf.

Final preparations are underway for testing the wet-ferrying process at Sloan Lake. One recommendation of the first test was to increase the clearance between the two DUKWs by six inches. Also, the test crew recommended that the DUKWs be fitted with larger rope bumpers. (General Motors)

Above: Although wet-ferrying tests of the light tank were a success, the army's real interest was in seeking ways to ferry its burgeoning inventory of medium tanks across water. On 18 September 1942, DUKW pilots 1 and 2 successfully wet-ferried an M4A4 medium tank across Sloan Lake at the Milford Proving Ground. (General Motors)

Left: DUKW pilots 1 and 4 move into position on each side of the M4 medium tank during a wet-ferrying test at Sloan Lake. For these tests, a coupling rig similar to that recently used on the M3 light tank was developed, but it was stronger in construction. (General Motors)

Below: The fourth DUKW pilot vehicle is configured for a vehicular ferrying rig, with four sets of couplings on the top edge of the hull and wooden planks attached horizontally to the side of the hull for bumpers. (TACOM LCMC History Office)

Once the wet-ferrying concept was proved, in early October 1942 means were developed to dry-ferry vehicles using two DUKWs linked together in catamaran fashion, with a cargo platform between them. Several rigs were tested; on this one, comprising two gutter platforms, a 6x6 cargo truck has been embarked. What appears to be an observation platform is on cargo bed of the truck. (TACOM LCMC History Office)

Right: The dry-ferrying rig shown in the preceding photo is observed from the front. Small numbers on the bows of the DUKWs indicate that pilot 4 is to the left and pilot 1 is to the right. (General Motors)

Below: With no truck aboard, clear details of the dry-ferrying rig at Sloan Lake are visible. The platform consisted of two gutters mounted on three cross struts, which both supported the gutters and joined the DUKWs catamaran style. Below the cross struts, vertical struts and tension wires added rigidity. (General Motors)

The dry-ferry rig is viewed from ahead. The extension of the gutter platforms to the front were hinged so they could be dropped down to serve as loading ramps for the vehicle to be ferried. When the rig was being operated on water, the ramps were raised, as seen here. (General Motors)

The platform ramps are lowered on the dry-ferry rig. Two parallel strips of a material with fore-and-aft grooves, probably a non-slip material, are fastened to the ramps. To the left is pilot vehicle 4, and to the right is pilot vehicle 1. (General Motors)

The dry-ferry rig is viewed from directly ahead. The extension of the gutter platforms to the front were hinged so they could be dropped down to serve as loading ramps for the vehicle to be ferried. When the rig was being operated on water, the ramps were raised, as seen here. (General Motors)

49

Chapter 9
The First 1,000

The mass production of any item – especially one as complex and unique as the DUKW – is a much more involved process than it might seem at first glance.

The manufacturing facility, in this case Yellow Truck and Coach's Plant 2 in Pontiac, Michigan, does not take in raw iron ore, silica, and rubber on one end, and push completed vehicles out the other end.

Rather, sheet steel of specific thicknesses (gauges), widths, and lengths are brought in, tires, in set quantities and sizes, steel wheels upon which to mount those tires, speedometers, volt meters, axles, engines, transmissions – the thousands of components that that make up each individual – must be purchased. And, of course, money and space are also factored in, and these materials must be scheduled to arrive so that they are available when needed on the production line, but not so early as to overwhelm the plant's storage capacity, nor eat up too much capital while collecting dust in a warehouse.

The production rate itself carefully considers economics. Skilled labor is required to produce the vehicles – a labor pool that had to be guarded carefully, especially during wartime. If production is too fast, then the workers run out of work before the government can approve the next order, or before the next shipment of critically limiting components, such as axles, can arrive.

If vehicles can not be produced, whether it be because of a lack of military authorization or as a result of outstripping the supply of a component, there is no need for a factory full of workers. If workers find themselves subject to frequent layoff, they find work elsewhere, meaning when the next order does arrive – the plant has no labor force with which to construct the vehicles.

Of course, before any of this begins to happen, tools, fixtures

The first production order of DUKWs was for 1,000 vehicles. Seen here is one of those DUKWs. The vertical windshield would soon prove to be a liability, as it was vulnerable to heavy waves. In June 1943, after chassis 2006, an improved, sloping windshield would be installed at the factory. (General Motors)

On DUKWs the spare tire was stored on the port side of the aft deck. Later, after chassis 2006, the spare tire would be repositioned on the starboard side of the aft deck. Alongside the driver's compartment, the cowl forms a sort of shroud over the port warm-air outlet, protecting the outlet and its door from waves. (General Motors)

and patterns must be created, and assembly lines set up, not only for the DUKWs themselves, but for the myriad of subassemblies and components – not only in the Yellow Plant, but also those previously mentioned subcontractors – bilge pumps, transfer cases, wheels, and propellers.

Added onto all of this are the spare parts – not only the field service spare parts, which sometimes the government orders on the same contract as the vehicles, and at other times orders as separate purchases, but also a sufficient number of spares to cover loss and damage during the manufacturing process. It is inevitable that there will be a certain amount of loss – parts will be dropped and broken, crushed, or otherwise damaged. In order to keep the assembly lines moving, and moving economically, a sufficient amount of spares must be available to cover these possibilities – spares that can only be ordered economically at the same time as the basic production parts order. Too many spares for these possibilities are wasteful – too few risks halting production.

For normal civilian production, Yellow could draw on its vast experience, as well as its ongoing sales through its dealer network. Service parts were ordered at the same time as production parts, and if the assembly line damaged or lost something, the Service department "sold" the needed parts to Production.

The DUKW, being a wholly new type of vehicle, meant that there was little historical data to aid in this. The directive issued within GM regarding this was as follows – major purchased units were to be ordered to meet actual requirements, small parts were to be ordered with an excess not to exceed 5 to 15 sets. Purchased parts which are ordered rough, to be finished by Yellow Truck and Coach, are to be ordered with 10 to 25 sets surplus, in order to allow for scrap and loss when finishing. Forgings were particularly difficult to obtain outside of actual production orders, and so the quantity of spares to be ordered was to be governed by the size of the forging and the quantity used per vehicle.

Even as Yellow Truck and Coach was preparing to build Tony McAuliffe's rush order for 600 DUKWs, on 22 August 1942 Captain Nail from Col. Van Deusen's office with the Quartermaster General called Yellow's A.A. Dodd with a question. The question was, in the event the current order for 2,004 DUKWs was increased, how many of the amphibians could Yellow produce working three shifts per day?

Roger J. Emmert, Yellow's vice-president factory manager, provided the answer, which was six trucks per shift, or 18 per day, equivalent to about 500 per month. The 28 August memorandum that detailed this quantity also revealed that assembly line production of the DUKW was expected to begin in late September or early October with a caveat – which was important. That was, "the freezing of the design as it now exists." The memo continued "Changes now being discussed, such as the use of these vehicles for handling heavy weights or for use as pontoon bridges should be introduced at a later point in production, or the contemplated production schedule will probably be set back an interval of time equal to the time taken to design changes and release new drawings."

Also as of 28 August there remained some problem areas in filling the initial 600 vehicle production run – specifically the steering gear, wheels, and tires. Saginaw was not going to be able to build steering gear off production tooling until 19 October, so it was decided that the first 10 production vehicles would have hand-made steering gear. Also, only Goodrich had molds capable of making the 11.00-18 tires for the DUKW, and they could only produce nine per day. U.S. Rubber was asked to tool up to make the DUKW tires as well.

To overcome a bottleneck with the production of the water propeller transfer case, 10 units of this item would have to be hand made as well.

A feature of early production DUKWs was an air-scoop door to the front of the cowl and immediately aft of the engine-access hatch on the forward deck. It is seen in the raised position here. The early-type unreinforced surf board mounted on a piano hinge is at the front of the forward deck. (General Motors)

This photo and the following series document the assembly of DUKWs under the first production contract for 1,000 vehicles at the old Coach Assembly Department at the GMC Truck & Coach Division, Pontiac, Michigan. Here, the two front wheel houses are secured to a drive-line tunnel-assembly jig, and a section containing the forward and rear drive-shaft tunnels is being lowered in place. (General Motors)

Clamped to a center-floor assembly jig are the two tandem wheel houses, with the propeller tunnel and the stern of the hull taking shape to the rear of the wheel houses. Intensive use was made of jigs, temporary braces, and various types of clamps in building the subassemblies. (General Motors)

By 2 October 1942 the 6th production hull was moving down the assembly line. The Chevrolet axles used on the DUKW, while looking like those used on CCKWs with Chevrolet axles, sometimes called "Corporation" or "Banjo" (due to their shape) axles, actually incorporated special seals and brake shoes. Proper DUKW axles were not yet available, so the assembly line was using CCKW axles to support the vehicles as they moved along the line, intent on replacing those axles with actual DUKW axles after the vehicles were completed. In a similar manner, the DUKW wheels had not yet arrived, and again CCKW components were temporarily borrowed from the CCKW parts stockpile to keep the DUKW assembly line moving.

Five of the hand-made steering gears had arrived, but further delays in beginning steering-gear mass production meant that at least another 20 would be hand made, which were slated for arrival by the 15th. With machine-made steering gears now not expected until the 25th, plans were made to make more by hand.

The DUKW cab utilized a few components found on the open cab CCKW – parts that were in short supply. Accordingly, Yellow Truck planned to make those by hand until Chevrolet or Budd had enough production capacity in place to supply the DUKW assembly line.

It was apparent by this time that deliveries of the DUKW were slipping behind schedule. Coincidentally, on 13 October Yellow Truck and Coach advised the Army that should they want DUKWs beyond the 2,000 then on order, as had been suggested by Captain Nail in August, Yellow must have an order immediately if those vehicles were desired before 1 July 1943.

On Monday, 26 October 1942, Roger Emmert held a meeting concerning the DUKW program and how production was supposed to move forward. At that time the initial delivery date was revised to 14 November. One of the items bringing about the delay was the Woods power take off, delivery of which was then expected 1 November. The decision was made to continue moving the vehicles down the assembly line and add the power take off after the vehicle was completed.

Another critical item was the transfer case, and Plant One had worked over the weekend, creating improvised tooling so that assembly could begin on the 27th, with the first six transfer cases moving to Plant Two for assembly into vehicles on Wednesday. Also short in supply was the malleable iron strut which would hold the water propeller shaft. Later in the day on the 26 October, 12 of the struts arrived from Albion Malleable Iron Company. Of those 12, three were serviceable as is, the other nine having slight defects that Yellow hoped to repair. Malleable iron components for the DUKW, as well as the CCKW, would continue to be problematic throughout production.

By this time the long-awaited axles had begun to arrive, with 18

At a wide-assembly welding-operation jig, welders fabricate the outer skin for the port side of a DUKW hull. The curved bow section is to the left. In the foreground, in the right background, and on chain hoists at the top are hull-side subassemblies. (General Motors)

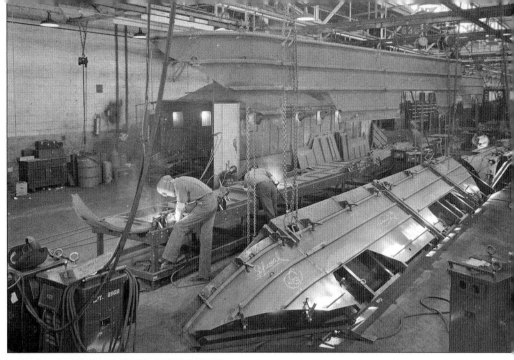

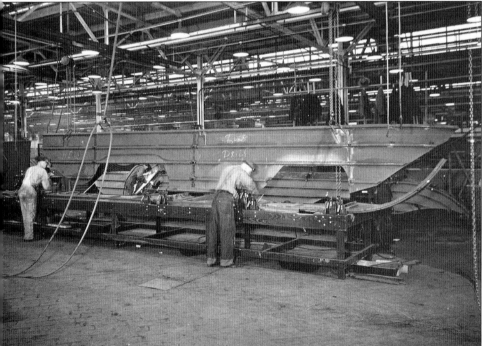

A starboard hull side is secured to the side-assembly finishing jig. The hat-channel rub rails have been welded in place, and several vertical joints in the hull panels are visible. The U-shaped lifting eyes have been welded to the top of the assembly, and serve as lifting points for the chain hoists. (General Motors)

In area 64H, GMC workmen are positioning a hull subassembly with wheel houses on a main framing jig. In the left background are several upended, nearly complete DUKW hulls. In the center background are some hull-bottom subassemblies. (General Motors)

53

At a main framing jig at GMC's Pontiac, Michigan, plant, with the stern of an under-construction hull in the foreground, workers are lowering into place a port side assembly. To the rear of the propeller tunnel, the tow pintle already has been installed. (General Motors)

Side panels of a DUKW are being attached to the bottom assembly, and workmen wearing face protection are using industrial spot welders to fasten the panels. Another welder is at work on top of the assembly in the background. (General Motors)

Several welders are at work inside a hull on a main framing jig, as viewed from the bow. Inside, the shapes of the wheel houses, the drive-shaft tunnels, and the propeller tunnel are visible. The inside of the skin is reinforced by vertical hat-section ribs. (General Motors)

A hull assembly is being lowered into the water test tank at GMC Truck & Coach Division, Pontiac. During this procedure, inspectors would check to see if there were any leaks in the joints. The water-test tank was empty when the hull was lowered into it. Water would then be pumped in to fill the tank and check for leaks. The frame that was temporarily attached to the front of the bow was engaged to an apparatus that held the hull down in the water to the fully loaded level. After the test was concluded, the water would be pumped out of the tank and the hull removed. (General Motors)

sets on hand and a further 125 sets to arrive during the week of the 26th, as were tires.

Tooling too continued to be a problem, with the missing critical tooling being those used to form the transfer case crossmember as well as the tooling for the combing. Authorization was given to work overtime and continue to fabricate not only these parts, but any parts required to complete the components for the first 200 vehicles. At the conclusion, the intent was to ship 50 DUKWs in November and 320 in December, just over 60% of what had been planned for back in August.

Shortages of materials were much broader than many believe looking retrospectively. An example is illustrated by the manner of shipping the DUKWs. Early on it was intended that the DUKWs be shipped in open rail cars, because it was felt their size would prevent them from being shipped inside a boxcar. (During this time frame, it was common practice to ship automobiles inside specially-equipped boxcars, some of which were loaded through the ends, and others through double doors in the sides. It would be the 1950s before the concept of hauling vehicles on multiple level flat cars, as is done now, came to the forefront.) The problem of shipping the DUKW on open cars, such as flat cars or inside gondola cars, was that the standards of the time required that the vehicles be covered with tarpaulins. Of course, virtually every US tactical vehicle being produced included a canvas duck cover, and duck was also used for the seat covers in almost every military vehicle. The result was that there was a nationwide shortage of canvas duck, which the government responded to by placing a freeze on the use of such material. Yellow Truck and Coach studied the situation and found a way that the DUKW could be loaded into a 40-boxcar, if done carefully by a skilled driver. In this way the initial DUKW shipments would be made.

In time, all these hurdles were overcome, and by 25 November 1942 production vehicles at last had begun to reach Provincetown, Massachusetts, the site selected by Palmer C. Putnam for further DUKW demonstrations and testing

A DUKW hull is in the water test tank, being checked for any leaks. If any were detected, they were noted and repaired before the vehicle proceeded down the assembly line. A "no loitering" sign on the rail around the tank warns that only designated employees were allowed in this area. (General Motors)

Welders work on the inside of the hull of a DUKW following its water test. The man to the left is holding an inspection light up to the hull and has a pencil in his right hand; he probably is checking for small openings in the hull that could admit water. (General Motors)

Two GMC employees use compressed air and liquid soap to check for leaks in the welded joints of a DUKW subassembly. An original notation on this photograph notes that it was an "obsolete soap test," indicating that a better method had been devised to check for small leaks. (General Motors)

Following a water test and the filling of any holes in the hull that could admit water, the chassis frame, viewed from the front end, is being lowered into the hull of a DUKW. The axle transfer case is already installed in the frame; the flange for the front drive shaft is visible below the frame. (General Motors)

A GMC workman is using a chain hoist to lower a DUKW hull onto the wheel, tire, and spring assemblies. Details of the front spring shackle and spring bracket are visible. The wheels are the Firestone CV 800 rims with side rings used on DUKWs after the 405th example. In the background, another worker is making adjustments to the tandem suspension. (General Motors)

Two men are welding the winch-cable eye to the center front of the hull, although the eye is not visible in this photo. This eye served as a guide for the winch cable when it was routed to the front of the vehicle. (General Motors)

Once the DUKW was nearly finished, it was subjected to another water-tank test to check for any remaining leaks. This example, being driven into the tank, has a type of surfboard for DUKWs with vertical windshields; released for production on 20 February 1943, it was installed on DUKWs before chassis 2007. When raised, it protected the windshield from battering by waves. Two round vision holes for the driver are in the surf board. (General Motors)

Another DUKW undergoes a water-tank test, whose purpose was to to test run the vehicle's propeller drive train. Every vehicle would undergo such a trial. This particular vehicle lacks the window surfboard seen in the preceding photo, but has the early-type unreinforced surfboard on the front of the forward deck. The front deck hatch is open, revealing the white interior. (General Motors)

Another nearly finished DUKW is in the water tank. This example features the late-type reinforced surfboard in addition to a vertical windshield and a windshield surfboard. A static test evidently is being conducted, with the propeller churning up water to the rear. (General Motors)

A DUKW in the water tank is viewed from aft. The churned-up water and the cable, secured to the tow pintle, holding the vehicle in place suggests that the propeller was being run in a static test. The tarpaulin is partially installed over the cargo compartment. (General Motors)

GMC mechanics make final adjustments to a DUKW before it leaves the Pontiac factory. The man to the left is working on the area under the rear deck, which has been removed. Next to this vehicle is a DUKW that appears to be completed, with the full tarpaulin and driver's compartment covers installed. (General Motors)

Left: A completed DUKW, one of the first 1,000 from the first contract for 2,000 vehicles, was photographed at Aberdeen Proving Ground, Maryland, on 10 March 1943. (General Motors)

Below: A soldier demonstrates the firing of a .50-caliber machine gun on the M36 ring mount on a DUKW at Aberdeen Proving Ground on 10 March 1943. The ring was situated quite high above the driver's compartment, but this allowed for easier use of the gun as an antiaircraft weapon. By 1945, the Table of Organization for Army DUKW companies specified 13 machine gun mounts and machine guns per 50-DUKW company. (General Motors)

Chapter 10
More Trials

With production of the DUKW well under way in Pontiac, training of DUKW crews got under way at Camp Edwards on Cape Cod. Yet still to be refined was the practical use of the amphibian and tactics regarding its use.

On 10 November 1942 pilots 1 and 4 and a detachment of Camp Edwards' Engineer Amphibian Command under Captain Friberg were dispatched from Camp Edwards at the southwestern base of Cape Cod Hook, 70 miles away to Provincetown, Massachusetts, located on the inner shore near the extreme northern end of the Cape.

Gradually over the next six days, seas up to six feet on the Atlantic side of Cape Cod Hook tested the surf ability of the DUKWs and their crews. Also tested was the sand performance of the DUKW. The sand in the Provincetown area was notable for its softness, but through trial and error it was found that 18 pounds of pressure in the 8-ply tires fitted to the pilots produced satisfactory results. Quicksand, however, was impassible by the DUKW regardless of tire pressure.

It was also during this period that one of the most useful and successful accessories for the DUKW was developed. Following a suggestion by NDRC Division 12 chief Hartley Rowe, a 5,000-pound capacity, stern-mounted A-frame was created. Utilizing the DUKW's rear-mounted winch as a source of lifting power, the A-frame rig allowed a DUKW to unload (or load) its companion vehicles in areas impassible by conventional material handling equipment.

One of the key concerns was getting the DUKW itself to the front. On 21 November tests conducted at Quincy, Massachusetts, proved that the 31-foot DUKW could be lowered through an LST's 30-foot deck hatch by lowering the DUKW at an angle of 30 degrees. The same day it was found that the DUKW had no trouble entering or leaving the LST at sea via the bow ramp. Whether the DUKW was moving bow or stern ahead made no difference in practicality.

On the same day as the LST tests, a detachment of the Engineer Amphibian Command began operating at Provincetown, utilizing the four pilot DUKWs.

Four days later the first four production DUKWs reached Provincetown, upping the detachment's roster to eight vehicles. The production vehicles were equipped with 10-ply tires, requiring that the tire pressure guidelines previously developed be revised, with a 2-3 pound further reduction in pressure recommended for sand use.

The importance of thorough and proper training of DUKW crewman became increasingly apparent, as on 27 November DUKWs 5 and 8 got badly stuck while returning from a late afternoon loading trial utilizing a 105-foot lighter. The tires of both vehicles were inflated in excess of the recommendations and the problems were compounded by other factors mentioned by Rod Stephens: "… (an) extremely unfavorable point was selected for landing and there was a lack of driving ability and judgment." Using the winches on two other DUKWs, the mired vehicles were extricated by Rod Stephens, Yellow Truck and Coach's Gil Roddowig, Captain James Mueller and Roger S. Warner, Jr. Warner at that time was Mr. Rowe's technical aide. The next year he would become Rowe's executive officer, succeeding Palmer Putnam in that position. That a man who would become so influential in the NDRC saw first hand the importance of proper and thorough personnel training would no doubt benefit the program in the future.

It appears, however, that some of this lesson was lost on the trainees, as the next day DUKW number 5 repeated this performance at noon. The situation on the 28th was compounded by a combination of the driver failing to rig a cover as the tide began to rise, and attempting to drive out by spinning the wheels, causing the vehicle instead to settle deeper in the beach. As a result, the mired vehicle was swamped by

The stern of an early-production DUKW is snugged up to the ramp of a landing craft. In the military campaigns to come, DUKWs would form a tight relationship with landing craft, particularly LSTs, which would transport the amphibious trucks to distant shores.

five-foot waves. The same four-man team as the day before recovered the vehicle using the winches from two other DUKWs, one rigged with a two-part tackle and the other using a three-part tackle.

Despite this strenuous activity, at 4:15 that afternoon Stephens and some others set out for Portland, Maine, with DUKWs 3 and 6, arriving in blackout conditions at 11 that night. The next day the vehicles entered the water after negotiating mud and boulders near the South Portland Shipyard. At 1:30 PM they left Portland, returning to Provincetown at 8 that evening.

Rescue of the crew of the *Rose*

Shortly after midnight the morning of 2 December 1942 one of the most oft repeated stories concerning the development of the DUKW began to unfold off Cape Cod. A Coast Guard Auxiliary, a yawl about 50-feet on the water line, which was on lookout for U-Boats, had gone aground off Highland Light. The winds were blowing 40 to 60 miles per hour, driving a hard rain and stirring up high waves. The crew of the vessel, which before military service had been known as the *Rose*, radioed Boston advising she was aground, but the crew was unharmed. Sea conditions, however, were such that the crew could not reach shore either by swimming or by means of lifeboat or raft. Coast Guard personnel from three stations had been dispatched, with breeches buoy gear as well as a surfboat. Upon their arrival, it was learned that the shoreline was too low to permit the use of the breeches buoy, and that the wind and current made use of the surfboat inadvisable.

Commander Allison of the Coast Guard placed a call to the Towne House, the beachfront hotel in Provincetown which was serving as quarters for the Provincetown detachment of the Engineer Amphibian Command. Responding to this call, around 1 a.m. Rod Stephens, Palmer C. Putnam, and Roger Warner, Jr., along with Commander Allison and fortuitously accompanied by noted maritime photographer Stanley Rosenfeld, left the Towne House with two DUKWs bound for the beach about one mile from Highland Light. Upon reaching the sand, tire pressure was reduced to eight pounds. The DUKW men briefly conferred with the Coast Guardsmen on the beach who told them that if they wanted to "try" to rescue the seven-man crew of the yawl, they were welcome to. It was decided that one DUKW, manned by Rod Stephens, Palmer C. Putnam, Commander Allison, and his Chief Silva would attempt the rescue. The other DUKW and crew would remain on shore unless summoned by the rescue crew.

Rod Stephens would later describe the rescue trip as "extremely uneventful," with the *Rose's* crew and their belongings returning to shore in less than six minutes. Back on land, discussions with *Rose's* skipper indicated it would be advisable to run out an anchor from the vessel into deep water. Stephens, Putnam, and Chief Silva, together with the skipper of the *Rose*, and a member of her crew, and accompanied by the photographer Rosenfeld, returned to the vessel and laid out the anchor.

In his biography *All of This and Sailing Too,* Olin J. Stephens II wrote: "Stanley was well equipped and brought back some pretty dramatic nighttime pictures of the rescue." These photos, now seemingly lost in the vast expanse of government archives, would play an important role in the future of the DUKW. Copies of these photos were immediately supplied to NDRC head Vannevar Bush, who took them to Secretary of War Henry L. Stimson, and told him the story of the rescue. Bush picked up the story of the photos and the rescue account in his book

Pieces of the Action: "Mr. Stimson took them to a Cabinet meeting and waited until Mr. Knox [Secretary of the Navy Frank Knox] was close by, and then told the President that this was probably the first case in history in which a naval vessel had been rescued by an Army truck. This eased off some of the opposition."

A major demonstration

As for the *Rose,* when the DUKWs and the crew of the *Rose* returned at 6:30 a.m., no trace of the vessel could be found. The remainder of the day, and the three following days, were spent preparing for a massive demonstration scheduled for 6 and 7 December. On the morning of the 4th, the various pieces of trial cargo were transferred from the 105-foot lighter that had been working with the DUKWs to the Liberty ship *John Carver* which had just arrived off Provincetown late on 3 December. Mooring lines were rigged alongside the Liberty ship as well, and the DUKWs practiced tying up. On the evening of the 4th the DUKWs were loaded onto the deck of the bigger vessel.

On 5 December the *John Carver* emerged from the sheltered harbor and headed out to sea. By the time the ship had been repositioned, there was only enough time remaining to launch one DUKW, a vehicle loaded with a 105mm howitzer. The DUKW successfully carried the cannon through the six- to eight-foot seas and ashore. Also that day new DUKWs 9 and 10 arrived from the factory.

Following a noon lunch, demonstrations began at "F Beach" near Provincetown at 1:30 and formally continued until 2:30, at which time individual rides and demonstrations were made for the roughly 40 U.S. Army Officers, four Navy officers, six Commonwealth officers and various Marine Corps, Coast Guard, Yellow Truck and Coach, Sparkman & Stephens. and NDRC representatives present – a total of roughly 80 men beyond those hosting the demonstrations, ranging from Major Generals to civilians. A pool of four Ford GPAs were available to officers who wished to observe the unloading of the Liberty ship up close from sea level.

Demonstrations continued the next morning when a battery of 105s was put ashore using four DUKWs. After traversing a four- to five-foot surf, the DUKWs came ashore, and at a pace of two minutes per cannon an A-frame equipped DUKW unloaded the artillery. The weapons were then connected to the towing pintles of the DUKWs that had brought them ashore and towed across the dunes. The day concluded with dinner and movies of amphibians in action at the Towne House. It was established that further trials were to be conducted in the Norfolk area as quickly as the DUKWs could be driven down.

The tests, training, and demonstrations – in sum, the DUKW experience – accomplished at Provincetown pointed to the need for further refinements in the vehicle design and production technique, and Rod Stephens spent the week after the demonstrations in Pontiac imparting his experiences to the Yellow Truck and Coach team.

The Provincetown operation was closed, and vehicles 7 through 10 were turned over to the Engineer Amphibious Command for its use at Camp Edwards and Sandy Hook. Vehicles 1 and 4 were dispatched to Pontiac for further improvements to their ferry fittings and DUKWs 2, 3, 5, and 6 were driven to Fort Story, near Norfolk, in preparation for operations that were set to commence there.

The testing at Provincetown pointed to the need for numerous changes that would have to be made before the DUKW would truly be fit for combat. Some of these changes were substantial, others

A DUKW is loaded into a 28-foot-long cargo hatch on a landing ship, tank (LST), offering a good view of the underside of the vehicle, including the front and rear suspensions, the front tow clevises, and the watertight housings for the front and front-tandem drive shafts.

The trials indicated a defined need for shielding the engine's ignition system from water. The somewhat crude sheet metal shield tested on the prototype is visible in this view. To the lower right are the radiator and fan. At the bottom are the oil filter and the crankcase breather and oil-filler tube. (General Motors)

Right: This photo of SS *John Carver* demonstrates the proper positioning of a Liberty ship to create satisfactory lee (absence of wind and its disturbing effect on the water) so a DUKW can moor in calm water alongside the ship: in this case, to the port side of the ship. To accomplish this, the stern of the ship was warped 10 degrees into the wind, either by a tug boat or by using the ship's anchor along with spring lines.

Below: DUKWs also would work closely with cargo vessels, particularly Liberty ships, developing highly efficient procedures for transporting supplies and men from ship to shore. This photo documents the correct method of mooring a DUKW alongside a ship, in this case the Liberty ship *John Carver,* using a spring line from the DUKW tied to a guest warp, the thick hawser rigged from bow to stern on the side of the ship.

Two DUKW pilots are stowed on SS *John Carver*: one on the main deck and the other, in the foreground, below a cargo hatch. If the tarpaulin bows were removed from the DUKW, it could be stored between decks.

A DUKW is being lowered by boom over the side of SS *John Carver*. Before the vehicle was lowered into the water, its engine was already being warmed up. Also, a spring line for mooring the DUKW to the ship is rigged before the vehicle is lowered.

Tossed by a choppy sea, a DUKW with the number 8 painted on the side holds alongside SS *John Carver* on the weather side of the ship. The guest warp can be seen running diagonally along the hull. Typically, the guest warp was at least 6 inches thick, and the spring line was 3.5 to 4.5 inches thick.

With the DUKW afloat next to the *John Carver*, crewmen on the vehicle are casting off the hoisting sling. This DUKW was carrying in the cargo compartment a 105mm howitzer. The tarpaulin hides most of the weapon except for the barrel.

Once the hoisting sling has been cast off, power has been applied to the DUKW's water propeller, resulting in tension on the spring line. Also, the driver of the DUKW is holding the rudder so as to keep the vehicle close to the hull of the Liberty ship.

DUKW pilot number 2 transports a 105mm howitzer ashore during a demonstration off Provincetown, Massachusetts, in December 1942. The U.S. Army provided four of these weapons for the use of the DUKW test team in its demonstrations.

During a demonstration at Provincetown in 1942, the DUKW in the background with one of the recently developed A-frame booms has removed the 105mm howitzer from DUKW number 6, and the weapon has been hitched to number 6. A movie camera crew is standing next to number 6.

It is rough going through ocean-side sand dunes for DUKW number 6, serving as a prime mover for a 105mm howitzer during the December 1942 Provincetown demonstrations. Eight DUKWs were available to the test team by that time.

Above: A cargo-compartment closure or surfboard installation on a DUKW is displayed. Made of waterproof plywood, it included a window with a canvas flap and two triangular side braces called wings. The closure and the wings were removable and were secured in place with pins. (General Motors)

Left: A closure assembly is viewed from the starboard side. The closures were discontinued with DUKW chassis number 4202 when it was found that they were being damaged during cargo handling and a shortage of waterproof plywood occurred. (General Motors)

The vertical windshield of the earliest DUKWs was highly vulnerable to damage when large waves struck it. Thus, experiments were conducted on means of protecting the windshield. A result was this provisional arrangement of a plate set at an angle in front of the windshield and supported by brackets. (General Motors)

In this experimental windshield surfboard, a slanting panel is positioned to the front of the windshield, with a room enough over it to see over, and four vertical stiffeners have been fastened to the windshield frame. Tests showed that this type of protection was inadequate, because waves could batter and damage the part of the windshield above the surfboard. In this case the windshield has been severly cracked from the impact of waves. (General Motors)

The final fix for DUKWs with vertical windshields was to add this surfboard, which extended to the top of the windshield. Mounted on two hinges, it was stored flat atop the engine-access hatch door and deployed by swinging it back against the top of the windshield. Two holes with wire mesh in the upper port corner of the surfboard allowed the driver a degree of forward vision. (TACOM LCMC History Office)

The bow surfboard and the windshield surfboard are deployed on DUKW registration number 70899, a vehicle produced in February 1943. The top of the windshield surfboard was fastened to the top of the windshield frame. Two braces held the bow surfboard in place. On-vehicle equipment includes a shovel, axe, mattock head and handle, and boat hook. (TACOM LCMC History Office)

Above: The following sequence of photos taken during surf tests illustrates the wrong way to deploy the plywood closure at the rear of the cargo compartment. On the vehicle to the right, the tarpaulin is not rigged over bows, so the closure will act as a giant water scoop when big waves wash over the vehicle on the way out. (U.S. Army Transportation Museum)

Left: The DUKW with the inappropriately installed closure is forging ahead into the surf. The excellent buoyancy of the bow compartment enabled the DUKW to enter heavy surf like this with a bow-up attitude. The other DUKW in the preceding photo is operating to the right; it has a duck insignia and the number 13 on the hull. (U.S. Army Transportation Museum)

Below: Now the DUKW with the inappropriately installed closure is in trouble. A 15-foot wave has crashed over the bow, and the closure will act as a scoop, keeping water in the cargo compartment rather than its intended purpose of keeping following waves from getting into that compartment. (U.S. Army Transportation Museum)

were minor. Rod Stephens traveled to Pontiac, Michigan, on 22-23 December to discuss with Yellow Truck and Coach the three lists of recommended changes, all of which had been approved by Colonel Tossy, Ordnance Department Purchasing and Contracting Officer on 14 December.

The four double-spaced, typewritten pages of List A consisted of 67 items enumerating changes applicable to all DUKWs. List B's two typed pages contained 47 items, comprising changes deemed critical for the first 100 DUKWs that were to be dispatched overseas for combat use. List C, also two pages in length, contained 33 items that detailed improvements urged for the next production run of vehicles.

The changes ranged from substitution of a Midland tire pump for the then-current Saylor-Beall unit, on to such details as zinc-plating the wheel-mounting studs.

The most noticeable changes in store for those 100 overseas-bound vehicles were the extension of the cargo coaming, the addition of a plywood back for the cargo enclosure, and the supply of a Danforth anchor to be mounted on the stern. The higher cargo coaming, in addition to keeping the cargo area drier, would also better retain loosely loaded cargo. It was suggested that the coaming be tapered, in

order to act as a guide when loading a DUKW via a sling.

Although introducing so many changes to vehicles already in production wreaks havoc on mass production, Yellow Truck and Coach was up to the task, and on 21 December their product engineering team began modifying the 100 overseas-bound vehicles in the Engineering shop. This work would not be complete until 1 February. On 3 October 1942, Major General C. C. Williams sent a letter to the NDRC, requesting the Committee tackle a new project, coded OD-92, entitled "Amphibian Trailers for 2½-ton Amphibian Truck." The liaison officer for the new "Restricted" project was Col. R. R. Robins with the Services of Supply branch.

Responding to this request, on 19 October 1942 Hartley Rowe submitted that the NDRC on 6 November should issue a contact to Yellow Truck and Coach in the amount of $36,000 to cover the design, drawings, and manufacture one of each of three trailers for use with the DUKW. One trailer was to have two wheels and a one-ton capacity; another was to also have two wheels, but with a two-ton capacity; while the third had the broader specifications of "maximum practical size of amphibious cargo trailer that may be towed behind the 2½-ton cargo vehicle."

Pursuant to early tests of DUKWs, the first 100 examples earmarked for shipment overseas received a number of modifications, including installation of a 4½-inch-high extension of the cargo-compartment coaming and a plywood closure at the rear of the cargo compartment, to prevent following waves from entering the compartment. It is believed that these DUKWs are some of those vehicles during modifications. A plywood closure is visible on several of the DUKWs. (General Motors)

Yellow Truck and Coach was agreeable to this proposal, with the stipulation that Yellow Truck would not be called upon to manufacture any further models. Ultimately, the decision was made that rather than issue a new contract, an existing contract would be modified to include the design, manufacture, and test of only the 2½-ton version of the trailer.

The two-wheel trailer was water tested in Ford's Rouge River Basin on 13 February 1943. The trailer, which was primarily of plywood construction, weighed 2,000 pounds and had a nominal capacity of 5,000 pounds. It was designed so that it could be towed by the DUKW while afloat and ashore.

While the additional cargo capacity was useful, the laden combination of the DUKW and trailer could make a water speed of only 2-3 m.p.h. Studies indicated much of this loss of speed was attributable to the fact that between the DUKW and the trailer there was enough distance to allow an independent wave system to form, thereby increasing the total surface wave that offered resistance to the DUKW/trailer combination.

Rod Stephens reported: "Basically the trailer idea would seem valuable only where there was short and favorable water operation in conjunction with most favorable landing site together with long and favorable land haul. This set up is greatly in variance with my conception of most military operations, for which reasons I am opposed to the trailer program."

On 28 May 1943 NDRC Technical Aide James A. Britton wrote to Major E. H. Holtzkemper, Chief of the Transport Vehicle Section, Development Branch, Tank-Automotive Center, concerning this project: "One trailer was built and tested. It is judged impractical in surf or heavy going. Accordingly, on our recommendation, the project was cancelled."

Almost a year later, on 8 May 1944, GMC shipped the sole trailer to Camp Gordon Johnston in Florida. In his cover letter concerning the shipment, GMC's Chief Engineer Charles O. Ball seconded Rod Stephen's findings, adding that the track of the trailer was too narrow for road operation, the brakes needed further development, repeated stops and starts would probably buckle the drawbar, and that the springs were too stiff. Ball concluded the letter with the ominous warning: "We are sending you this information so that you will not expect a vehicle which is 'ready to go', since even assuming very favorable water conditions and careful, experienced operators, considerable hazard is involved."

During the interim between the first and second production lots of the DUKW, an experimental amphibious trailer designed by Sparkman & Stephens was built for use with the DUKW. It was a two-wheel, 2½-ton vehicle with a boat-shaped hull and a tarpaulin supported by five bows. (General Motors)

The trailer was built of plywood and had an extended, tripod-type hitch at the front. It had tail lights, and to power them, electrical cables, visible here, are routed from the rear of the DUKW to receptacles on the front of the trailer. (General Motors)

Above: Like the DUKW, the trailer had a flat, inclined bow. Vertical stiffeners were on the bow, and longitudinal stiffeners, in line with the bow stiffeners, were on the bottom of the hull. The trailer had an overall length of 176 inches, and it was 96 inches wide and 85 inches high to the level of the deck. (General Motors)

Left: On 13 February 1943 a DUKW has the trailer under tow in preparation for tests of the trailer in the Rouge River Ship Basin at the Ford Motor Company plant in Dearborn, Michigan. With the tarpaulin removed from the trailer, it can be seen that a coaming was present on the deck to help prevent water from flowing into the trailer.

The DUKW tows the experimental trailer through the Rouge River Ship Basin during tests on 13 February 1943. The trailer weighed 2,000 pounds and had a capacity of 5,000 pounds. During tests, the trailer slowed down the DUKW by about half and significantly diminished the DUKW's maneuverability on water.

Right: The DUKW with the experimental plywood trailer under tow passes a Ford ore boat in the Rouge River Ship Basin. During the tests, it was found that the DUKW with the trailer had a poor turning radius, and propeller wash got into the trailer's cargo compartment because the distance between the trailer and the DUKW's stern was too short.

Below: Because the DUKW trailer's liabilities outweighed its benefits, GMC and the army did not pursue the concept seriously.

The DUKW pulls the trailer out of the Rouge River Basin. The relative sizes of the trailer's cargo space and the cargo compartment of the DUKW are visible. The hinged closure at the rear of the DUKW's cargo compartment has been stored in the lowered position. (Benson Ford Archives)

Chapter 11
The Duck Proves Its Worth

The water box, which had previously been shipped from Michigan to Provincetown, where it sat unused, was subsequently sent on to Fort Story, Virginia, where it was put to use load testing the tank ferrying equipment. The quick dump valves on the box could allow its entire 40,000 pounds of water to be discharged in 13 seconds should one of the DUKWs become distressed.

This may have been particularly of concern since only four DUKWs were equipped for use with the ferrying apparatus, and one of these had been damaged in a road accident. An overzealous driver put the DUKW into a skid while making a turn on an icy road, causing the DUKW to slide from the roadway and demolish a 10-foot tall brick-and-concrete gatepost, heavily denting the bow, wrecking the surf shield, and littering the DUKW's hood with debris.

The wreck did not seem to disrupt the watertight integrity of the hull, so the ferry tests went on as planned. Following the successful salt water trials in moderate surf with the water boxes, the DUKW crews were emboldened to drive the apparatus, laden with 42,000 pounds of water, up on to and along the beach, which they successfully did. Thus spirits were good for an actual demonstration of wet-ferrying a Sherman tank – a display planned as part of the comprehensive field test of the DUKW abilities and comparison to the LCVP. The LCVP, or Landing Craft, Vehicle, Personnel – or more popularly referred to as a "Higgins boat" – would be the classic landing craft used during World War II, with images of the bow ramps dropping and troops rushing up

beaches from the 36-foot vessels etched in America's psyche.

The DUKWs in this test were a mixed lot of four driven down from Provincetown, including pilot models No. 6 (from Yellow Truck and Coach Engineering) and No. 22 (straight from the assembly line). An arrival of equal or perhaps greater import to the program was that of Dennis Puleston of Sparkman & Stephens, who was assigned to DUKW field work on 21 December 1942 and promptly dispatched to Fort Story. Puleston would spend the next 19 months doing DUKW field work, engaging with the U.S. Army and Marines, as well as the forces of Great Britain, in virtually every theater where the DUKW was in use. In addition to providing engineering and manufacturing change recommendations, Puleston was also heavily involved in establishing DUKW training schools, starting with 34 crews in Fort Story.

The field tests began on 3 January 1943 when 10 preloaded DUKWs and 10 preloaded LCVPs departed the transport *Harry Lee* (AP-17 – reclassified as Attack Transport APA-10 on 1 February 1943), which was anchored ¾ miles off shore. The task was to transport the cargos of the DUKWs and the LCVPs to a supply dump 150 yards from shore, behind the first row of sand dunes. To unload the cargo from the LCVPs, a team of 100 men formed a "bucket brigade" from the surf to the shore, where a sled, pulled by a pre-positioned tractor, would move the cargo to the final inland dump position. By contrast, the DUKWs were unloaded at the dump site over the side using "hog

For purposes of doing load tests on various ferry rigs for DUKWs in rough water, parts of discarded ferry platforms were assembled into a platform to hold a water box. When the water box was filled, it simulated various loads, obviating the need to risk actual vehicles on the platform. (National Archives)

trough" slides developed in the field by a Lt. Raymond.

At the end of 27 minutes the DUKWs had brought in 40 tons of cargo. The LCVP team required about 90 minutes to bring in 30 tons. Perhaps equally important, many members of the LCVP team were wet, exhausted, and had this been a combat situation, would have been in extremely exposed positions. To further cement the difference in performance – all of which was witnessed by Admiral Henry Kent Hewitt, Commander, Amphibious Force, Atlantic Fleet, and his staff – many of the LCVPs had trouble withdrawing from the beach.

To add insult to injury for all involved, in heavy seas on 4 January the DUKWs reloaded and returned their cargos to the *Harry Lee*, in preparation for the major exercise scheduled for Sunday, 5 January, for the benefit of a larger group of Army and Navy officers. The LCVPs were unable to operate on the 4th because of the water conditions – and on the morning of the 5th they had still not been able to pick up their cargo. So the DUKWs ferried the LCVP cargo back out to the ship that morning prior to the demonstration. During this exercise the first known DUKW sinking occurred. In his report on the incident, Rod Stephens wrote: "…Ensign McLean, who had constantly shown poor judgment and lack of cooperation, overloaded his DUKW with about 9,000 pounds of cargo, much of which was in the rear end of the cargo space. He was directed by someone on deck to the weather side of the *Harry Lee* where he lay alongside for 45 minutes in spite of a 4 to 5 foot sea created by 25 mile breeze. He failed to rig the tarp and kept afloat only by virtue of good pump capacity. At the end of the 45 minutes when the motor stalled for unknown reasons, the water gained fast and he swamped in 60' depth."

With the Ensign rescued and the cargo repositioned, the exercise was ready to begin again, although with some twists. The LCVPs were augmented by two 50-foot tank lighters, while the dry ferry rigs on the DUKWs were used to put ashore a 2½-ton 6x6 (CCKW) carrying a Jeep in its bed, as well as a half-track, in addition to replicating the

The forward spreader bar on the water box test rig is viewed close-up. The water box on this test rig was fabricated especially for this project. It was fitted with a plywood box that held 40,000 pounds of water and was included quick-release valves that could empty the box in 13 seconds should the DUKWs become endangered. (General Motors)

In early November 1942, DUKW pilots 1 and 4 were dispatched to Provincetown, Massachusetts, to run water-box tests. Later, pilots 2 and 3, seen here, were also fitted with a water box and conducted tests with it. Pilot 2 is the closer DUKW. (National Archives)

The DUKW pilots with the water-box test rig are viewed from off the port aft quarter of pilot 2. Of interest are the large number 2 on the side of the hull, the much smaller number 2 to the rear of it, and the draft marks painted toward the front and the rear of the side of the hull. (National Archives)

Left: Pilots 2 and, in the foreground, 3, are proceeding through the water with a full water box. The box apparently is full, as the DUKWs are drawing a lot of water. Pilot 3 has its surf board raised, displaying the damage incurred a few days earlier in a collision with a masonry gate post. In the distance, above DUKW pilot number 3, another DUKW is following. (National Archives)

Below: Pilot DUKWs numbers 2 and 3 make a test run with a water box. The vehicles are churning up a noticeable wake. At least 11 men are visible in the photo. (National Archives)

Testing proceeds with a water box suspended between DUKW pilots 2 and 3. A man is standing atop the water box holding a flexible hose that is discharging water, possibly from one of the DUKW's bilge pumps. (National Archives)

cargo handling chores of 3 January. The results were the same – the DUKW flotilla landed 30 tons in 20 minutes, while the landing craft managed 20 tons in an hour. One DUKW using the hog trough system discharged a 6,000-pound cargo in a minute and a half using a five-man crew, including the driver. A testament to the success of the DUKW that day came when Commander Walter C. Capron requested DUKWs pick up his shivering men from the surf. Capron, a member of the Coast Guard, was assigned to the staff of the Army Engineer Amphibian Command and directed the Army's first school on beach landing-craft operations.

On 6 and 7 January there took place the wet-ferry testing of the Sherman tank in the sea. The first test involved taking the tank from land to the ship, then positioned a mile off shore, where the ship's cargo handling davits lifted the tank from the ferry. It was then returned to the DUKWs, who returned the tank to shore. Further testing involved use of a tank lighter to bring the armored vehicle to

a bar, with DUKWs then transporting it across soft spots to shore. All operations were satisfactory up to waves of about 2½ feet, but the limited reserve buoyancy of the three units (two DUKWs and tank) meant that any trouble would spell disaster, and this marked the end of the wet-ferry efforts.

All this very serious work was occasionally relieved by lighter moments. In his book, *Pieces of the Action,* Vannevar Bush recounted one such incident involving Palmer C. Putnam. Bush recalled: "One very cold day he demonstrated the DUKW to a group of officers on a beach in Virginia. Ten officers and I stood in the truck as it rolled down the beach; a vicious surf was pounding in. 'Gentlemen,' said Put, 'I am sorry we have no surf this morning. It was excellent yesterday, but has subsided so that I can give you only a weak demonstration: Driver, take her out to sea.' After some time with this sort of thing a rather wet group of officers got ashore and headed for a drink. Put smiled and said he had hoped for better surf."

The pilot DUKWs with the water box rig are parked on a beach following a test run. The water is being emptied from the water box using the quick-release valves on the bottom of the box: note the large cascade of water issuing from the bottom of the box. (National Archives)

In early January 1943, the scene of DUKW demonstrations shifted to Fort Story, Virginia. The attack transport USS *Harry Lee* (AP-17) was placed at the disposal of the DUKW test team, to experiment with ship-borne transportation, loading, and unloading of DUKWs and cargo-handling procedures. Stowed on deck are landing craft, with which the DUKWs competed during efficiency demonstrations. (U.S. Army Transportation Museum)

USS *Harry Lee* is rigged for DUKWs to moor alongside her. Running along the hull is a guest warp: a heavy cable to which the DUKWs could be moored with spring lines. The original caption for this photo noted that the guest warp was "improperly rove off" and "should not be triced up." (General Motors)

The photographic crew of the DUKW test team took this close-up photo of USS *Harry Lee* during demonstrations off Fort Story to show how the guest warp was triced-up with lines, contrary to proper procedures. During her period with the DUKW test team, the ship was anchored three-quarters of a mile off shore. (U.S. Army Transportation Museum)

During a DUKW-loading operation by USS *Harry Lee*, a spreader bar bears and distributes the weight of two cargo drafts, or loads, in order to load the DUKW with a full, 5,000- to 7,000-pound load in one operation. The exercise showed that 25 DUKWs could fully discharge 8,000 tons of cargo from a Liberty ship lying one-half mile offshore in 26 hours. (U.S. Army Transportation Museum)

A DUKW numbered 233 on the side of the hull is hoisted out of the water by a boat davit on USS *Harry Lee* off Fort Story, Virginia. Although the official report of the DUKW test team does not specifically mention this incident, it apparently was a test to gauge the ability of the davits to handle DUKWs. Apparently nothing came of the experiment. (General Motors)

One of the DUKWs employed in the demonstrations at Fort Story appears to be departing from the side of the *Harry Lee.* During a demonstration on 5 January 1943, one of the DUKWs proved its usefulness as a lifesaving vehicle by rescuing several members of the shore party who were stranded in the water. (U.S. Army Transportation Museum)

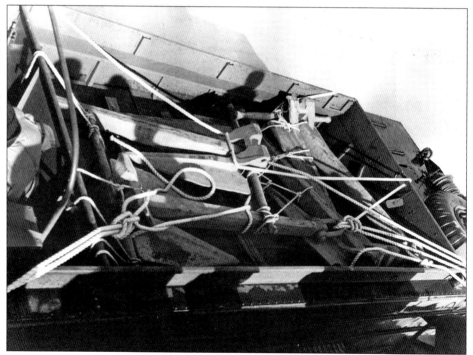

Right: The DUKW test team took this photo to document an improperly loaded cargo compartment. Too much weight was distributed to the rear of the compartment, resulting in low freeboard at the stern. One of the test team's DUKWs sank off Fort Story because of such faulty loading along with the absence of a tarpaulin over the cargo compartment. (U.S. Army Transportation Museum)

Below: A procession of eight DUKWs comes ashore at Fort Story, Virginia, during demonstrations of the vehicles in January 1943. The ship lying in the distance apparently is the USS *Harry Lee.* (U.S. Army Transportation Museum)

Right: A DUKW comes ashore during the Fort Story demonstrations in early January 1943. Bows for a tarpaulin over the cargo compartment are stowed at the rear of that compartment. During these demonstrations, one DUKW would sink, in part because its tarpaulin was not rigged while operating in rough seas. (National Archives)

Below: Ten DUKWs were used in the January 1943 demonstrations at Fort Story, Virginia, and all ten of those vehicles are lined up on a beach. In a competition against 10 LCVs on 3 January, these DUKWs vastly outperformed the landing craft in bringing ashore cargo. (National Archives)

A naval officer at the center of the photo inspects DUKWs on the beach at Fort Story. The disk-type wheels on the first 405 DUKWs, one of which is particularly clear in this photo, had "L" type rims with lock rings. Subsequent DUKWs had "CV" rims with side rings. (National Archives)

Above: The DUKW test team demonstrates a procedure in which crewmen slide cargo down devices called hog troughs as the vehicle moves along in a supply dump. By this procedure, it was estimated that one DUKW and a few crewmen could accomplish a task that otherwise would require up to 50 men. (National Archives)

Right: A line of crates marks where the moving DUKW in the background has discharged its cargo on a beach at Fort Story. Men in the cargo compartment of the vehicle are still discharging boxes using a hog trough. (U.S. Army Transportation Museum)

Two DUKWs conduct a dry-ferrying demonstration alongside USS *Harry Lee* off Fort Story, Virginia, on 5 January 1943. Loaded on the platform between the two DUKWs is a GMC CCKW 6x6 truck. The number 102 is on the side of the hull of the closer DUKW. (National Archives)

Above: The two DUKWs dry-ferrying the CCKW are underway off Fort Story. The truck is high and dry, but the DUKWs are drawing quite a bit of water. During dry-ferry tests, it was determined that the maximum load was approximately 30,000 pounds. (National Archives)

Left: The dry-ferry rig with the CCKW on it is parked on the sand. Of interest is the broken surf board on the bow of the nearer DUKW, pilot number 2, which was smashed when the driver hit a brick gate post at Fort Story on 5 January 1943. The board it is lashed together with rope as a temporary fix. (National Archives)

The CCKW is at the bottom of the fold-down ramps of the dry-ferry rig at Fort Story. On each side of the ramps is the bow of a DUKW, with the headlights and headlight guards visible. (National Archives)

Left: The two DUKWs with the attached dry-ferry rig are observed from the front on the beach at Fort Story. From this angle, the vertical struts attached to the bottoms of the horizontal compression struts, or spreader bars, are visible. (National Archives)

Below: The forward ends of the platforms of the dry-ferry rig have been raised in this photograph. Two strips of non-slip material, to assist vehicles in gaining traction when driving up the platforms, are visible on each platform. Faintly visible on the side of the bow of the DUKW to the right is U.S. Army registration number 4209658. (National Archives)

With the USS *Harry Lee* riding at anchor in the background, two DUKWs come ashore dry-ferrying a CCKW with a Jeep loaded in its cargo compartment. The nearer DUKW is number 658. (General Motors)

Above: The CCKW with the Jeep loaded in the back is on the ramps of the dry-ferry rig at Fort Story. To the left is a half-track that was used in a dry-ferry demonstration, and in the background is an A-frame. (U.S. Army Transportation Museum)

Left: A hoist sling is attached to the Jeep riding piggyback on the CCKW used in the demonstration of the dry-ferry rig. A DUKW, numbered 257, with an A-frame boom to hoist the Jeep is backed up to the CCKW. (National Archives)

DUKW 257 has hoisted the Jeep used in the dry-ferry demonstration at Fort Story. The A-frame in harness with the DUKW's winch could lift the Jeep, weighing approximately 2,300 pounds, with ease. (National Archives)

Left: As viewed from the rear, an M2 half-track is secured to the platform of a dry-ferry rig at Fort Story. Tarpaulins were often rigged on the DUKWs during the January 1943 demonstrations to keep water from the often rough seas out of the cargo compartments. (U.S. Army Transportation Museum)

Below: The M2 half-track is viewed from the rear as it is being maneuvered on the ramp of the dry-ferry rig. The vertical struts mounted on the bottoms of the horizontal spreader bars incorporated screw-type fittings with handles, for adjusting the tensioning cables. (National Archives)

At Fort Story on 5 January 1943, two DUKWs were equipped for dry-ferry operations with an improvised rig consisting of materials typically found aboard ship. The trial was successful, with the vehicles transporting ship to shore an M2 half-track weighing approximately 20,000 pounds. (TACOM LCMC History Office)

The same dry-ferry rig seen in the preceding photo – in which two DUKWs are coupled closely side-by-side with an M2 half-track secured sideways over their cargo compartments – is viewed at sea from astern on 5 January 1943. It appears the DUKWs are joined by coupling devices on their hulls, fore and aft. Tensioning cables are arranged in criss-cross fashion at the sterns.

The dry-ferry configuration with the two DUKWs linked side-to-side is viewed close-up from the side of the port vehicle with the half-track on board. Vertical wooden sills were mounted on the outboard sides of the cargo-compartment coamings, with lateral timbers on top. On top of those timbers were pieces of lumber for the half-track to rest on. (General Motors)

Right: An M5 Stuart light tank is loaded aboard the platform of a dry-ferry rig supported by two DUKWs. Weighing 30,800 pounds empty, this tank pushed the limits of the dry-ferry rig's safe capacity of 30,000 pounds. The nearer DUKW is pilot number 2 with its broken surf board. (U.S. Army Transportation Museum)

Below: The M5 Stuart light tank proceeds down the ramps of the dry-ferry rig. During the ferry experiments, several designs of platforms were developed, including one with a detachable ramp at the rear and one with a teeter ramp, whereby the entire platform pivoted to form its own loading ramp. The platform with the two hinged front ramps was the final design. (National Archives)

An operation of some sort is being performed on a dry-ferry ramp. A DUKW with an A-frame boom is backed up to the ferry rig, and the man at the right is securing to the hoist-cable hook a rope tied around tie-down loops on the platform. The ramps have been removed from the front of the platform. (National Archives)

At Fort Story, Virginia, on 6 and 7 January 1943, wet-ferry tests were conducted with DUKWs and an M4 medium tank. The wet-ferry rig with the tank is seen here moving alongside USS *Harry Lee*. In the background are another DUKW and a Higgins 50-foot tank lighter employed in the tests. (National Archives)

A dry-ferrying operation of an M4 medium tank is underway at Fort Story. Only the turret of the tank and the top of the hull are visible above the water. During the first trial, on 6 January, the DUKWs ferried the tank from shore to the *Harry Lee*; a boom on the ship hoisted the tank; and then the tank was lowered and reconnected to the DUKWs. (National Archives)

The wet-ferry rig with the M4 medium tank coupled to it is observed from aft. Two men on the rear deck of the tank are making adjustments to the fittings. The small ferrying trunk fitted to the rear of the tank and the rear spreader bar connected to the DUKWs are visible. (National Archives)

Left: The DUKWs with their M4 medium-tank charge have entered the water at Fort Story, and, judging from the wakes they are kicking up, the vehicles are now under propeller power. The soldier in the tank's commander's hatch is signaling by hand to the man on the stern of the starboard DUKW. (National Archives)

Below: During the second wet-ferry trial of the M4 medium tank at Fort Story, first the tank was loaded into a 50-foot lighter, which proceeded to an offshore bar and grounded itself firmly in the sand, as seen here. In the left background, a DUKW stands by. (National Archives)

Above: Once the 50-foot tank lighter was grounded off the sand bar, the ramp was lowered and the M4 medium tank disembarked from the craft. The tank then parked a few yards off the shore of the bar, and its crew awaited the arrival of two DUKWs. (U.S. Army Transportation Museum)

Left: Next, the lighter moved away from the tank, and two DUKWs were positioned to each side of the M4 medium tank and effected a hookup for a wet-ferry rig. Here, one DUKW is adjacent to the port side of the tank, and the other DUKW is moving in. (U.S. Army Transportation Museum)

Below: The DUKWs have achieved a wet-ferry connection with the "stranded" M4 medium tank and are moving it to the bar, bearing much of the tank's weight. Subsequently, the rig would cross over the bar and the body of water between the bar and the mainland. (U.S. Army Transportation Museum)

Above: The DUKW-M4 medium tank wet-ferry rig comes ashore, the tank now supporting its own weight. The turret of the tank and the 75mm gun barrel are visible between the two DUKWs. The entire shuttle by dry-ferry rig had taken about ten minutes. the bar and the mainland. (U.S. Army Transportation Museum)

Left: The DUKW wet-ferry rig with the M4 medium tank is observed from the front after arriving on the beach at Fort Story. The lack of much clearance between the sides of the tank and the hulls of the DUKWs is apparent. (General Motors)

Following the wet-ferry demonstration at Fort Story, the port DUKW has been disengaged from the side of the tank and has driven away, and the starboard DUKW is in the process of being disconnected from the tank. the bar and the mainland. (U.S. Army Transportation Museum)

Chapter 12
Experimental Development

It will be recalled that early on in the DUKW development process, it was requested that the use of the DUKW as a support for a floating bridge be explored. Beginning on 21 January 1943 Yellow Truck and Coach engineering began the design of a truss that would permit two DUKWs to be coupled together stern to stern, providing a stable, self-powered and self-maneuvering float.

To connect the DUKWs, a pair of girders were fashioned to span the vehicles, and each girder was then split midway between the sterns. Two pins in each girder section could then be used to reconnect the sections rigidly. Screw jacks were provided with which to elevate the mating ends of the girders to permit alignment despite different DUKWs riding at different levels in the water.

Two sets of these girders were constructed, and the equipment was tested in Crystal Lake near Pontiac. While effective, it was found that the pair of DUKWs when coupled had poor speed and maneuverability in the water.

Hence, an alternate design was tried, this time connecting the DUKWs bow to stern rather than stern-to-stern. This arrangement was much more satisfactory, proving much superior in water maneuverability, and by all indications capable of doing the task for which it was designed, although it was not adopted. The appearance of this open truss arrangement differed significantly from that of the original solid-sided girder design.

However, there were a few noteworthy incidents in the testing of the apparatus. In an effort to examine the performance of the equipment under severe overloading in the water a unique test was developed.

Left: Since planners considered the possibility of using DUKWs as self-propelled pontoons for supporting rafts or bridges, experiments were conducted in linking two vehicles in alignment. In the first tests, the DUKWs were linked stern-to-stern with solid trusses attached to the tops of the hulls. (Sparkman & Stephens)

Below: The next configuration in the experiments with DUKWs as pontoons was bow-to-stern. The solid trusses were replaced by framework trusses, attached to the tops of the hulls to hold the two vehicles rigidly in alignment. (TACOM LCMC History Office)

Above: This appears to have been a test of the second type (bow-to-stern) of DUKW pontoon rig to investigate the rigidity of the connections and the trusses. Although the front end of the forward DUKW has been driven over the cliff, the tops of the hulls are in alignment. (TACOM LCMC History Office)

Left: During tests of the second DUKW pontoon rig, an M4 medium tank has been lowered onto the trusses to check the ability of the rig to withstand heavy loads. A third DUKW with an A-frame is secured to the pontoon rig with a beam, probably for purposes of stability. (TACOM LCMC History Office)

The M4 medium tank on the DUKW pontoon rig is viewed from farther aft. The rear deck of the closer DUKW is almost awash. The idea of using DUKWs as self-propelled pontoons was not advanced past the test stage, in part because of the demand for the vehicles for other purposes. (TACOM LCMC History Office)

Ford Motor Company graciously provided the use of its Rouge Basin, a large traveling crane and an M4A3 Sherman tank. The two coupled DUKWs, along with a third, rigged to act as an outrigger to prevent toppling, were maneuvered beneath the crane, which then lowered the tank onto the truss.

When about 60,000 pounds of the tank's 66,000-pound weight was on the truss, the decks of the DUKWs were awash, and the entire affair was being subjected to a load of about 100% beyond what its designed capabilities. However, once the load was removed and the vehicles and trusses examined, no evidence of permanent set or or improper design was found.

The tandem DUKW apparatus was also tested at the Bridge and Test Section of the Army Engineers at Imperial Dam near the Arizona/ California border. While the tests were satisfactory, they failed to raise interest in the equipment as designed. However, four DUKWs equipped with the trusses were tested as a heavy ferry for moving medium tanks. The test was successful until the tank driver became confused and drove off the end of the raft, the tank sinking to the bottom of the Colorado River.

On the other side of the nation, at Camp Edwards, in February 1943 a different type of test was being conducted, utilizing a new technology. Demonstrations were held at Fort Story, Virginia, and Camp Edwards, Massachusetts, concerning the use of infrared equipment during nighttime landing-boat operations. The Fort Story operation involved a DUKW and a GPA, with the GPA using IR driving lights and image tube to locate landmarks and place IR marker lamps ashore and auto-collimating reflectors along a trail through the woods, then returned to base. The DUKW, using its own IR driving lights and image tube, found the landing spot defined by the GPA and followed the trail through the woods. All went as planned during the Fort Story test, except that the GPA could not operate in the heavy seas, and thus all the markers were placed without the GPA entering the surf.

For the Camp Edwards test two DUKWs were employed rather than a DUKW and a GPA, and the test went off as expected, with General Noce, Commanding General, Engineer Amphibian Command and his Chief of Staff, Colonel Trudeau, aboard the lead DUKW, serial number 353-158. During the Camp Edwards tests the General Electric lighting apparatus performed exactly as expected, as did the RCA binocular image tube provided for the driver. The equipment provided a level of visibility for the driver, as well as crew using hand-held image tubes, comparable to that which would have been possible with conventional headlights, while remaining invisible to others.

To investigate the possibility of using infrared (IR) illumination in conducting landing operations at nighttime under blackout conditions, a demonstration was conducted at Fort Story on 7 February 1943 using a DUKW specially fitted with two 400-watt fixed IR headlights and one 600-watt movable searchlight by the windshield, as well as small IR tail lights and binocular vision tubes for the driver. (National Archives via Jim Gilmore)

Infrared beach marker lamps such as this one were placed at strategic spots on the beach for the Fort Story demonstration. The use of IR illumination as a means of conducting tactical operations was in its infancy and was not used extensively in World War II, but later its use would become widespread. (National Archives via Jim Gilmore)

Chapter 13

The Balance Of The First Order

Delivery of the initial 600 production vehicles, which were requested urgently by Col. McAuliffe for delivery by 31 December 1942, was finally completed in early February 1943. Yellow Truck and Coach then turned its attention to the remaining 1,404 vehicles of the government's initial production contract. These vehicles would encompass many of the lessons that had been learned through the weeks of testing and trials.

Reports, from NDRC specialists such as Palmer Putnam and Roderick Stephens, as well as military observers, along with Yellow Truck and Coach's own engineers were funneled to the Company's product engineering department, who then addressed the issues raised. Once a solution had been found to a given problem – either in Pontiac or in the field – a Motor Transport Engineering Recommendation (M.T.E.R.) was issued. Each MTER had a unique number, but some MTERs addressed multiple problems within multiple systems of the vehicle. Many of these recommendations then required approval of the Ordnance Department of the Army to implement, as they would impact parts interchangeability or would conflict with Ordnance Department standards. Once approved by Ordnance, the changes were then passed to production control, who would secure the necessary materials or make changes to existing purchase orders, secure any needed tooling changes, and schedule the introduction of the change to the assembly line.

The MTER system was used not only on the DUKW as a whole, but also on its powerplant, the GMC 270-cubic-inch, 6-cylinder engine. The 270 was the cornerstone upon which the AFKWX, CCKW, ACKW, and the DUKW were built – as well as being a key part of the GMC's post-World War II civilian truck line. Yellow Truck and Coach built its engines in their Plant 4, in Pontiac, Michigan. Engine production occupied 102,638 square feet of this 324,683 square foot building in late 1941, the rest being consumed by the company's service department. General Motors had bought these buildings on South Saginaw St. (now known as Woodward Ave.) in April 1937. The buildings had previously been part of the Wilson Foundry Machine Shop – Wilson Foundry of course is familiar for its work on Jeep engines, which was carried out at another facility long after GM bought the properties discussed here.

A study conducted by GM, at the behest of the War Department in October 1941, revealed that Plant 4, working 22½ hours per day, could produce a maximum of 23 270-cubic-inch engines per hour, although the practical limitation was 21 engines per hour. The blocks themselves were built by the Pontiac Motor Company at their foundry operations on Montcalm St., only a few blocks away from Yellow's Plant 4. Cylinder heads were initially produced by Ferro Foundry in Cleveland, Ohio, but this was later supplemented with additional cylinder head casting by the Buick Motor Division of GM. From the standpoint of Yellow Truck and Coach, the limiting factor in engine production was the machining time required on the various engine components.

The serial number for these engines, which is stamped into a pad near the distributor, begins "270." However, all 270s are not alike, not even all the military engines. In fact, the manuals list no fewer than 20 different variations of the 270, four of which are specific to the DUKW (Models SN3214, SN3229, SN3380, and SN3477). Significant,

Shown here is an example of a DUKW, U.S. Army registration number 701223, of the second production order, serial numbers 1006 to 2006. The principal identifying characteristics of this series was the presence of both the vertical windshield and a new cargo-compartment coaming, which tapered higher toward the rear. The tarpaulin hides the tapered coaming in this series of photos. (General Motors)

Above: The same DUKW is viewed from the aft port quarter. The front wheel house has a cover, but the rear wheel house lacks one. Reinforced covers for the forward wheel houses were released for production on 19 January 1943; these had a rub rail at the bottom, as seen here. (General Motors)

Right: At the rear of this DUKW from the second production order, the Gar Wood winch is at the upper center. It was a worm-type winch, shaft-driven from a power take off. To each side of the winch, mounted on the rear deck, is a tail light assembly with a brush guard. U.S. Army registration number 701233 is on the stern. (General Motors)

Up to serial number 2005, a spare tire was stowed on the port side of the aft deck of DUKWs, and two holders for 5-gallon liquid containers were on the starboard side of that deck. After serial number 2005, the positions of the spare tires and the liquid containers were reversed. The oblong object on the bracket below the starboard tail light was a tow-chain link. (General Motors)

Right: The tarpaulin over the cargo compartment of the DUKW, as seen on U.S. Army registration number 701233, was intended to keep waves from rushing into the compartment and possibly swamping the vehicle. At the rear of the tarpaulin was the waterproof plywood closure, mounted on hinges. (General Motors)

Below: Three reflectors were mounted on the side of the DUKW in the forward, center, and aft positions. In addition to the tilted, U-shaped lifting eyes toward the rear and the front of the top of the hull, a mooring eye was positioned on each side of the top of the hull adjacent to the front of the cargo compartment. (General Motors)

The wheels on the DUKWs of the second production order (and actually including DUKWs after the 405th example) were "CV" rims with side rings, characterized by numerous hex nuts around the rings. The cover for the driver's compartment included side curtains with oval plastic windows. (General Motors)

Above: DUKW registration number 701233 is viewed from its forward starboard quarter. Stored on the starboard side of the forward deck is a manually operated bilge pump, a standard accessory on DUKWs. (General Motors)

Right: The windshield surfboard is visible in the lowered position on top of the engine access hatch on registration number 701233. A headlight assembly and brush guard is on each side of the forward deck. All-glass sealed-beam headlights were adopted on 27 March 1943 to protect the filaments from water in heavy seas. (General Motors)

This photo and the following series of photos document some of the second DUKW production lot under construction. Here, a welder is affixing a davit eye, for handling the vehicle by ship's davits, to the forward deck, while other workers adjust the surfboard and install other fittings. (General Motors)

A DUKW undergoes its first water-tank test for proper operation of the propeller and rudder and to check for water leaks in the hull. The propeller is churning up the water in the background. (General Motors)

A DUKW is being put through its final final water test and inspection. The propeller is being tested, and the cable holding the DUKW in a static position throughout the test is visible to the rear. (General Motors)

visible changes, such as to the water pump, air compressor drive, and carburetor resulted in new engine model numbers (in addition to the associated MTER), while less major changes, such as the change in air cleaner clamp screw from a slotted, Fillister head to a hexagon head with Philips engagement, merited only an MTER change (#44).

Well over 1,000 MTER changes to vehicle and engine were approved during the production of the DUKW, many of them only days apart, certainly wreaking havoc on the orderly model of "mass production" familiar to the automotive industry.

That so many changes were made was not indicative of faulty original design or production, but rather were a combination of a relatively new concept in vehicle – an amphibian – and lessons learned with the Ford GPA program. With the GPA, NDRC had conceived the vehicle, Ford had built it, and then NDRC turned it over to the Army, washing its hands of it. With a lack of Army personnel trained to use the DUKW, coupled with the rigid and slow system for providing feedback to the manufacturer existent within the Army structure, the bulk of the GPA production was completed before trouble reports made their way to Ford engineering, leaving little actual time to correct faults. This situation is one reason that the GPA program is retrospectively viewed as a failure.

Having learned from this, the NDRC/OSRD retained an oversight position on the DUKW until production and use were well on their successful way, only turning the project over to the Army in 1944. This arrangement allowed for much faster – in some instances same-day – feedback from the field to GM engineers regarding problems and recommended solutions. While causing no end of headache for those involved purely in production, this arrangement did result in a vehicle seen as an unqualified success.

The DUKW uses the Clark Equipment Co. Model 204 VO-319 transmission, a selective sliding gear design with five forward speeds and one reverse, with the fourth speed being direct drive (that is, with a 1:1 gear ratio), and the fifth speed being overdrive. The gearshift lever has high gear to the driver's far right and up. First, second, and sometimes third gears, as well as reverse were used in conjunction with the marine propeller transfer case. (National Archives via Jim Gilmore)

Newly painted DUKWs are undergoing detail work in the final-assembly area underneath a patriotic poster. The tapering coaming around the cargo compartment, higher at the rear than at the front, which was introduced with the second production lot, is seen to good advantage. (General Motors)

Two DUKWs at station 6 in final assembly, seen in the preceding photo, are receiving final touches. A man on the platform is resting his hand on the opened canvas side curtain of the DUKW to the left; this was a hinged assembly with a plastic, oval window. (General Motors)

On the final assembly line, DUKWs are being prepared for rolling out. On the DUKW to the center, the engine-access hatch door is in the open position. To the left are completed DUKWs with their tarpaulins fully installed and lashed down. (General Motors)

The DUKW production engine was the GMC Model 270, a four-cycle, six-cylinder, in-line gasoline-powered unit. As seen from the right side, the oil filter is on the side toward the front, to the rear of which is the crankcase breather and oil filler. (General Motors)

The fan belt and water pump are on the front face of the DUKW engine, which is viewed here from the front. The oil filter is to the left. Above the engine to the right is the carburetor, topped with the air cleaner. The generator is to the lower right. (General Motors)

Early in the testing of the DUKW, Hartley Rowe suggested that it would be advantageous to have an A-frame boom on board. So equipped, one DUKW could be used to unload other DUKWs in the absence of a crane. However the DUKW with A-frame could not unload itself. The bottoms of the A-frame were secured to brackets on each side of the Gar Wood winch, whose wire rope was reaved through the A-frame pulley. At the end of the wire rope was a short section of lead chain and a hook. (General Motors)

The early production DUKW engine can be distinguished by the shiny die-cast carburetor visible just beneath the black air cleaner. The shiny object mounted just atop the intake manifold is the governor. DUKWs were equipped with governors to limit engine speed, particularly important during marine operations, when oftentimes the hand throttle was set to maintain the engine speed. Under those conditions, should the operator forget to close the hand throttle before shifting gears there was considerable risk of over speeding the engine. The governor prevented such an eventuality. (General Motors)

Engine Data

ENGINE MAKE/MODEL	GMC 270
NUMBER OF CYLINDERS	6
BORE	3-25/32 inches
STROKE	4 inches
CUBIC INCH DISPLACEMENT	269.5
HORSEPOWER	91 @ 2750
TORQUE	216 lb-feet @ 1400
GOVERNED SPEED	2,750 r.p.m.
WEIGHT, without accessories	572 pounds

Above: At the rear of the engine is the bell housing, enclosing the clutch and flywheel. Bolted to the bell housing is the transmission, above which are shift and parking brake levers. Toward the bottom left of the transmission is the Gar Wood power take off, a dual two-speed and reverse design. An air duct is attached to the belt-driven generator, mounted near the front of the engine beneath the exhaust manifold. Later-production engines dispensed with the air duct attached to the generator, and used a more rugged and salt-water resistant cast iron carburetor. (General Motors)

Left: Jutting from the side of the engine block (seen here from the right rear) aft of the oil filter is the ignition shield. Below and slightly aft of the ignition shield is the engine starter assembly. (General Motors)

Chapter 14
Factory School

In addition to numerous field schools that OSRD and the military established, both in the United States and abroad, General Motors operated schools to train personnel in both the DUKW and the 270 engine.

These schools trained not only instructors for the military schools, but also the many General Motors Field Representatives who worked with various military commands. GM field personnel worked, often for extended periods of time, at the Stateside military installations at Fort Ord, California; Charleston, South Carolina; Camp Gordon Johnston, Florida; Camp Edwards, Massachusetts; as well as at overseas locations in the European and Pacific Theaters. The field reps, in addition to providing the most up-to-date expertise to military maintenance personnel, also facilitated rapid feedback to the factory concerning new problems and solutions.

To train DUKW maintenance personnel in the mechanical intricacies of the new DUKW, some of them were sent to General Motors service school. Here, A GMC instructor at the Detroit Zone quarters teaches the procedure for mounting and dismounting the tandem suspension. (General Motors)

DUKW mechanics in the making are disassembling components of Type 270 engines at GM service school at the Detroit Zone quarters. In the background at a podium is the instructor. On the shelves alongside the windows is an assortment of tech manuals, parts lists, and other references. (General Motors)

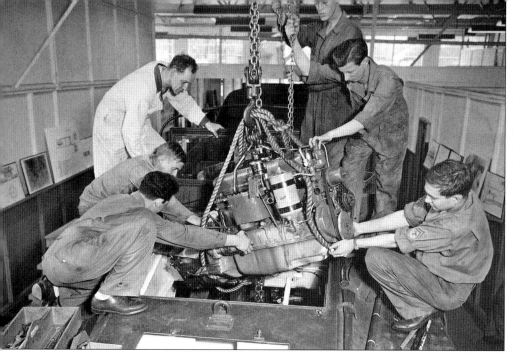

Trainees at GM service school, Detroit Zone quarters, are manhandling an engine over the engine hatch of an early DUKW with vertical windshield. The engine hatch door has been completely removed for accessibility. (General Motors)

More of the DUKW is visible in a view from another angle of the same group in the preceding photo, including the U.S. Army registration number, 701632, a vehicle completed in late April or early May 1943. Details of the reinforced surfboard are visible. The radiator fan is lying on the deck to the lower right. (General Motors)

A GMC service school instructor in the white overalls supervises as U.S. Army mechanics check the engine connections and steady the engine while two soldiers man the chain hoist. Instructional drawings and photos are on the shelves to the sides. (General Motors)

A DUKW's land and marine drivelines and suspension have been removed from the chassis frame, probably for training purposes. To the far left is the marine-propeller transfer case and shift lever, as well as the belt-driven forward bilge pump. The chain-driven aft bilge pump sits on a crate at the lower center. (General Motors)

Drive shafts – required for the axles, the marine propeller, and the winch – are displayed here. Three waterproof drive-shaft housings were supplied for the front axle and the two tandem axles, and these appear at the top. (General Motors)

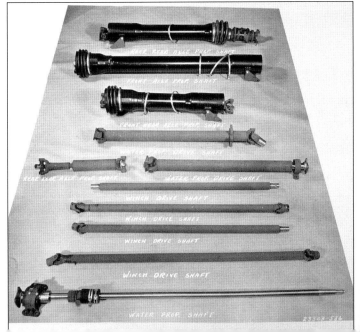

Above: This photograph of the engine, drivelines, and suspensions of a DUKW chassis was the basis for technical drawings in TM 9-802, the technical manual for the DUKW. It shows the winch, the rudder, the marine propeller, drive shafts, steering and brake gear, and other mechanical components. (General Motors)

Below: The same engine, driveline, brake, and steering components seen in the photo to the center left are viewed from the rear. A good view is provided of the Chevrolet-designed and produced axles used on all DUKWs, as well as some CCKW cargo trucks. These axles, sometimes referred to as "banjo" or "corporation" style, were produced in both "standard" and "high traction" models. While cargo trucks were produced using both styles, the DUKW used the high-traction version exclusively. (General Motors)

105

Chapter 15
Massive Production

At an urgent meeting at the Yellow Truck and Coach plant on the evening of Friday, 9 January 1943, R. J. Emmert asked R. A. Crist to take immediate steps to requisition material for 5,000 more DUKWs. Contract conclusion for the vehicles was imminent. Another meeting was held the next morning (Saturday) in Crist's office with a Mr. Matson of the company's Control Division regarding scheduling.

Yellow Truck and Coach President Irving Babcock expected to get a purchase order any day, and therefore a verbal approval was given to proceed, as there was to be no gap between the completion of the order for 2,004 vehicles and the start of the new 5,000 DUKW order that was to be finished by November. Such a gap would have meant the dismantling of the DUKW assembly line (in order that that space could be used for other production), and the dispersion of the DUKW assembly line workers, some of them highly skilled and all specially trained, to other jobs, including some outside of the company – with the distinct possibility that some could be drafted.

To do this, and meet the anticipated 1 November deadline, an ambitious production schedule was laid out, with production ramping up to 30 vehicles per day. Additional tooling would be required to meet this demand, which would mean additional work for the already burdened tool room at Yellow Truck and Coach.

Surprisingly, given the past problems with steel, at this point in time the biggest bottleneck anticipated was the marine plywood used in the cab and cargo compartment of the DUKW – over 1.25 million square feet of it. Other critical items required to fill the 5,000-vehicle order were 150 pounds of welding rod per vehicle; 14,536 tons of carbon steel; 281 tons of alloy steel forgings, and 22 tons of hot rolled alloy steel bars.

The entire forecasting process, especially when it came to purchased parts and components, was compounded by the vast number of ongoing changes being made to the design. Just two days earlier, the extensive trials had been held at Fort Story, yielding a new list of improvements to be incorporated in the vehicles. The professionals in the Pontiac offices were burning the midnight oil trying to hit a moving target with these forecasts.

Among the most visible changes that the new order would incorporate were a new, sloping, wave-resistant windshield, a relocated spare tire, and the addition of a central tire inflation system.

As it turned out, much of this effort was in vain, as no purchase order was forthcoming. Rather, in frustration on 22 January, Yellow Truck and Coach's Mr. Livingston sent the following telegram to Palmer C. Putnam at the OSRD office in Washington:

"Retel January 7 we have received no additional releases on DUKWs……Even if release is received immediately it will be impossible at this late date to line up without break in production. All preparations have been made….All to no avail."

Putnam responded on the 26th with the following telegram:

The following series of photos documents DUKW production at GMC Truck & Coach Division, Pontiac, Michigan, in the final months of 1943. This vehicle, U.S. Army registration number 7018326, exhibits the slanting windshield with clear side wings introduced with DUKW serial number 2007. This design could withstand heavy waves much better than the original vertical windshield. (General Motors)

The late-type slanting window is viewed close-up from the port side of a DUKW. The triangular side windows may have offered limited visibility to the sides when the cargo compartment cover was installed, but they added structural strength to the windshield. (General Motors)

The slanted windshield with side wings was released for production on 24 June 1943; an installation is viewed from the front in a photo dated 18 July 1943. Pioneer tools are stowed on the port side of the forward deck and a manual pump on the starboard side. (General Motors)

"Reurtel this was read to General Moses, War Department General Staff G-4, General Dillon, Deputy Chief of Transportation, Colonel Gallant, War Department, General Staff Operations Division. In response Operations informs me that an order for 1000 is now in the hands of Chief of Ordnance. Whether this is (a) tide over order or the total order for the time being I am not informed. Please confirm to me by mail what revision in the production schedule is necessary in order to avoid a shutdown."

On 13 February the Letter Purchase Order mentioned in Putnam's telegram reached the desk of A. A. Dodd. This purchase order was indeed for 1,000 vehicles, not the 5,000 previously anticipated, and these were to include all the design changes approved up to that time, as well as 10 lots of spare parts. This order was handled as a supplement to contract W-374-ORD-2849.

Production control began immediately modifying all of its paperwork downward from 5,000 to 1,000 and releasing the company's orders to outside vendors. Still, the delay on the part of the government in issuing a new order spelled trouble, particularly since the delay was combined with the long list of modifications that required countless drawings to be changed by Engineering, and that had to trickle down to purchase orders to vendors. All of these processes took time. In a 29 March 1943 report, Mr. Matson of Yellow Truck and Coach's Production Control Division wrote "…it does not now look humanly possible to get material in time to eliminate a gap in production."

The government was pushing for the balance of the initial 2,004-vehicle order as quickly as possible, while good automotive

Bow subassemblies are under construction on jigs. On the example to the right, the pockets for the forward tow-hook shackles are visible, and the round object to the right of the welder's elbow is a hull drain valve, one of several to allow bilge water to drain out after the vehicle comes ashore. (General Motors)

In this view of the DUKW chassis-frame assembly line, shift levers for the axle transfer cases and their linkages are installed. The Oberdorfer bilge pump is present on the two nearest frames, but lacks the pulley and belt, as seen in the preceding photograph. The frame rails are unpainted and crossmembers are black. (General Motors)

Having passed the vented painting "booth" at GMC Truck & Coach in late 1943, the chassis frame assemblies in the foreground are now painted. Transfer cases are installed. To the port side of each axle transfer case, and connected to the case by a belt, is the Oberdorfer forward bilge pump, built on DUKWs to chassis 4201. (General Motors)

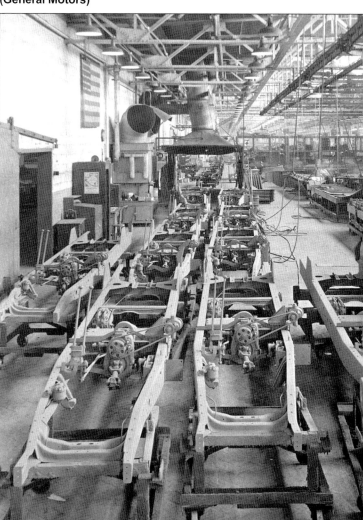

business practice dictated that the pace of production of that order be slowed from 12 per day to a pace that would correspond with being able to begin production on the new order for 1,000 vehicles. Ultimately, the need to maintain continuous production won out, and production was slowed to 10 vehicles per day on 12 May 1943. It was then revised upward to 16 per day, beginning on the last day of that month.

Although the Central Tire Inflation System was released for production by Engineering on 17 February 1943, shortages of key components meant that while the body parts for the CTIS were added beginning at chassis 2006 (USA registration number 7014883 – produced in late June), the complete CTIS package was not installed until chassis 3006 (USA registration number 7019096 – produced in early October). Modification parts kits were to be shipped to the field to complete the earlier vehicles. In Rod Stephen's report to the OSRD dated 15 August, 1943, concerning his activities in July, Stephens wrote: "July 2, 3, 4. Pontiac. Pleased to learn of additional procurement. Displeased to learn that priority rating not adequate to get present deliveries complete as to central inflation." Given that the DUKW was being built under the highest possible production rating – this bottleneck is truly indicative of the difficulties encountered by GMC in securing components.

At least the long-running problem of protecting the windshield from the surf had been solved. Numerous failures eventually made way for an entirely new windshield design, one of heavy glass with sloping front and sides. This design negated the need for the cumbersome and often ill-fated shield that previously had been used. At the rear of the DUKW, the internal fuel tank and external spare tire were both shifted from the driver's side of the vehicle to the starboard side, which produced the desired result of making an unladen DUKW rest on an even keel.

All three of the DUKW's axles are readied for installation in the axle installation area at GMC Truck & Coach. In the foreground, front-axle assemblies, identifiable by their steering knuckles, are being prepared for installation on DUKWs. The two axles at the back are rear axles. All three axles were banjo-type, single-reduction units, with a gear ratio of 6.66:1. The axle shafts were a full-floating design. (General Motors)

Using a chain hoist, a mechanic lowers a GMC Model 270 engine to the chassis frame of a DUKW. The job is greatly simplified by the fact that the forward deck of the hull is not yet installed. A cooling-air intake is mounted on the rear of the generator. (General Motors)

Assemblies comprising the side and rear walls of driver's compartments, with extensions at the front to the engine compartment, are under construction at GMC Truck & Coach Division in late 1943. A cowl is under construction in the foreground. (General Motors)

An assembly including the cowl and the driver's compartment/engine compartment box is being lowered into a DUKW hull. The crosspiece to which the hoist chain is attached is the cowl, which will form the exposed part of the driver's compartment below the windshield. (General Motors)

In the foreground, a front deck assembly is under construction on a jig. Lying on the floor to each side of the jig is a deck subassembly consisting of the fender and the side panel of the deck, for installation on the next deck to be assembled on the jig. (General Motors)

Workmen at GMC Truck & Coach Division manhandle a front deck assembly into place. Once it is exactly where they want it, they will remove the wooden two-by-four under the deck and lower it into its final position. It is then fastened with special ¼-inch bolts every three inches. These unusual bolts have both a hex head and a Philips slot. (General Motors)

A DUKW under construction in late 1943 is observed from its starboard aft corner. The inverted-U-shaped object toward the left is the aft davit eye, which, with the forward davit eye on the forward deck, allowed ship davits to raise or lower the DUKW. (General Motors)

A welder attaches the cable eye to the front center of the hull. This fitting, also referred to as the bow fairlead, served as a guide for the winch cable when the cable was extended to the front of the DUKW. This cable eye was not to be used for mooring or lashing-down the vehicle. (General Motors)

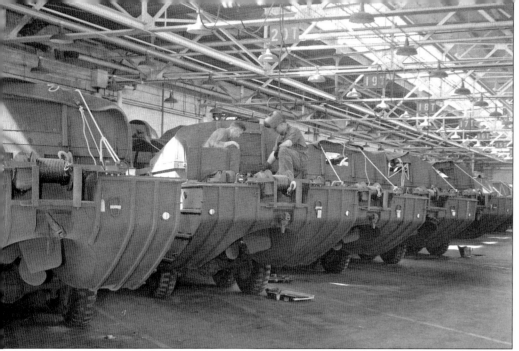

DUKWs are lined up for hull conditioning and final assembly. The marine propellers are now installed on their shafts. The two five-gallon liquid container holders now were on the port side of the aft deck; the spare tires, not yet installed here, were now on the starboard side. (General Motors)

Right: Two DUKWs are situated in paint booths at GMC's Old Coach Paint Shop, ready to receive their finish. The aft deck of the DUKW to the right has been detached and is propped-up against the plywood closure at the rear of the cargo compartment. (General Motors)

Below: Freshly painted DUKWs on lines numbers one through three are ready to leave the paint shop. Signs next to the doors warn against the use of welding torches or open flames in that room. Wheelhouse covers are leaning against the bows of the DUKWs. (General Motors)

A woman worker at GMC Truck & Coach works on a late-type, slanting windshield assembly in late 1943. The windshield wipers are already installed. These would have had pneumatic motors: DUKWs before serial number 2006 had one vacuum-operated and one hand-operated wiper. (General Motors)

A DUKW is on the inspection ramp on the final assembly line, and an inspector is checking the bottom of the hull and the rear axle. The propeller is not installed yet. At this stage of assembly, the plywood closure was a lighter color than the hull. (General Motors)

A GMC Truck & Coach worker conducts a water test on a nearly complete DUKW using a hose. This was to test the watertightness of the hatches on the forward deck. With the introduction of the new slanting windshield, there was no longer a need for the windshield surfboard. (General Motors)

A worker at GMC Truck & Coach is installing standard tools and equipment on a DUKW. He is securing an axe above the shovel. On his cart are life jackets, coiled ropes, chains, a snatch block, and other items to be stored onboard the vehicle. (General Motors)

During final assembly, a worker is securing in place a Danforth anchor on the aft deck. The spare tire is now stowed on the deck. A hook is fastened to the end of the winch cable. Five-gallon liquid containers will be stored on the holders later. (General Motors)

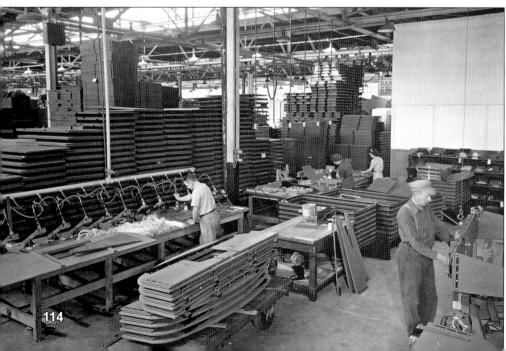

Several operations are going on in this photo of an area at GMC Truck & Coach in late 1943. In the foreground, cargo-compartment closures are being constructed. In the background, workers are stenciling floor boards and fabricating tool boxes. (General Motors)

Above: This is the final-conditioning line at the front of the GMC Truck & Coach factory in late 1943. To the right, DUKWs are nearly prepared for rolling out. To the left, CCKW 6x6 cargo trucks stand ready for shipment. (General Motors)

Right: This magnificent photo documents workers making last-minute adjustments to DUKWs at Final Assembly Department 2907. Workers and supervisors with checklists are very much in evidence as other employees scramble to put the finishing touches on the DUKWs. (General Motors)

Below: Row upon row of finished, late-type DUKWs with slanting windshields are neatly parked at GMC Truck & Coach around late 1943, ready for delivery to the armed forces. Interstingly, each one has what appears to be an identical light-colored paint smudge on the engine hatch cover. (General Motors)

A new DUKW loads into a railroad gondola car at the factory. The tight clearance between the car sides and the DUKW, which is larger than most wheeled vehicles, is evident. In the background is an automobile boxcar, which was the preferred shipping method for DUKWs as there was no need for a tarpaulin to protect the vehicle while in transit, and cotton duck was a critically short item during much of the war. (General Motors)

A DUKW completed in January 1944 is viewed with the tarpaulins and bows removed in a photo taken at the GMC Truck & Coach Division on 24 January 1944. The serial number was 5137 and the registration, though smudged, is 7018226. The improved transfer case was installed beginning at serial number DUKW353-2506, and offered greater reverse speed when afloat. (General Motors)

A 24 January 1944 file photo provides a three-quarters front view of a DUKW with the slanting windshield with triangular side wings. This vehicle, like the ones in the preceding two photos, were fitted with covers on all four wheel houses. This DUKW had enhanced water performance as compared to DUKWs produced just a few months earlier due to its two-speed marine propeller transfer case. (General Motors)

An official photo by the Ordnance Operation, Engineering Standards Vehicle Laboratory in Detroit dated 3 May 1944 shows a DUKW with a ring mount with a Browning .50-caliber machine gun M2 installed to give the crew an antiaircraft defense. (General Motors)

Central Tire Inflation System

Beginning with chassis serial number 2006, the first vehicle of the second government production purchase order, DUKWs began to be equipped for a central tire inflation system (CTIS). This system, while common on military vehicles, and even some civilian vehicles today, was unusual when it began to appear in June 1943. With CTIS, the driver can inflate and deflate the tires without leaving the vehicle cab. In the case of the DUKW, which would be moving from sandy beach to firmer conditions, such a device was ideal, and avoided the time-consuming manual inflation/deflation process that had been used up to this point.

In the early 2000s various sources began to cite Frank W. Speir as the developer of this equipment. To date no documentation has surfaced to support this claim.

The files of the Office of Strategic Research and Development, now held in the U.S. National Archives, contain correspondence, both internal within that organization as well as between OSRD and General Motors, concerning the application for patents related to the DUKW (which was permissible under the terms of the contract). Eight invention disclosures were made – none of which was for a Central Tire Inflation System.

The Central Tire Inflation System was mentioned, however, extensively.

In a letter dated 13 June 1944, G. C. Helmig of GMC writes to Carlton C. Davis, OSRD, concerning Central Tire Inflation: "From our investigation of the latter it was concluded that the tire inflation system was fairly well developed in the prior art. The system as a whole comprises pipe line leading to the several tires from a valve control at the driver's seat coupled to a compressed air storage tank. A conventional air compressor is driven by the engine to charge the storage tank and each of the several pipe lines has an individual hand valve, also located in the driver's compartment, whereby each line can be isolated from the system. A pressure gauge on the instrument panel indicates the line pressure and the main control valving includes two valves, one of which communicates with the storage tank with the several lines for tire inflation purposes and the other valve enables the

lines to be opened for deflation purposes. As a part of the pipe lines a flexible hose runs between the spring supported chassis and the hub of each wheel with a special type of rotary seal at the hub and from which a hose leads to the tire tube stem."

"With the exception of the rotary seal structure and hub assembly all of the individual units, such as the compressor, the storage tank, the valving and the piping are conventional items. The rotary seal structure employed is similar to that shown in Williams patent 2,107,405, owned by Scovill Manufacturing Company, and permission to use the structure for governmental purposes and free of royalties was given to us by Scovill. It many be added further that subsequently we were advised by Detroit Ordnance District that the Government had negotiated a royalty free license for the duration running from Scovill directly to the Government."

"The system as a whole appears to be substantially that shown in a number of expired patents, of which the following are examples:

Mercader	770,531
Brown	946,717
Rivers	1,016,896
Meyers	1,322,196
Hutchinson	1,794,900

In view of the foregoing no patent was filed on the tire inflation system and the result of our investigation is given to you in order to clear your record."

Following up on this, on 16 June 1944, John G. Roberts, Patent Counsel for OSRD, wrote to Hartley Rowe, head of Section 12, "In view of the contractor's attitude relative to the closeness of this development to the prior art, it does not appear to me that a formal invention report should be made by the contractor."

Regardless of his role in the development of CTIS, Frank W. Speir did play a major role in amphibian development. In addition to authoring the official report on the use of the DUKW in Italy and Sicily, after World War II he was Project Engineer of the Army Amphibious Warfare Program, the unit charged with developing the next generation of amphibians, including the Superduck and Drake.

The control panel for the CTIS was attached to the starboard side of the DUKW's instrument panel. Unlike the early control panel illustrated earlier, the production version included, left to right, the control lever; the tachometer; an air-pressure gauge, and a tire-pressure gauge, with ranges for sand or mud, coral, and highway conditions. (General Motors)

The CTIS finally adopted for production with chassis serial number 2006 had a single air hose connected to a rotating gland on each wheel hub, enabling the driver to adjust the tire pressure from his control panel while in motion or at rest, on land or in the water. Rigid struts protected the air hoses. (General Motors)

Flashlight in hand, a factory worker inspects the connections on a CTIS hose on a DUKW. The air hoses were vulnerable, and if one was severed, the tire it was connected to would go flat. However, as long as the hose remained intact, it was possible to keep a shot-up tire sufficiently inflated to operate. So effective was the central tire inflation system that during testing at Camp Seely 14 bullets - seven each from a .303 and a .45 - were fired into a single tire, resulting in 28 holes. However, the system had no difficulty maintaining 25 pound inflation pressure on the holed tire as well as all others. (General Motors)

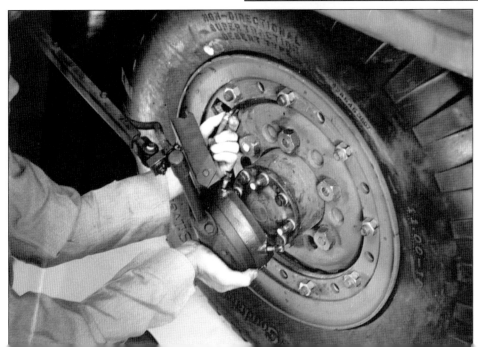

The tire-inflating device of the CTIS, normally attached to the wheel hub, could be detached for maintenance. The mechanic is holding the detached tire-inflating device in his right hand and the hose from the inflating device to the valve stem in his left hand. (General Motors)

Chapter 16
Additional Equipment

The initial assault on a beachhead is often what decides the overall success of an operation, and heavy, close firepower is frequently the deciding factor in determining the advantage. To provide such close support, a meeting on 13 February 1943 brought together representatives of the NDRC, Yellow Truck and Coach, and the California Institute of Technology. The last-named institution was involved in the development of a 4.5-inch barrage rocket, and it was hoped that a launch mechanism for such rockets could be devised that would fit into the DUKW cargo bay.

GM's Engineers devised a launcher consisting of 144 barrels in 12 groups of 12 barrels. Because of blast pressure difficulties, this was later reduced to 120 barrels divided into 12 groups of 10 barrels, each on a 45-degree angle. The rockets were muzzle loaded and electrically fired. Within each group of 10, the lower ends of the barrels were housed in a trough that conveyed the rocket blast to the rear of the DUKW against scoops that deflected the blast up and out of the cargo compartment. Perforations below the rocket heads minimized the blast pressure, preventing blast pressure from firing rockets from dislodging as-yet unfired rockets, thereby disconnecting their firing circuitry. A metal shield was installed over and behind the driver's compartment, protecting the crew from the exhaust of the departing rockets, which were launched at half-second intervals creating a ripple effect.

As the rockets were intended as barrage weapons rather than precision munitions, the 45-degree launch angle satisfactorily minimized any dispersion caused by the launch from a DUKW pitching in the sea. The launchers were demonstrated at Camp Pendleton, California ,and Camp Gordon Johnston, Florida, and based on the success of these trials, GMC made a limited number of sets for field testing, subsequent to which another firm was contracted for series production of the launch apparatus.

Wake Suppression

The wake of any vessel is often easier to spot than the vessel itself, and this is particularly true at night. Hence it was no surprise that in March 1943 work began at the Woods Hole Oceanographic Institute on developing a wake suppression kit for the DUKW. The device took in sea water, mixed it with a suppression fluid, and discharged the solution by spraying it by the front and rear of the DUKW. Additionally, it was suggested that the cargo tarpaulin be dragged behind the vehicle, covering the propeller wake, and that an apron be suspended from the bow to conceal the bow wave. Despite the modest success of this project, no follow-up work was done.

Landing Mat

In May 1943 Tri State Engineering of Washington, Pennsylvania, developed a device for spreading a landing mat from a DUKW. As those

Following a conference between GMC officials and representatives of the National Defense and Research Council and the California Institute of Technology in February 1943, GMC developed a version of the DUKW armed with 120 4.5-inch rocket-launcher tubes. The production version was designated the 4.5-inch multiple rocket launcher T44. (National Archives via Jim Gilmore)

The rocket tubes were arranged in structurally rigid, fore-and-aft groups of 10, with 12 groups of five-foot-long tubes abreast and supported by cross-beams at the front and rear. The rockets could be fired at split-second intervals, barrage-fashion. This example has the early-type blast shield for the driver. (TACOM LCMC History Office)

The early-type rocket-laucher DUKW is viewed from the front. To the rear of the driver's compartment is the blast shield, which protected any personnel in that compartment from injury when the rockets were fired. The top of the shield was secured with rope lashings at the corners and the center. (National Archives via Jim Gilmore)

The early-type rocket-launcher DUKW is observed from aft, showing the rear cross-beam. Not visible in these photos were the collector trough, a structure underneath the blast tubes that conducted the rocket blasts aft, and the scoops, which then conducted the blasts out of and away from the cargo compartment. (National Archives via Jim Gilmore)

Above: The early-type driver's shield of the rocket-launcher DUKWs was replaced by this version, with full protection over the driver's compartment. Part of the extensive electrical wiring harness for firing the rockets is visible at the front of the tubes. (TACOM LCMC History Office)

Right: The late-type driver's shield incorporated a framework for added strength. Each of the launcher tubes was fabricated from two half-round steel sections, spot-welded together. Toward the bottom of each tube were perforations to reduce the blast pressure, which otherwise could dislodge unfired rockets. (TACOM LCMC History Office)

The 120 rocket tubes were fixed at a 45 degree angle. The 4.5-inch fin-stabliized rockets were loaded by inserting them into the tops of the tubes and allowing them to slide down into place. For maintenance or repairs, a row of 10 tubes could be removed as a unit, or all 120 tubes could be pulled as a package. (General Motors)

The control box for the 4.5-inch multiple rocket launcher T44, on the floor in front of the passenger's seat in the DUKW, had controls for firing the rockets and selecting the number of them to be fired at a time. There was no sighting mechanism for the launchers; the vehicle was maneuvered to train the rockets on target. As the tubes had fixed elevation, the rockets were fired at a specific range to put them on target. (General Motors)

This DUKW with 4.5-inch multiple rocket launcher T44, assigned to an engineer unit, had defensive armament in the form of a pedestal-mounted .30-caliber machine gun on each side of the driver's compartment. (US Army Engineer School History Office)

The same engineer DUKW with barrage rocket launchers seen in the above photo comes ashore. The machine gun pedestals extended about a foot below the top of the hull. On this example, the windshield and side wings have been removed. (US Army Engineer School History Office)

involved with the DUKW well knew, driving vehicles – particularly wheeled vehicles – across soft sand required skilled operators and reduced tire pressure. If massive attacking armies were to be equipped with DUKWs, this requirement for highly skilled operators was impractical. One means around this problem was the use of a mat to distribute the vehicle's weight over a far greater area than the mere contact surface of its own tires or tracks. The British did extensive testing of such devices mounted on tanks.

It was envisioned that a DUKW equipped with the Tri State device would land prior to the beaching of landing craft. The DUKW crew would select a suitable landing site, and as the vehicle exited the surf they would pull the mat from its folded position atop the rear of the DUKW, over the top of the vehicle and down ahead of the front wheels.into position ahead of the front wheels. Once the DUKW began driving on it, the mat would automatically unfold over the beach wherever the DUKW went.One DUKW was expected to be able to lay between 200 and 400 feet of mat, depending upon conditions. To date no documents have surfaced suggesting that this apparatus was employed in combat during World War II. It was, however, used in Korea.

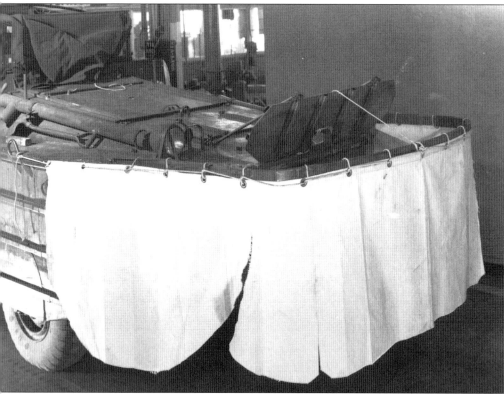

In March 1943, a wake-suppression kit was developed for the DUKW, and six copies were made. It involved spraying a chemically treated sea-water solution in front of the bow and behind the stern. Seen here are fabric panels lashed to a frame protruding in front of the bow to hide the bow wave. (TACOM LCMC History Office)

In May 1943, Tri State Engineering, of Washington, Pennsylvania, developed a mat-laying apparatus for the DUKW. It consisted of a curved frame over the driver's compartment and bow, over which woven-wire matting was dispensed. (TACOM LCMC History Office)

Above: The matting was stored on the rear of the DUKW, folded, accordion style. The front of the matting was brought under the front tires, and the forward motion of the vehicle caused the matting to move forward as the DUKW rolled over it. (Sparkman & Stephens)

Left: A DUKW with matting dispenser is viewed from the front. The prime use for such matting was to form prepared ramps at coastal or riverine landing sites, so vehicles would not get bogged-down in mud or sand. The matting also could be used to form temporary airfields when DUKWs performed aircraft-ferrying operations. (Sparkman & Stephens)

In a view from inside the driver's compartment of a DUKW with a matting dispenser, a man in the assistant driver's seat is grasping a control lever, apparently linked to a brake to control the playing-out of the matting. At the bottom is a type of CTIS control panel. (Sparkman & Stephens)

Chapter 17
Made In Missouri

On 19 May 1943 the Ordnance Department asked Yellow Truck and Coach to issue a proposal to build a further 1,196 DUKWs for delivery before the end of 1943. In drafting a response, once again the critical problem was maintaining a rate of production for the orders in hand (at this point in time, the DUKWs on the assembly line were those that were a part of the first production contract – although materials had been ordered, the third 1,000 DUKWs that constituted the second production contracts had not yet begun assembly) that would permit continuous operation of the assembly line, and employment for the skilled workers. The chief problem with achieving this goal was the ability to get components – particularly steel – for 1,196 vehicles in a timely manner.

It was anticipated that final assembly of vehicles in such a new order would begin in September. To achieve that aim, the company would need to begin fabricating 400 sets of sheet metal in July, followed by another 400 in August and 396 in September. Demand on the nation's steel mills at the time, however, was such that the bulk of the steel capacity for July and August was already committed. Compounding this problem, the Priority Rating proposed for this order, as well as the third 1,000-DUKW order, was only AA-2X, rather than the AA-1 of the initial order, meaning that higher-priority projects could interrupt the flow of materials and components.

A meeting was held at the Yellow Truck and Coach plant on Friday, 28 May, between company officials and Col. Van Duesen and his staff concerning this situation, as well as the question of Yellow Truck and Coach's maximum amphibian production. The company's response to the latter was that if any coach (bus) production was to be retained – and the materials for this production as well as the government

When the military's demand for DUKWs exceeded the GMC Truck & Coach Division's capacity to produce them, a second assembly line for these amphibian vehicles was opened at Chevrolet's plant in St. Louis, Missouri. This photo is the first in a sequence showing DUKWs under construction at the St. Louis plant. (National Archives)

authorization were already in hand, the shop facilities would be limited to three hull assembly jigs from which nine assemblies per eight-hour shift could be produced, giving a maximum of 18 per day. Van Duesen was cautioned, however, that due to materials and manpower shortages (absenteeism typically ran about 5%), 16 per day was a more reasonable number to actually plan for. This rate of production would require about 1,000 men, from hull assembly to final inspection and shipping of the vehicle. To increase production to 20 per day working two nine-hour shifts would require an additional 250 men. To reach 22 vehicles per day would require two 10-hour shifts and another 50 men beyond the 250 already referred to, because it was felt that the long shifts would increase absenteeism. Assembly of a DUKW required 576 man-hours, 747 including sheet metal fabrication.

At this same meeting, it was agreed to immediately send Yellow Truck's K. E. Turner to the War Production Board in Washington with the Controlled Materials Plan application (CMP-4A) requesting the materials for these 1,196 in the third quarter of 1943. Turner returned to Pontiac Sunday with an approved plan for 80% delivery in the third quarter, with the balance in the fourth quarter.

Still, Production Control cautioned the other parties that the AA-2X rating proposed for both this order and the 1,000-vehicle order already in hand would need to be raised to AA-1 in order to secure all the needed materials in a timely manner, and that a large number of things would even require the reserved-for-emergencies-only AAA rating. The latter was particularly the case for July and August alloy steel. All of this work of course was being done before the age of computer and email, and it was estimated that it would take the Production Control and Purchasing departments the entire month of June to complete the voluminous paperwork for this order.

The monumental effort taken to this point was done prior to any official order being placed – but that order, Contract W-374-ORD-6523, finally arrived on Monday, 7 June 1943. Irving Babcock, President of Yellow Truck and Coach, called Production Control at 2:45 p.m. that day to advise them of this and give them the go ahead for the 1,196 vehicles plus spare parts. He also passed along the news

As viewed from overhead, Chevrolet workers are installing a chassis frame in the hull of a DUKW. The view is facing forward, with the aft tunnel at the bottom of the photo. Mounted on the frame between the two men toward the front of the port side of the hull is a Gould forward bilge pump; this type replaced the Oberdorfer pump after chassis number 4201. (National Archives)

A DUKW undergoes a propeller test in the water tank at the St. Louis plant. Chains secured to the aft corners of the vehicle hold it in check as the propeller is put through its paces. Two men in the cargo compartment are monitoring conditions there. (National Archives)

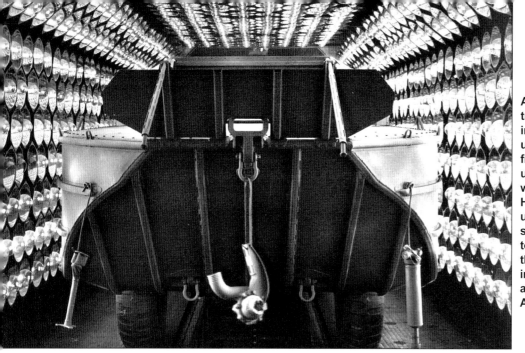

A newly painted DUKW is undergoing treatment by banks of infrared drying lights in a drying booth at St. Louis. Coming up with proper paint for the DUKW was fraught with difficulty. Early production used standard military automotive finishes, which quickly wore and rusted through. Hence a new paint system was developed utilizing a rust-inhibiting primer. At the same time a non-skid deck coating began to be applied. Dangling from the bow in this photo are several DUKW components, including a drive shaft (right) and a Higgins aft bilge-pump assembly (center). (National Archives)

Right: Workers at Chevrolet's St. Louis plant are putting the final touches on several DUKWs. Tarpaulins have been installed over the driver's compartments. Forward and aft wheel-house covers are installed. The round stickers visible on several of the windshields read "EXPORT." (National Archives)

Below: Newly minted DUKWs drive down a paved ramp and enter the water at a basin at St. Louis for tests under more extended conditions than available in the factory's water tanks. They will be checked for any problems such as leaks or performance issues. (National Archives)

Above: A DUKW splashes into the water with force during tests in a basin at St. Louis. Several civilians are in the front of the cargo compartment for the ride. Not all accessories have been stored on the vehicle yet; for example, the manual bilge pump is absent. (National Archives)

Right: During outdoor water tests at St. Louis, a DUKW chugs along with several wooden crates – probably containing on-vehicle material (OVM) packed in crates for shipping – stacked in the cargo compartment. A U.S. Army registration number is stenciled on the stern but is illegible. Liquid containers are not yet stored on the aft deck. (National Archives)

Below: Saint Louis-produced DUKWs are nearing readiness for delivery. Temporary markings, probably inspectors' marks, are written sideways on the bows. Standard tools and accessories are yet to be stored on the vehicles. (National Archives)

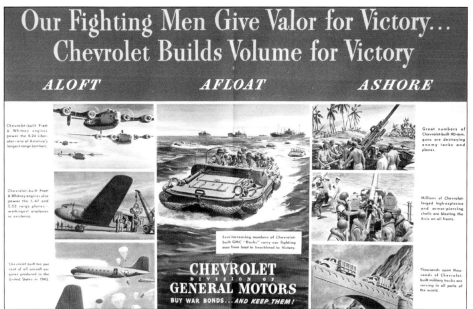

Although almost forgotten today, that Chevrolet produced almost half of the DUKWs was no wartime secret, as this period advertisement clearly indicates. A painting of a DUKW transporting troops during an invasion landing forms the centerpiece in an advertisement promoting Chevrolet's contributions to the war effort: a nod to the work of the St. Louis plant in producing these amphibian vehicles.

that this order was rated AA-1, and that the previous order was also rerated to AA-1. He also advised that Mr. Whitworth, Contracting Officer, Detroit Ordnance District, had advised them they could deal directly with the War Production Board without an intermediary, and that every possible aid would be given in securing AAA ratings for trouble items. Internally, Yellow Truck and Coach combined the order for these 1,196 vehicles with the earlier order for 1,000 vehicles on Sales Order TC-200568.

Production Control sprang into action, and by working around the clock, completed all the requisitions, a task originally forecast to take a month, by 4 p.m. Wednesday – a display of remarkable dedication.

The problem created for production by the ongoing deluge of proposed changes flowing from Ordnance and OSRD field operations is illustrated in a memo from R. A. Crist, Yellow Truck and Coach Production Control Manager:

"In connection with Engineering Notifications which we have received since Engineering learned we were making a buy and which I am holding on my desk for the time being (in which they ask us to hold up material) I mentioned to you that I proposed not to make any hold-up until were received the changed or new parts; otherwise we hang ourselves before we get started, and my position is that we cannot meet the program laid down for us with this kind of handling. When, as and if the changes come through we will analyze the particular material involved at that time, determine if the material is actually affected, and at that time determine the point at which the change can be made without interruption to production. Point is that we must allocate our material allotments immediately – otherwise they are lost to us – any holdup without a release of new material would jeopardize the whole program."

So by 26 June 1943, output schedules had been set up to ship all 4,196 DUKWs then on order by the end of 1943. On 2 July came word that an additional 3,600 DUKWs, plus 36 sets of spare parts, were sought on contract W-374-ORD-6900. Half of this order was to be delivered by the end of March 1944, with the remaining 1,800 to be finished in June 1944. Thus the cycle outlined above began again. For vehicle assembly to start in January, hull fabrication had to be underway in December, with steel, of course, arriving prior to that.

Steel continued to be a problem. Under ideal circumstances, Yellow

Early Pontiac-built DUKWs

Contract W-374-ORD-2849

Sales Order TC-200449

Serial Numbers	Registration Numbers
6 to 602	70104 to 70700

Sales Order TC-200450

Serial Numbers	Registration Numbers
603 to 901	70701 to 70999
902 to 2005	701000 to 702103

Contract W-374-ORD-6523

Sales Order TC-200568

Serial Numbers	Registration Numbers
2006 to 4201	7014883 to 7017290

Contract W-374-ORD-6900

Sales Order TC-200585

Serial Numbers	Registration Numbers
4202 to 6601	7017291 to 7020891

Sales Order TC-200587

Serial Numbers	Registration Numbers
7802 to 11878	7022093 to 7026169

Early St. Louis-built DUKWs

Contract W-374-ORD-6900

Sales Order TC-200586

Serial Numbers	Registration Numbers
6602 to 7801	7020892 to 7022091

Sales Order TC-200588

Serial Numbers	Registration Numbers
11879 to 14778	7026169 to 7029069

Within each sales order the serial numbers and registration numbers increase correspondingly.

Truck and Coach would supply a steel mill with an order for steel rolled to various widths and gauges, which would then be rolled to order, minimizing the amount of sizing that had to be done at the Truck plant. However, the orders outlined above were given to Yellow Truck and Coach at such late dates (compared to the required delivery dates) that rather than getting steel rolled to order, Yellow had to settle for whatever steel could be found, in mills or warehouses, and then sheare it to size in the Company's sheet metal shop. The volume of this work exceeded the plant and manpower capacity of Yellow Truck's sheet metal shop, so outside firms were contracted to do much of this work, increasing the amount of handling of the steel as it was shipped in and out of the plant, and adding to the already enormous paper trail.

With word coming in September that an order for 6,977 more DUKWs was in the offing, a meeting was set up with Fisher Body – Pontiac and Chevrolet – St. Louis, in hopes that an arrangement could be reached whereby GMC – as Yellow Truck and Coach had become on 20 September – would build half of the forthcoming DUKW orders, with Fisher and Chevrolet each building 25% of the future orders. By 1 October Fisher Body had been eliminated from the program, and so it was decided that production of the future DUKW orders would be split equally between GMC's Pontiac plant, the former Yellow Truck and Coach plant, and Chevrolet, St. Louis. The Government's deal was with GMC, and Chevrolet was GMC's subcontractor – hence, vehicles built in both plants were being bought from and delivered by GMC – and their nameplates did not bear the Chevrolet name.

Due to material shortages, the DUKW production program, as of 8 September 1943, stood as follows:

The order for the third 1,000 vehicles on Sales Order TC200568 was all past due.

The contract for 1,196 vehicles also on Sales Order TC200568 was being rescheduled.

The contract for 3,600 vehicles was being rescheduled.

The two new contract supplements in the amounts of 3,600 and 3,377 vehicles, were pending.

To balance production between Pontiac and St. Louis and meet the schedules requested by Ordnance, GMC issued a contract to Chevrolet to produce 4,100 DUKWs in St. Louis. These included 1,200 vehicles on Sales Order TC200586, which were part of the contract for 3,600 vehicles, and Sales Order TC200588, which covered 2,900 of the 6,977-vehicle order pending.

GMC supplied Chevrolet considerable data, and such key DUKW project people, as Production Control Manager R.A. Crist and OSRD contractor Rod Stephens, went to St. Louis to familiarize Chevrolet personnel with the project. Under the terms of the agreement, Chevrolet would assemble DUKWs, but the DUKW sheet metal would be fabricated by GMC or outside vendors. The overall schedule called for Pontiac to produce 600 complete vehicles per month, with Chevrolet assembling a further 400 vehicles per month, meaning GMC's sheet metal department – aided by some outside vendors – had to turn out 1,000 sets of DUKW sheet-metal components, plus spares, per month. The DUKW components furnished by GMC to Chevrolet were shipped to St. Louis by rail, and transit time had to be built into the schedule as well, along with allowances for in-process materials.

Chevrolet was expected to have its first nine DUKWs on wheels and practically complete by 20 November, with 100 to be built in December and 300 in January, finally hitting the 400 vehicle per month stride in February.

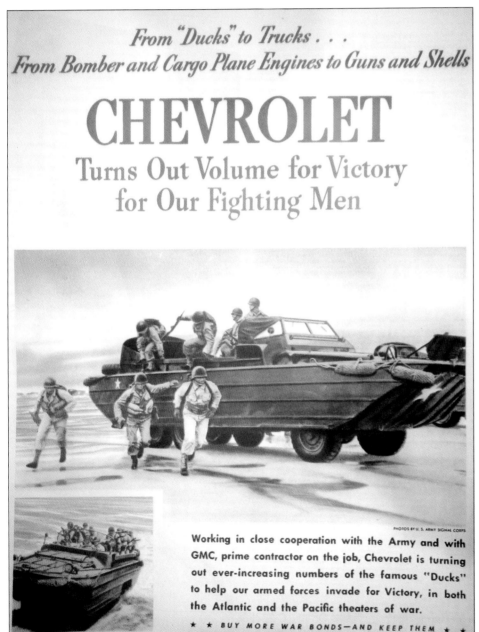

From "Ducks" to Trucks . . .
From Bomber and Cargo Plane Engines to Guns and Shells

CHEVROLET
Turns Out Volume for Victory
for Our Fighting Men

PHOTOS BY U. S. ARMY SIGNAL CORPS

Working in close cooperation with the Army and with GMC, prime contractor on the job, Chevrolet is turning out ever-increasing numbers of the famous "Ducks" to help our armed forces invade for Victory, in both the Atlantic and the Pacific theaters of war.

★ ★ BUY MORE WAR BONDS—AND KEEP THEM ★ ★

The troops have come ashore in the illustrations on another Chevrolet ad promoting the company's role in supplying the U.S. Armed Forces with fighting equipment. The ad copy took care to point out that GMC was the "prime contractor on the [DUKW] job." (Steve Preston collection)

Chapter 18
Special Cargo Handling

As the use of the DUKW began to grow, it was increasingly seen as a versatile vehicle, which with little modification could serve in a variety of roles. A number of accessories were developed for use with the vehicle, some of which were mass produced, while others remained one-off.

Howitzer Harness

On 3 January 1944 work began on an apparatus that would allow the 105mm Howitzer M2A1 to be fired from a position in the DUKW, whether the DUKW was at sea or ashore. The apparatus created to do this is known as a howitzer harness – a fitting name given that it was required to restrain the weapon in six different directions while firing, as well as transmitting the forces of both transport and recoil to the appropriate places in the DUKW structure. The firing loads, with a Zone 7, or maximum charge, amounted to 12,000 pounds horizontally and 6,000 pounds vertically. This was complicated by the necessity that the cannon trails be spread when firing – but closed to provide a better configuration for transport.

An improvised harness was created and test fired on 6 January. On 25 January a completely engineered pilot arrived at Aberdeen Proving Ground, having been completed by GMC in Pontiac only days before. After test firing at Aberdeen, the vehicle was driven to Fort Story for further evaluation. After receiving data indicating that the

blast pressure would have no ill effects on the driver, such firing was tried, successfully. Interestingly, the blast effect did require that when mass production of the howitzer harness kit began in late April 1944, the kits included Lucite head lamps as well as additional hatch hold downs. A pair of sighting rods were added to aid the driver in broadly laying the weapon. The bulk of the harness kit consisted of metal bound planks for trail support at the coamings, and other timbers to hold the weapon in position.

Litter Carrier

It was discovered at some point that the width of the DUKW cargo coaming was such that a standard army litter would conveniently span the cargo bay. Furthermore, the height was such that litters so arranged would be suspended at an appropriate level above patients resting in litters placed on the cargo deck. The only problem with this arrangement was that jostling of the DUKW, either on the road or at sea, could cause the upper litters to slip off the coaming, dropping litter and patient on the lower level of patients. To remedy this, a wooden guard rail with metal bracket system was designed which, attached via wing nuts, could be quickly installed or removed. When not in use, these guard rails were stowed beneath the cargo deck boards. A DUKW so equipped could evacuate litter-borne casualties. Dennis Puleston proposed such a system, including conducting a study of an

From early in its development, one of the key roles envisioned for the DUKW was as a means to transport 105mm howitzers from ship to shore or across rivers. In early January 1944, work commenced on a means of mounting a 105mm howitzer M2A1 so that it could be fired from the DUKW afloat or on land. Here, a 105mm howitzer has been mounted in the cargo compartment of DUKW registration number 70108. (Patton Museum)

A 105mm howitzer is stored in the cargo compartment of a DUKW. Above the rear wheels are the spade and the lunette at the rear of the right trail. The piece is lashed down with wires around the tires.

Right: There was barely enough clearance for the wheels of the 105mm howitzer M2A1 in the cargo compartment of the DUKW; here, the lug nuts of one of the wheels are digging into the steel coaming, damaging it. A permanent fix for the cramped wheel fit would have to wait for a post-WWII Modification Work Order.

Below: The same DUKW with 105mm howitzer seen in the preceding photo cruises offshore. Rope lashings called the harness are secured from the rear of the trails of the howitzer to the mooring eyes at the upper center of the hull. The surfboard is erected on the bow in readiness for encountering waves.

A 105mm howitzer M2A1 is secured to a DUKW, its wheels on chocks. Before the piece could be fired, it was necessary to spread the trails. A kit for a DUKW-mounted, fully firing 105mm howitzer was developed in less than a month, and production kits were available in May 1944.

A makeshift 105mm Howitzer M3 installation in the cargo compartment of a DUKW is viewed from the rear. The weapon, designed as a light howitzer for airborne troops, was photographed in the Rome area on 13 June 1944. Both wheels have been detached. (National Archives via Jim Gilmore)

U.S. Army DUKWs display their ability to transport a variety of weapons and vehicles. They are loaded with, from foreground to background: a 57mm antitank gun; a 75mm howitzer; a quarter-ton Jeep; and an M-29C Weasel tracked amphibious vehicle.

arrangement, at the Amphibian Vehicle Training School in Charleston, South Carolina, forwarding a detailed plan on using a DUKW to evacuate 12 litter patients to the OSRD offices on 4 April 1943.

Coincidentally, the Research and Development Division of the Surgeon General's Office had requested that two DUKWs be shipped to the Medical Department Equipment Laboratory at Carlisle Barracks, Pennsylvania, for similar purposes. Work began on this project on 31 March 1943, and by 15 April the request had been complied with, and approval had been granted for the Medical Department to work directly with the Engineer Amphibian command to expedite completion of this development.

One of the advantages of this system, of great interest to the Surgeon General, was that the DUKW could pick up the wounded near the front lines and transport them to ships off shore for medical care, with the ship's gear lifting the entire DUKW to the deck, minimizing the amount of handling and jostling the patients were subjected to.

On 17 April 1943 Puleston's plans were forwarded to the Surgeon General. His plans included a loading diagram, along with a suggestion that pins or clips be used to limit the movement of the litters. The Medical Department was loathe to modify the thousands of litters already in service so as to accept pins, and was concerned that removable clips, four per stretcher, would easily be lost in the haste of evacuation.

The Medical Department tried various means of using rope or line to secure the litters in place before settling on a plan that involved removable stops, which were to be attached to the DUKW rather than the litter. Such an arrangement was designed by the Medical Department and tried at Camp Edwards. General Motors, however, basing itself on a design submitted by the Equipment Laboratory, extensively redesigned the litter stop arrangement, producing one that ultimately was placed in production.

When production of this apparatus finally was approved on 17 May 1944, the decision had been made to produce 2,500 of the kits for issue to units already using DUKWs in the field, and that they would be furnished together with all new DUKWs leaving the assembly line in the future.

One of the DUKW's primary duties was the evacuation of casualties, and its amphibian capabilites gave it great efficiency in that area. Here, G.I.s are posing as the lower layer of patients in a DUKW. Next, a top layer of litters holding patients will be arranged sideways on the tops of the coamings.

Litter patients are stacked two layers high in the cargo compartment of a DUKW. The problem with this arrangement was that the rails of the top litters, which rested atop the coamings, could shift around, causing the patients to fall on those below them.

To alleviate the problem of litter rails shifting and sliding on the coamings, a system was devised for lashing the rails in place with a light line wrapped around the handles and routed through tie-downs on the side of the coaming, as demonstrated here.

Once the litter patients were loaded into the cargo compartment of the DUKW and the top litters were lashed down, the canvas top has been placed on top of the bows, and the canvas closure has been installed on the aft bow. Next, the sides of the tarpaulin will be lowered and lashed in place.

To remedy the problem of litter rails moving off the coamings while transporting patients, a fix was developed involving boards mounted parallel to and outboard of the tops of the coamings. These boards acted as stops to keep the litters from moving.

The litter stops are attached vertically to brackets on the upper parts of the side coamings of the cargo compartment. With these stops installed, litters for six patients could be placed atop the coamings. (Reg Hodgson)

The rails on the litter-stop assemblies are of painted wood. When not in use, the assemblies were removed and stored in the hull under the front left panel of the cargo compartment deck. (Reg Hodgson)

Litter stops are installed on this DUKW. The handles of the two litters to the right (A) are correctly placed atop the coamings, butted against the litter stops. The litter stop noted as B has been detached and lowered. If the vehicle was driven like this, the litters would shift, dropping one end of the litter and the patient into the cargo compartment and onto the patients in the lower level litters. (National Archives via Jim Gilmore)

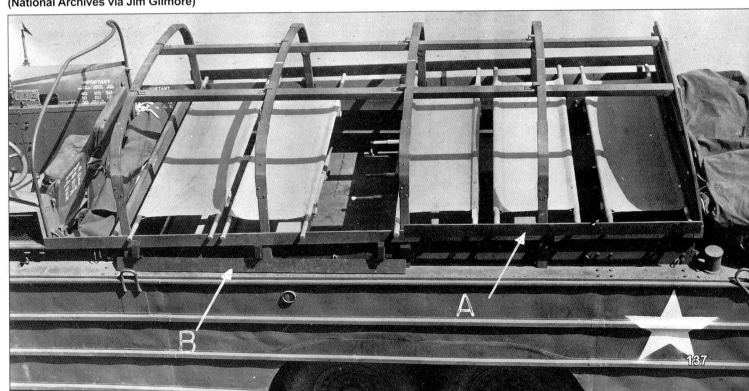

A-V frame

One of the most useful accessories developed for the DUKW was the previously discussed A-frame. The chief disadvantage of the A-frame was that the DUKW could not unload itself – that is, an A-frame equipped DUKW could unload companion DUKWs, but for that DUKW itself to be unloaded the A-frame had to be transferred to another vehicle. This also obviously inhibited solo DUKW cargo handling operations. To counter this, it was suggested that the A-frame be modified to form a V-frame, mounted with the joined end down, one leg of the frame standing vertically, secured by guy wires to the DUKW structure, while the second leg served as a davit boom. Some even suggested that a winch be added to this assembly so that the boom could be raised or lowered, while as with the A-frame the DUKW's rear power winch provided the lifting force.

Sail

A peculiar side benefit of the V-frame arrangement was tried by a group of GMC employees without government direction or authorization. These employees discovered that one leg of the V-frame could be secured in the machine-gun mounting clamp located behind the driver's seat, while the other leg, positioned perpendicular to and near the top of the former would suspend the cargo canvas, which formed a makeshift sail. The GMC employees felt that such a rig would be useful should a DUKW engine become disabled, or if a stealth landing approach was needed. Although this rig was successfully tested in a lake near the GMC plant, it not only was not adopted, the experiment was not officially sanctioned, and thus NDRC ordered that reference to these experiments be purged from the official published histories.

Above: The A-frame of a DUKW is being tested in a photograph dated 29 August 1944. The weight it is hoisting is marked 2,000 pounds. Stay cables from the forward lifting eyes to the top of the frame tubes of the A-frame supported and held the structure static when deployed for hoisting. (General Motors)

Left: Experiments were conducted with several V-frame cranes consisting of a kingpost and a boom mounted at the rear of the cargo compartment of a DUKW. While this rig would have given the DUKW the ability to self-load or -unload cargo, it is not clear if it saw much operational use. (General Motors)

The DUKW-mounted A-frame hoisting a 2,000-pound weight is observed from the rear. To accomplish the lift the winch cable was routed through a pulley at the top of the A-frame. The first DUKW A-frame was improvised from timbers during a demonstration of a pilot vehicle at Provincetown, Massachusetts. (General Motors)

Seen from aft, a V-frame crane installation on a DUKW lifts a steel tub filled with sandbags. Four cable stays stabilize and strengthen the kingpost; their bottoms are fastened with clevises to the aft lifting eyes and to the horizontally oriented eyes welded to the rear corners of the hull. (General Motors)

GMC employees who were also sailing enthusiasts adapted the V-frame to serve as a mast in August 1944, with the cargo cover acting as a sail. The mast was secured in the socket provided for a machine gun mount. The mast was the boom with a sheave at the top, while the yardarm was two boat hooks lashed together. Such a rig would have been for emergency-only use. (General Motors)

Chapter 19

Production Peaks

Early in December 1943 the Ordnance Department issued Contract W-20-018-ORD-2164, calling for an additional 2,600 DUKWs. On Christmas Eve 1943, Plant Manager Dodd authorized the procurement of materials for these vehicles and associated spare parts. GMC managers proposed that 700 of these vehicles be built in St. Louis, with the remaining 1,900 to be built in Pontiac. The plan was approved and a purchase order issued to Chevrolet Central Office accordingly on 13 January 1944.

It was proposed too that the purchasing of the materials for these 2,600 DUKWs be tied to the purchase of materials for 76,657 trucks authorized in the same time frame. However, these purchases were delayed because of some problems with the truck program, and on 18 February GMC President Irving Babcock authorized the purchase of the DUKW material independently, having been pressured to do so as fabrication of the sheet metal for these vehicles would have to begin in August, from steel delivered in July. We have already seen examples of the long lead time and difficulty with steel orders.

On the same day, the production schedules were revised and the distribution of production between Pontiac and St. Louis was revised, taking into account both contract W-274-ORD-6900 and the new W-20-018-ORD-2164. The intent of this change was to make production of contract -6900 wrap up in both Pontiac and St. Louis during September.

The adjustments to Sales Orders were as follows:

TC-200587, Contract -6900, Pontiac production increased by 300 units to 4,477

TC-200588, Contract -6900, St. Louis production decrease by 300 units to 2,500

TC-200613, Contract -2164, Pontiac production, decrease by 300 units to 1,600

TC-200614, Contract -2164, St. Louis production, increase by 300 units to 1,000

As can be seen, the total production at the two facilities remained the same, these changes were done purely to make the paperwork and the transition between contracts cleaner.

This was the plan with which both GMC and Chevrolet operated until 3 May 1944. On that date a request was received from Ordnance with modified delivery dates. Had the originally forecasted production rates been adhered to as well as the newly requested delivery dates, the result would have been no DUKW production during December 1944, a situation untenable for General Motors. To compensate for this and maintain continuous production at both facilities, it was decided to slow DUKW production in Pontiac, freeing up labor to build buses.

So, the Sales Orders were again changed as follows:

TC-200587, Contract -6900, Pontiac production decreased by 400 units to 4,077

TC-200588, Contract -6900, St. Louis production increased by 400 units to 2,900

TC-200613, Contract -2164, Pontiac production, decreased by 300 units to 1,300

TC-200614, Contract -2164, St. Louis production, increased by 300 units to 1,300

Further, at about the same time the Detroit Ordnance District requested a proposal to deliver an additional 2,589 DUKWs, with spare parts, during the first six months of 1945. General Motors corporate policy at the time prevented its operating units from ordering materials in excess of nine months in advance of need. To work within that policy, yet meet the military demands, internally GMC broke this arrangement into two lots – one for 1,300 vehicles, whose materials could be ordered immediately upon execution of the contract, and another for 1,289 vehicles, the materials for which could be ordered at

The following sequence of photographs documents DUKWs produced in August and September 1944. On this vehicle, the front wheel house cover is removed, allowing a view of the central tire-inflation system connections. The "sling here" stencils below the lifting eyes became a production standard in November 1943. (General Motors)

Above: An important but hard to discern recently added feature on the August-September 1944 DUKWs was the addition of small tabs with holes in them to the sides of the hull, for hanging the tire-inflation devices when performing maintenance on them or tire changes. One hanger was above the forward wheel house, and two others were to the front and rear of the aft wheel house. (General Motors)

Left: A tarpaulin partially covers the driver's compartment of this DUKW, just recently off the assembly line in the August-September 1944 time frame. When the canvas top for the cab and the tarpaulin were installed, the driver's side vision through the triangular side windows was somewhat restricted. (General Motors)

The DUKWs produced in the late summer of 1944 incorporated a number of recent modifications, most of which were subtle, such as an improved paint treatment that minimized the chances of corrosion, a measure released for production on 27 February 1944. (General Motors)

Left: The white waterline-load markings on the port and starboard sides of the stern were released for production on 17 January 1944. They were intended to provide a visual way to judge the weight of the cargo and the trim of the vehicle while afloat. (General Motors)

Below: The forward and aft wheel house covers had horizontal stiffeners in line with the rub rails on the hull. The wheel house covers were attached to the hull by means of cotter pins inserted vertically through holes through the hull rub rails and the covers' stiffeners. (General Motors)

On the each side of the cowl of the slant-windshield DUKWs was a pointed holder that the window rested on when in the lowered position. On the outboard side of each of these holders was a hold-down clamp to secure the windshield when in the down position. (General Motors)

Above: A DUKW negotiates a very rough, concrete obstacle course, probably at General Motors' proving grounds. This course tested the ability of the suspension to withstand severe flexing. (General Motors)

Left: Details of the bow and the forward deck of a late-summer-1944 DUKW are displayed. This version of the surfboard was metal, with four hat-channel reinforcers on the top side. The surf board was equipped with four heavy-pin-type hinges. Early surfboards had piano hinges. (General Motors)

The reinforced surf board is viewed from the driver's compartment, showing the braces that held it erect and the cautionary stencil on the board. The forward hull hatch was locked in the closed position by two hinged channel sections secured by wing nuts. (General Motors)

The driver's compartment of a late-summer 1944 DUKW is viewed. On the coaming to the right are three plugs for letting water out of the bottom of the hull; they were stored here when on land. On the opposite coaming are three hull drain plugs. At the center of the dash board is the compass, in this case the Pioneer model. The kapok seat cushions doubled as life preservers. (General Motors)

With the driver's seat cushion removed, visible inside the base of the seat is the bilge-pump valve manifold. Three levers from the manifold protrude through cutouts at the front of the seat base; these levers were added after chassis serial number 4201 and were used to selectively pump-out the center and aft compartments of the hull. At the bottom is one of two brackets for a machine-gun ring mount to the rear of the driver's compartment. (General Motors)

The assistant driver's seat cushion is removed in this view of the starboard side of the driver's compartment. Both of the ring-mount brackets to the rear of the compartment are at the bottom. To the front of the steering wheel is the CTIS control panel. Below the compass is the map compartment. A first-aid kit is to the starboard side of the dash board. The floor panels in this compartment were removable and were fabricated from plywood. (General Motors)

The Pioneer compass is a product of Eclipse-Pioneer, a division of the Bendix Aviation Corporation. On this example, the side plate of the compass has been removed, showing some of its inner mechanisms. (General Motors)

a future date to stay within the policy limitations.

On 20 July 1944, the order for the 2,589 DUKWs with spare parts materialized in the form of Contract W-20-018-ORD-6053, and on 24 July Mr. Babcock authorized the purchase of 1,300 sets of components. Production Control and Purchasing had completed all the necessary paperwork in advance, and needed only to fill in the applicable contract number prior to submitting the orders. A rate of production of 24 vehicles per day was agreed upon with the Detroit Ordnance District, to be divided more or less equally between Pontiac and St. Louis. Shipment of this order, as well as all previous orders, was to be complete by the end of August 1945. These 1,300 vehicles were placed on two sales orders, TC-200632 for Pontiac for 700 vehicles, and TC-200633 to St. Louis for 600 vehicles.

Almost a month after Babcock's 24 July authorization to purchase, the time was approaching that the remaining 1,289 sets of material needed to complete the new order could be ordered without violating GM policy. Mr. Babcock held a meeting in his office on 24 August 1944, during which he directed that those materials be ordered on or about 1 September 1944. Production of these 1,289 DUKWs was to be divided on sales orders TC-200635 for 650 units in Pontiac and TC-200636 in St. Louis for 639 vehicles.

Contract W-20-018-ORD-6053 was modified on 8 December 1944 when a contract supplement requesting a further 358 vehicles arrived. These too were split between Michigan and Missouri, with sles order TC-200676 going to Pontiac for 206 vehicles, and TC-200277 picking up the remaining 152 for St. Louis.

Yet another modification to the contract arrived near mid-month, this one adding a further 3,700 DUKWs, plus spare parts, to the order, to be delivered by the end of December 1945. Once again, in order to work within GM policy, this was divided into a group of 2,000 and a group of 1,700. Requisitioning of the materials for the 2,000-vehicle group was combined with that for the earlier 358-vehicle supplement,

A powerplant is lowered into the hull of a DUKW, which like its sister beside it, is seen under construction on 16 March 1945. The small metal tab for holding the tire-inflation device when detached from the front wheel hub is faintly visible below the second rub rail from the top of the wheel house. (General Motors)

with the balance being held in abeyance. The DUKW-peculiar spare parts for all 40 sets of spares on the contract supplement were also requisitioned at this time. At the time, it was planned that output of these 2,000 vehicles would be split equally between Pontiac and St. Louis.

On 23 February 1945, yet another new order appeared, this one from a new source – the United States Navy. This order, the first directly from that branch, was for a modest 240 vehicles, and GMC linked it to the requisitions for the 1,700 vehicles remaining of the 3,700 vehicle supplement issued in December. Both the 1,700-vehicle and the 240-vehicle orders were split evenly between Pontiac and St. Louis in the scheduling.

On 19 April 1945, Supplement 10 of Contract W-20-018-ORD-6053 was entered into the mix. This supplement called for still more DUKWs – 3,149 more to be specific, which were to be completed by the end of May 1946. Once again, in order to keep the production line flowing continuously, the pace of output for 1945 was slowed, with 568 DUKWs previously scheduled for 1945 delivery moved into 1946 so that there would be no gap in production while awaiting materials to arrive. Production rates were established at 24 per day through August, 28 per day from September through December, and then up to 30 per day as of 1 January 1946. These numbers are the combined GMC/Chevrolet total, with it being expected each would contribute one half.

The new order was scheduled to be split 1,569 to Pontiac and 1,580 to St. Louis. Requisitions for the materials with which to construct the additional amphibians were issued immediately.

On 17 May 1945 the Army announced that the slowing of production planned in order to prevent a gap between orders was not acceptable, and instead wanted the rate of delivery increased, with a total of 819 more vehicles to be delivered in 1945 than had previously been scheduled. Material shortages meant that this could not be met, so as a compromise the delivery schedule existent prior to the April 19 order was reestablished, and every effort would be made to advance material deliveries to prevent a gap from forming between that schedule and the new order for 3,149 vehicles.

With the fall of Germany, the Allied victory seemed imminent, and U.S. industry and consumers were anxious to resume production of goods for the civil market. Trucks and automobiles were weary from years of heavy wartime service, a situation recognized by the government as well, which was agreeable to the resumption of some production for the commercial market.

Within General Motors one of the impacts of this was a reallocation of resources. Chevrolet, which in addition to building DUKWs had also been building large quantities of CCKW 6x6 cargo trucks under contract for GMC, was anxious to resume building cars in St. Louis. GMC was equally anxious to resume building trucks.

To achieve these goals, it was decided that at the end of August 1945 DUKW production in St. Louis would cease, with all amphibian production being carried out in Pontiac. Similarly, CCKW production in Pontiac would halt at the same time, with all such trucks being assembled in St. Louis.

To meet this goal, sales orders changes were issued as follows:

TC-200714, Contract -6053, Pontiac production increased by 528 units to 1,528.

TC-200715, Contract -6053, St. Louis production decreased by 528 units to 472.

TC-200725, Contract -6053, Pontiac production increased by 970 units to 1,940.

TC-200726, Contract -6053, St. Louis production cancelled 970 units.

TC-200752, Contract -6053, Pontiac production increased by 1,580 units to 3,149.

TC-200726, Contract -6053, St. Louis production cancelled 1,580 units.

These carefully laid plans were soon wrecked when Chevrolet pushed to get out of the DUKW business a month early. After much debate, Chevrolet prevailed, requiring further schedule revisions. To achieve this, St. Louis monthly DUKW production for June and July was increased by 100 amphibians each month. This would leave St. Louis 97 DUKWs short of the requirements, and those 97 were cancelled from the Chevrolet purchase order and added to Pontiac's September 1945 production schedule.

The production schedule in effect for Pontiac, was thus scheduled at 21 amphibians per day through August, then upping to 30 per day for September (to pick up the 97 DUKWs lost by the early closure of the St. Louis assembly line), then shifting to 26 per day for the last three months of 1945 in order for Pontiac solely to meet the Army's delivery schedule.

As with so many plans carefully made by GMC's personnel, this one did not last long, because on 23 June the company elected to shift the annual inventory date from the end of September to the end of August, changing the number of working days in each those months.

All of this changed again on 3 August 1945, when with victory over Japan appearing imminent, the Detroit Ordnance District contacted GMC and cancelled the contract supplement for 3,149 DUKWs. This was not a Contract Termination (which would come later), but a cancellation of the extension. GMC's purchasing department spun into action, canceling orders for steel and other materials. After this cancellation there remained 1,721 DUKWs scheduled to be built in 1946.

Twelve days later, on 15 August 1945, GMC received Notice of Termination of contracts for DUKWs and CCKWs from Detroit Ordnance District. By this time, Chevrolet, St. Louis had already completed production of DUKWs, although some remained on their property, unshipped. Permission was granted for Chevrolet to ship all the completed vehicles to the government.

Things were different in Michigan, however. Production Control Manager noted the situation as follows:

"….Pontiac GMC T&C plant was "full of Ducks." There were 14 assembled back of the paint shop, 16 in the paint shop, and 16 in Final Assembly after paint, a total of 46 in process – PLUS 140 Built but not Shipped, of which 39 were in Final Conditioning and 101 in Warehouse OK'd. Permission was secured from Contracting Officer to complete the entire 186 vehicles and ship them as complete units. This job was hurriedly organized and the last shipment made in the month of August prior to inventory on August 31st."

As a result of the termination, numerous DUKWS on various extensions of contract -6053 were cancelled, specifically 1,177 authorized 20 December 1944, 1,940 authorized 20 February 1945, and 3,149 cancelled on the 16 April 1945 authorization. A total of 21,147 DUKWs had been built.

To wrap up the DUKW production program, as Crist's wrote: "On September 29, 1945, Mr. Blevins put thru the final sales order change requests, which spelled finale for the DUCKS. By that time we were pitching the remains of Ducks in the gondola scrap cars."

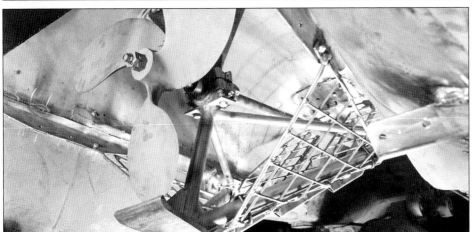

A worker makes adjustments to the tandem suspension of a DUKW secured at a tilted angle on the assembly line. Already installed are the central tire-inflation system fittings on the wheels. Hanging from the bow is the main panel of the aft deck, including the hatch door, as well as two drive shafts. (General Motors)

When launching forward from a landing-craft ramp, or when coming ashore, the DUKW's propeller was vulnerable to damage. This photo shows a solution at the GMC plant on 14 February 1945. Many DUKWs were fitted with similar guards in the field. (General Motors)

Late St. Louis-built DUKWs

Contract W-20-018-ORD-2164

Sales Order TC-200614
Serial Numbers	Registration numbers
16079 to 17378	7030370 to 7031670

Contract W-20-018-ORD-6053

Sales Order TC-200633
Serial Numbers	Registration Numbers
18079 to 18678	7033020 to 7033619

Sales Order TC-200636
Serial Numbers	Registration Numbers
19330 to 19968	7033621 to 7034178

Sales Order TC-200677
Serial Numbers	Registration Numbers
20175 to 20325	7034260 to 7034413

Sales Order TC-200715
Serial Numbers	Registration Numbers
21951 to 22325	7034617 to 7034991

Late Pontiac-built DUKWs

Contract W-20-018-ORD-2164

Sales Order TC-200613
Serial Numbers	Registration Numbers
14779 to 16078	7029070 to 7030369

Contract W-20-018-ORD-6053

Sales Order TC-200632
Serial Numbers	Registration Numbers
17379 to 18078	7031670 to 7032369

Sales Order TC-200635
Serial Numbers	Registration Numbers
18679 to 19329	7032370 to 7033020

Sales Order TC-200676
Serial Numbers	Registration Numbers
19968 to 20174	7034411 to 7034616

Sales Order TC-200714
Serial Numbers	Registration Numbers
20326 to 20773	7034992 to 7035439

All DUKW serial numbers include a DUKW353 prefix. Within each sales order the serial numbers and registration number increase correspondingly.

Banks of infrared lights hasten the drying and curing process on this freshly painted DUKW in a drying booth at the factory. On the aft deck on each side of the Gar Wood winch is a mount for an A-frame. These mounts are shaped like a leaf-type door hinge. A tow-chain link is dangling from a retainer chain. (General Motors)

Holding a paint sprayer, a painter in white overalls steps back to admire his work at GMC's Truck & Coach Division on 16 March 1945. Pieces of masking tape with Olive Drab overspray are stuck to the stern of the center vehicle, and masking paper is on the aft deck. The DUKWs display blue-drab U.S. Army registration numbers: from left to right, they are 7031961-S, 7031971-S, and 7031968-S. The "S" in the registration numbers indicated that the vehicles were equipped with radio suppression. (General Motors)

Three unidentified General Motors employees stand beside DUKW registration number 7035370. Leaning against the cowling of the DUKW is a sign reading "The Last DUKW," however government and GM records indicate the registration number of the final DUKW purchased was 7035439. Given the sudden termination of the DUKW contracts and the hurried completion of DUKWs in the final stages of assembly, it is entirely possible that the DUKWs were not accepted by the government in the sequence they were produced. (General Motors via Robert McDowell)

Chapter 20

DUKW Goes To War

The first operational use of the DUKW was at Nouméa, in New Caledonia, in March 1943 – a mere 11 months after the project began. As we have seen, even with the accelerated pace of development and testing, the unique nature of the DUKW meant that considerable training of the using troops had to be accomplished during those 11 months as well. Not only did the OSRD aid in establishing schools for DUKW personnel, OSRD further took it upon itself to develop tactics that took advantage of the DUKW's capabilities, and these tactics of course had to be relayed to the military authorities.

As seen earlier in this book, the first Army personnel trained with the DUKW was a small group at Camp Edwards, Massachusetts. Personnel from this cadre were drawn as instructors when the Army Transportation Corps school opened at Fort Story, Virginia, in January 1943. The War Department asked that OSRD assign an advisor to the Transportation Corps DUKW school until July 1943.

The DUKW school soon outgrew the facilities at Fort Story, and in April 1943 the school was moved to the Isle of Palms, near Charleston, South Carolina, where it remained until late in the war, when it was relocated again to Camp Gordon Johnston, Florida – despite OSRD objections. The school remained in Florida until spring 1945, when activation of DUKW companies in the U.S. stopped.

While roughly 70 companies and several battalion headquarters were processed through the Transportation School, there were still requirements for additional schools. DUKW-related schools also operated at Ford Ord, California; Fort Pierce, Florida; Camp Edwards,

Massachusetts; and Camp San Luis Obispo, California. General Motors continued to train mechanics both in Pontiac as well as other locales.

Camp Gordon Johnston was unsuitable for use as a DUKW training center, in the eyes of the OSRD. The beaches there featured smooth water and firm sand, neither particularly a challenge for DUKW crews nor an accurate reflection of the circumstances that crews would face in combat. The difficulties were compounded by the fact that there was no port of embarkation near the camp. Thus, students were given instruction on school-resident vehicles, and then shipped into theater with different vehicles. The students had no sense of ownership of the vehicles upon which they trained, and consequently class after class abused and neglected the school-resident DUKWs.

During World War II, army personnel were sorted according to Army General Classification rankings. The classification system considered education as well as social experience and ranked personnel into classes I through V. Class I represented men of higher intelligence – to qualify as an officer candidate a man had to fall into Class I or Class II; whereas Class V personnel were considered to have the lowest intelligence.

In a strange contrast to the development of the DUKW – which as we have seen involved some of the nation's best minds – the Army chose to fill the many of the DUKW training classes with men classified IV or V. The 1946 Summary Technical Report of Division 12, NDRC, said concerning Camp Johnston, "The curriculum did not take heed of the fact that the percentage of 4's and 5's (War Department

A DUKW is parked at the Amphibious Training Center, Camp Gordon Johnston, near Carabelle, Florida, on 14 January 1943. Three months later, the the Transportation Corps moved its facilities for training DUKW crews from Fort Story, Virginia, to Camp Gordon Johnston. Temporarily written on the bow of this DUKW are "OK" and "anchor." (National Archives)

After a day's training exercises at Camp Gordon Johnston on 8 July 1943, DUKWs and several GMC CCKWs are parked on the beach. The engine-access hatches are open on all of the DUKWs parked along the fence. These fences were erected around the assembly area to keep out drifting sand. (General Motors)

classifications) among the trainees was several times higher than the percentage of such groups in the Army as a whole."

While the initial truck companies were made up of white personnel with either truck driving or stevedoring backgrounds, by fall 1943, most of the companies at Camp Johnston consisted of black enlisted men and white officers. Dennis Puleston, arguably the key OSRD man involved in training both in the U.S. and abroad, wrote in his autobiography *The Gull's Way,* "We began organizing DUKW companies. These were made up largely of personnel from port battalions out of the Transportation Corps. The enlisted men in these companies were all Negroes, with white officers. Many of these men had never seen the sea before, but for them the opportunity to operate their own vehicles, instead of merely being stevedores working in the holds of ships was a big step forward. They took great pride in their vehicles; they were allowed to give them their own chosen names. Each company was assigned twenty-one DUKWs, with a mobile machine shop to go along with them."

The prejudices of the day hampered training. Again, quoting from the Summary Technical Report of Division 12, NDRC: "About half of these trainees were Negroes from the North. As was the case in other Southern camps, the morale of the men suffered from the necessity of conforming to the particular restrictions which they faced whenever they left camp. Such a situation would presumably have been less serious had the training camp been located in the North, or on the West Coast. It was actually less serious, in fact virtually nonexistent, in the overseas training camps, where the nearness of combat largely minimized many race prejudices. As a result of overseas training or retraining, Negro DUKW crews recovered in their morale and acquitted themselves at least as well as white crews. In some cases they did better."

The Summary Technical Report continued: "In Europe, they received high praise for their work on the Normandy beaches; at Iwo Jima they made more tonnage under fire than did white companies; and in the heavy surf at Tinian they were unsurpassed even by the best

Two soldiers stand for vehicle OVM equipment general inspection in front of their DUKW at Fort Ord, New Jersey. The equipment includes items such as snatch blocks, tarpaulins, ropes, a hydraulic jack, grease gun, life jackets, a ring buoy, and assorted implements. Such inspections were common and assured that no spares or equipment was missing. (General Motors)

African-American G.I.s practice unloading DUKWs by A-frame at the Aquatic Park, adjacent to Fort Mason in San Francisco, on 10 March 1944. The two vehicles in the foreground have identification numbers 32 and 33, while the DUKW in the background is numbered 24. (General Motors)

white Marine Corps units."

Beyond Camp Gordon Johnston, a significant school was established at Fort Ord, at the request of the Commanding General, Second Amphibian (later Engineer Special) Brigade. OSRD set up and operated an intensive training course during the ten days prior to the sailing of the brigade. The crews were trained during the day, and at night Ordnance Depot personnel under supervision of GMC field representatives modified the unit's 50 DUKWs bringing them up to the latest standards.

The first overseas DUKW school opened in North Africa in April 1943 prior to the invasion of Sicily. One officer from that school later trained both U.S. and British DUKW companies in Sicily and Italy.

The Chief, Combined Operations (British) had shown an early appreciation of the potential value of the DUKW, and at his request, OSRD personnel began a training program for Commonwealth forces in May 1943. The objective was to train 50 officers and noncommissioned officers who would become the instructors who would train a 100-vehicle DUKW company to land in Sicily in early July 1943.

The British school was set up at Camp Dundonald, Scotland – although a lack of DUKWs required that the initial training be conducted with CCKW trucks. The first two DUKWs arrived only two days before the conclusion of the training program. Training and assistance carried on right to the last moment, however, with OSRD personnel supervising the creation of a dozen A-frames even as the DUKWs were being loaded onto the transports taking them to the front.

Providing further assistance to the Commonwealth, in December 1943 at the request of the Supreme Allied Commander, Southeast Asia Command, a DUKW school was established at Juhu, in the western area of Bombay (now Mumbai), India. This school trained several Royal Army Service Corps companies in preparation for operations on the Arakan coast of western Burma (now Myanmar).

Dennis Puleston arrived in the Ellice Islands (now Tuvalu) in September 1943 to train Marine Corps DUKW drivers prior to the invasion of Tarawa – although ultimately the DUKW was not used in that operation.

As preparations for the Allied invasion of France began to ramp up, the need for thoroughly trained units in that area became critical. Hence, another British Army school was established at Towyn, West Wales. A U.S. Army Transportation Corps DUKW school was established at Mumbles, South Wales, with the British Navy providing a cargo ship with which crews could practice mooring and cargo handling. The Bristol Channel, in which it was anchored, was rough – at last allowing the green crews to experience conditions very different from the smooth waters of Camp Gordon Johnston.

The critical need for these field schools is borne out by this passage from the Summary Technical Report of Division 12, NDRC, "… an OSRD representative was also responsible for giving last-minute training to six Negro companies which had arrived from the United States only 10 days before D-Day. These companies were being staged near the port of Cardiff before shipment for the French invasion. Several of their officers reported to the port command to which they were attached that almost the only DUKW training their men had received was at a DUKW school in the United States, where they were taken for rides, about 18 men to a vehicle, with an instructor at the wheel of a DUKW."

Back in the Pacific, the east coast of Oahu was the location of a DUKW school established during the summer of 1944. That facility included a pier constructed to simulate a cargo ship that was used to train crews in cargo handling. In the area was soft sand, coral reefs, and heavy surf, making this a near-ideal training location for the Theater's DUKW crews. It operated through August 1945, training Army, Navy, and Marine Corps DUKW personnel.

According to statistics compiled by the OSRD, about 90 percent of all DUKW operations were conducted by DUKW companies, most of them amphibian truck companies of the U.S. Army Transportation Corps. The early Table of Organization (TO) set strength at 178 enlisted men, six officers and 50 DUKWs. In May 1944 this was changed to 173 enlisted men and seven officers. In both cases, the company was intended to operate around the clock. However, it was found that there were not enough men at this strength level to provide

On the same date as the preceding photograph was taken, a DUKW bearing the vehicle identification number 28 prepares to take on a sling-load of crates from a cargo ship lying off the Aquatic Park in San Francisco. The waterline load markings on the stern were officially added to DUKWs beginning in January 1944. (General Motors)

24-hour service. The OSRD reported that such service requires 4.2 men per DUKW, with 15 men in the company being mechanics, rather than the 11 mechanics called for by the TO. Many times the amphibian truck companies were organized around an amphibian truck battalion headquarters of 12 enlisted men and four officers.

U.S. Marine Corps DUKW companies, which began forming at Camp Linda Vista, on 15 December 1943, had an organizational structure similar to that of the Army companies, although the Marine units had more mechanics. In the British Army, the DUKW companies were formed from men drawn from Royal Army Service Corps general transport companies – the qualifications for which were far higher than was the case for their U.S. counterparts. Each company had 120 DUKWs, with a further 12 in reserve, and 470 men.

Almost from the outset of the DUKW program it was apparent that few within the rigid structure of the U.S. Army appreciated the capabilities of the DUKW, perhaps even fewer saw its potential, and it seemed, almost none grasped the importance of training. This became even more evident when in March 1943 55 DUKWs were sent to

Arzew, Algeria, along with four officers and 100 enlisted men from the Fort Story DUKW school. Even before the newly arrived vehicles had been serviced and tested, four of the DUKW-trained officers and many of the enlisted men were redistributed to units having nothing to do with the amphibians. With an almost complete lack of personnel trained with the DUKW, maintenance suffered. Upon hearing of this, the OSRD appealed to the War Department Assistant Chief of Staff, G-4, logistics, who dispatched a qualified DUKW officer to set up a training course. However, the earlier poor maintenance meant that there were few DUKWs that this new school could use, the result being that this class of men – who were serve as a training cadre for additional DUKW crews in the Mediterranean – were themselves poorly qualified.

The situation deteriorated further in April when General Patton, upon visiting and seeing a demonstration of the DUKW, requested additional vehicles and crews to use in the Sicilian invasion – meaning that the quality of training dipped even further. A few of the 55 vehicles were allocated to train two companies of British DUKW men.

A DUKW school opened on Oahu in the summer of 1944. As compared to the stateside schools, this facility had the advantage of featuring the coral reefs, soft sand, and heavy surf DUKW men would have to contend with in the Pacific. DUKW operators, regardless of branch, were trained at this facility through August of 1945. (National Archives)

Sicily

From this stage, the DUKW's first operational use in the Mediterranean was the 10 July 1943 invasion of Sicily. On the east coast, the British mounted a force of about 300 of the amphibians, divided between two RASC companies, as well as a temporary group with only modest training. U.S. forces mustered 700 DUKWs as part of three Quartermaster truck battalions and three engineer combat regiments.

D-Day for this invasion found the waters calm, but by that evening the weather had turned bad and for the next two days the weather was too inclement to use landing craft to transport cargo. The DUKW men shouldered this burden, and for those days and the next, DUKWs transported 90% of the tonnage put ashore. Despite this Herculean effort, which considerably impressed General Dwight Eisenhower, OSRD representatives felt that the DUKWs reached only 25% of their potential in this operation. The tonnage capability of the amphibian units was hampered by the location of supply dumps 15 miles inland, necessitating long road hauls. Poor staffing at those dumps brought delays in unloading, and the use of DUKWs for even longer hauls. In some instances DUKWs brought aviation fuel right to the newly captured airfields, with fuel being transferred from the DUKWs into waiting aircraft. Some DUKWs took supplies to front-line troops – in fact the Germans captured 20 during such an operation. The British use of the DUKW also was troubled, as seen in this passage from the Summary Technical Report of Division 12, NDRC, "The main problems were the utter lack of cooperation from the Navy and the vast amount of waste motion trying to find cargo to haul. The need for efficient centralized control system became so apparent that the first DUKW-control system was evolved then and there."

The same report summarized the troubles of the Sicilian operation in this way:

"1. The ignorance of the capabilities and limitations of the DUKW's exhibited by ranking officers of both Army and Navy caused a great deal of loss both of tonnage hauled and vehicles themselves.

2. Control of DUKWs is a complicated problem, and one which greatly affected their efficiency. Naval cooperation was very poor, and DUKWs were too often used for unprofitable work.

3. Dumps were located too far inland, and DUKW efficiency was reduced by the resultant long road hauls.

Above: A DUKW with a full load of cargo backs onto the ramp of a landing craft in North Africa on 2 July 1943. The supplies were for the 3rd Infantry Division, which in a little over a week would be participating in the Allied landings on Sicily. (National Archives)

Below: A U.S. Army DUKW enters the water while another one in the right background crosses the water as crews practice for the invasion of Sicily at a beach at Arzew, Algeria, on 6 June 1943. The DUKWs were under the command Lt. Gen. Mark Clark's Fifth Army. (National Archives)

Several of the DUKWs training at Arzew, Algeria, come ashore during exercises on 6 June 1943. General Dwight D. Eisenhower requisitioned 400 DUKWs for the Sicily operation in March 1943, and they performed well in the training maneuvers in Algeria. (National Archives)

Above: A force of eight DUKWs is coming into the landing beach at Arzew, Algeria. The availability of many DUKWs for the Sicily Campaign had a significant influence on the planning and execution of the campaign, greatly facilitating the movement of supplies. (National Archives)

Right: Another photo in the series taken at Arzew on 6 June 1943 shows DUKWs preparing to assemble on the beach. Because of these vehicles' impressive performance at Arzew, Eisenhower and his generals ordered many more for the Mediterranean theater. (National Archives)

Below: DUKW crewmen take a break during pre-invasion training maneuvers at Arzew, Algeria, on 6 June 1943. Vehicle numbers, 91 to 94, are visible on the first four vehicles. On three of the DUKWs, the engine-access hatches are secured in the open position. (National Archives)

DUKW crewmen go about their duties aboard their vehicles during the 6 June 1943 training exercise at Arzew. In a few weeks, the invasion of Sicily would begin, and these crews would be testing the capabilities of the DUKW in real combat situations. (National Archives)

4. Tables of Organization and Equipment were hopelessly inadequate to provide the maintenance needed for operation around the clock. Four men were found to be about the right number to handle each DUKW, but this number was virtually never available."

All this being said, even the heretofore most adamant opponents of the DUKW were impressed with its utility. Word of this success reached Washington, resulting in the following scenario, recounted in Vannevar Bush's *Pieces of the Action:*

"…I was lunching with (War Department) Secretary Stimson in the dining room of the Joint Chiefs of Staff. Vigorous conversation was going on all over that room: The Dukw (sic) had just been very successful in Sicily. Mr. Stimson said something about it and wanted to know who it was in the Army who was primarily responsible for the success. He knew it was my organization that did the development. I told him 'General Devers tested it under conditions that probably exceeded his orders, and Tony McAuliffe encouraged it. But,' I said, 'officially the Army opposed its development and your representative on N.D.R.C. voted against it.' He said, 'Who was that?' And I said, 'General Williams, but he acted under orders.' He said 'Why do you tell me all this?' And I said, 'Because it is your Army.'"

Messina Straits

On 3 September 1943, the British 8th Army used DUKWs as it assulated the mainland of Europe across the Straits of Messina. These straits are noteworthy for having the second swiftest currents of any European waters. Naval authorities insisted that it would be impossible for DUKWs to cross in the narrowest section where the current speed was fastest.

So, a crossing location with a 2- to 3-knot current was chosen, even though it required a run of seven miles across water. At dawn of D-Day, the entire force of 300 British DUKWs successfully crossed the Straits. In time, during this operation more than 12,000 individual DUKW crossings were made without one failure.

While the crossing was smooth, operation upon reaching the other side was initially problematic. Narrow congested streets coupled with the relatively large size of the DUKWs led to traffic jams. Ultimately, a bulldozer was used to cut a road speically for the DUKWs.

With the invasion underway, experiments determined that DUKWs could easily cross the fastest currents in the Straits of Messina. However, by that time the location of the dumps and the DUKW routes had been established and no regular trips were made on the shorter route.

After the British 8th Army moved north, the DUKWs followed, working the ports of Vibo Valentia and Sapri. Two platoons had been temporarily held back at the Straits, and when time came for them to move up to Sapri, the stage was set for a unique operation. The 11.00-18 tires of the DUKW were a unique item, and in critically short supply. To minimize wear, it was decided to swim the two 36-DUKW platoons to Sapri. The 150-mile trip took two days, with all 72 DUKWs arriving under their own power, marking the longest overwater mass swim of the vehicles.

Salerno

Operation Avalanche, the main invasion of Salerno by the U.S. 5th Army, began on 9 September. Two U.S. DUKW battalions made the Salerno landing against very strong enemy opposition. The initial landings by DUKW were to have taken place on Green Beach, but when the DUKWs arrived in position at 0500 they were met with fierce opposition. (Because it had been hoped to achieve surprise with this landing, no pre-invasion bombardment had been carried out – a

A DUKW enters the surf at Arzew while another proceeds through the water. While observing DUKW training maneuvers at Arzew in April 1943, Gen. George Patton was enthralled with their performance and ordered hundreds more for the Sicily Campaign. (National Archives)

move opposed by Admiral Kent Hewitt – the Germans greeted the arriving Americans first with a hail of munitions.) After a 30 minute delay, about half of the 60 DUKWs off Green Beach were able to make shore under cover of smoke.

The 60 DUKWs at Yellow and Blue Beaches faced similar circumstances, and ultimately were diverted to Red Beach, combining with those planned to land there for a total armada of about 150 of the amphibians coming ashore there. Because of the lack of cover, a great many DUKWs were struck by shell fragments and direct fire but these vehicles were cannibalized to put others back in operation.

This cannibalization was typical of what would be faced by many DUKW units through the end of the war. Concerning maintenance and spares during the Italian operations of the DUKW units, the Summary Technical Report of Division 12, NDRC, had this to say:

"The spare part situation up to this time was critical, for not more than 10 per cent of needed supplies were available. The fact that so many vehicles were kept running was a triumph of ingenuity and very hard work."

The report continued further on: "Under pressure to build up DUKW strength for the forthcoming Anzio landing, practically all vehicles were withdrawn from use by December. The next 6 weeks of frantic work by ordnance exposed the terrible toll taken by the lack of maintenance during the previous summer. As fast as DUKWs were "rebuilt" and put into a pool, other previously repaired DUKWs would be found inoperative. In fact, of 20 such DUKWs taken to Salerno for embarkation, 16 were rejected by ordnance inspectors."

Among the handful of DUKWs that were not withdrawn for service for these repairs was a small group that participated in an end run around the mouth of the Garigliano River. While this operation started well, on the last return trip, many vehicles became mired in the shallow mud in the center of the river. Despite considerable efforts to recover the stranded vehicles, several were permanently lost. While it had been well-known that the DUKW performance was poor in mud, this was the first operational loss due to mud in the MTO.

Anzio

Operation Shingle, the Allied landing at Anzio, began on 22 January 1944 and continued through 6 June 1944. This operation showcased the poor maintenance to which the DUKWs in the region were subject. Working side by side with two U.S. DUKW battalions was one RASC Company which used DUKWs of the same age and

mileage; yet on D+4, the British deadline was only 14 per cent, whereas the U.S. deadline stood at 55 per cent. Correcting this deficiency took the services of six ordnance companies, either in whole or in part.

As would be excepted, during the initial assault DUKW cargo consisted primarily of guns, ammunition, rations, and fuel. In the following months all types of cargo weighing up to four tons were brought ashore in DUKWs. The Germans, aware of the importance of DUKWs, made special efforts to disable them. A favorite strategy involved the use of antipersonnel bombs and shells, which were all too effective. One vehicle, however, remained in service after having received more than 200 holes in its hull.

Up to this time it can be said that the full potential of the DUKWs had not been utilized. Control was improving, but lack of cooperation from the Navy remained a large factor in producing poor tonnage reports.

In an effort to remedy this problem, four Transportation Corps amphibian truck companies were formed under the control of the 147th Quartermaster Battalion Headquarters. Each company of two battalions formed earlier had had a T/O of 110 men, but a paper battalion of 120 men had been divided between these two so that each company actually had more than 170 enlisted men. The 147th therefore had about the same number of men per company but far better maintenance facilities. Beyond this, special authorization was received for additional equipment and the companies normally handled all repairs through third echelon.

In his October 1943 study of DUKW operations in Sicily and Italy, Major Frank Speirs reported that DUKWs needed a complete overhaul after 300 hours of operation in that Theater. The report further remarked: "That nine hundred vehicles should have to be kept running for a period of from four to seven months without a single DUKW replacement part is shocking, especially in a combat zone."

Southern France

The invasion of southern France began on 15 August 1944. All DUKWs were handled by three battalions, since it had been found impractical to have small numbers in the hands of Engineer Corps regiments. Each battalion landed 100 extra "old" DUKWs. Of their basic 200 Table of Equipment [T/E] vehicles, 20 were also "old" and the remainder were just off the assembly line and equipped with the new controllable central tire inflation system. A considerable number of 40mm, 57mm, and 105mm guns were landed, the latter so rigged

A cargo net full of boxed supplies is lowered onto a U.S. Army DUKW from a Liberty ship off shore near Licata, on the southern coast of Sicily, for transportation to a supply dump in July 1943. The white star national insignia is at the stern. The circular surround is typical of vehicles used during various landings in Europe. (Imperial War Museum)

that they could fire from inside the DUKW. One "suicide" DUKW was also included, prepared to blow itself up in order to breach a concrete sea wall in case other means failed.

So essential were A-frames that one-half of all T/E DUKWs were equipped with locally manufactured versions in order to rapidly unload artillery. After the assault phase, one company of the A-frame equipped DUKWs was detailed to work supply dumps due to a shortage of cranes. Thus only three companies actually hauled cargo, while the fourth used its A-frames to load and unload all sorts of vehicles.

The three companies hauling cargo easily moved 5,000 tons per day, or 33 tons per DUKW per day, when ships were available. Again, Navy cooperation was generally lacking and about 30 per cent of all DUKW hours were unproductive. As the main Army moved north, the DUKWs went into Marseilles and worked the east end of the port. Here many of the problems previously experienced at Messina returned: the DUKWs tied up traffic throughout the city and the shore-to-dump time became fantastically high. In ccontrast to the situation at Messina, it was not possible to cut special DUKW routes through Marseilles.

As the Army reached Épinal, it was believed that DUKWs should be available for possible river crossings, and the 147th came to Lyon to practice in the Rhône River for an eventual crossing of the Rhine. The swift current and uncertain bottom texture made for conditions completely different from any that the 147th had been met before. Initially, a cable crossing rig seemed to offer the only practical solution, and all drivers were trained to use it. In time, further experiments were made and through experience it became evident that free-ferrying was a better method, in spite of the fact that drivers required very intensive training in this technique.

The two 7th Army DUKW battalions were so trained in preparation of a proposed crossing of the Rhine. Two DUKWs actually had used this method earlier in connection with a Commando raid nine miles north of Strasbourg on 28 December and thus became the first Allied vehicles to cross the Rhine.

Also at this time, experiments were conducted on the firing of 3-inch antitank guns without special harnesses. The 3-inch antitank gun was undoubtedly the heaviest artillery piece fired from a DUKW. With the gun held in place by the winch cable and with no special rig other than wheel blocks, its use on the DUKW was found to be feasible. Interestingly, during the first few rounds, the gun appeared to be more accurate in a DUKW than when in normal ground position – a phenomenon due to the absence of settling of its wheels.

Left: In the Sicilian Campaign, DUKWs fulfilled one of their prime missions in the port of Licata: ferrying supplies where port facilities had been heavily damaged. Although piers and a causeway had been badly damaged, DUKWs were able to keep supplies moving in. (Imperial War Museum)

Below: On the morning of the first day of the invasion of Sicily, 10 July 1943, a camouflage-painted DUKW comes ashore. This DUKW was fitted with an SCR-299 mobile communications unit in the cargo compartment and a ring-mount .50-caliber machine gun. (NARA via Steve Zaloga)

A DUKW transporting a load of .50-caliber ammunition approaches the beach at Gela, Sicily, during the invasion landings. Straight ahead of this DUKW is another one, approaching the beach at an angle. (National Archives)

On D+2, two DUKWs on the beach at Scoglitti, Sicily, take on supplies from an LCT and an LCM on 12 July 1943. Without cranes to assist in the operation, the materials are being brought on over the sides of the vehicles by hand. (NARA via Steve Zaloga)

At Gela, Sicily, a DUKW carrying a load of oil drums comes ashore next to a landing craft. The DUKW was destined for a nearby supply dump. The tarpaulin over the driver's compartment of the vehicle offered some shade to the driver from the hot Mediterranean sun. (National Archives)

A DUKW stands by on the beach at Scoglitti, Sicily, as infantrymen disembark from LCI-196 on D+1, 11 July 1943. The rear of the DUKW bears the symbol of the 1st Armored Division, the number 1 followed by a triangle. (National Archives via Steve Zaloga)

Left: As a DUKW's A-frame is being used to unload cargo from a Higgins landing craft at Gela, Sicily, on 12 July 1943, the weight of the slung load is causing the front end of the vehicle to pop up, and G.I.s are striving to hold down the front end. (Jim Gilmore collection)

Below: On the third day of the invasion of Sicily, 12 July 1943, Gen. Bernard Law Montgomery, standing in the driver's compartment of a DUKW, waves at a group of British soldiers en route to Syracuse. The "HD" code on the cowling indicated the British 51st (Highland) Infantry Division.

Cheerful-looking British troops in a DUKW proceed down a road in Sicily on 12 July 1943. The British acquired approximately 2,000 DUKWs, and Operation Husky, the Sicily Campaign, marked their first use of the DUKW in combat.

A U.S. Army DUKW transports supplies from the docks up the principal street of Porto Empedocle, on the southern coast of Sicily, on 25 July 1943. Various illegible markings are present on the bow of the DUKW. (National Archives)

Once the Allies had secured Sicily, the British employed DUKWs in ferrying supplies from that island across the Strait of Messina to the Italian mainland. Here, British DUKWs are lined up in the city of Messina, Sicily, preparing to transport fuel across the strait.

161

The British fielded a variety of gun trucks called portees, and it was natural that they would mount guns on their DUKWs, such as the 6-pounder antitank gun installed in the cargo compartment of this example, registration number WS-10574. The barrel of the gun is to the driver's right, and the shield of the gun is behind him.

The crew of another DUKW 6-pounder portee, numbered WS-10575, conducts exercises in North Africa prior to the invasion of Sicily. A canvas cover is fitted over the 6-pounder's barrel to protect it from dust. A number, apparently 847, is stenciled on the front of the cowl to the starboard side of the driver's compartment.

G.I.s struggle to hold down the front end of a DUKW down as it lifts a load of crated grenades in a sling with its A-frame. The scene is on a beach near Salerno on 9 September 1943. A large name that is illegible is painted around the national insignia, and a smaller name, apparently Marie, is painted toward the center of the hull. (General Motors)

Above: A British Army DUKW comes ashore at Gallico Marina, Italy, with a full complement of Jerrycan liquid containers destined for the Eighth Army. The vehicle accomplished this after crossing the Strait of Messina. The code "D3" is painted on the side of the hull. (Jim Gilmore collection)

Left: The Italian port of Reggio, with its heavily damaged facilities, posed yet another scenario where the DUKW proved its worth in moving supplies in a seemingly impossible situation. A U.S. Army DUKW, registration number 70267, with what appears to be a British crew chugs through Reggio harbor.

A wounded British soldier on a litter is being loaded onto a DUKW for medical evacuation in Italy on 15 December 1943. The name Rosalind is painted on the driver's compartment coaming. On the side of the hull are the bridge classification number, 9, and the registration number, L-5216140.

British DUKW driver E. W. Kelly scrubs the forward deck of his camouflage-painted vehicle on the beach at Fossacesia, Italy, on 15 December 1943. The registration number of the DUKW was L-52161407. The name Pat was painted on the front of the driver's compartment coaming, and Hilda Margaret is painted on the hull.

Troopers of the 509th Parachute Infantry Battalion conduct a training exercise in a formation of DUKWs in the Bay of Naples, Italy, on 24 January 1944. The nearest DUKW is armed with a ring-mount .50-caliber machine gun, and stenciled on the hull is "1 Detroit." (National Archives)

In late January 1944, DUKWs are backing up into landing ships, tanks, at Salerno Harbor, Italy, in preparation for the Allied landings at Anzio. The DUKW to the right has an A-frame boom in the travel position. To the right is LST-381.

Several DUKWs deliver supplies to the beach at Anzio, Italy, on 14 April 1944. The closest DUKW has just emerged from the water, its hull still wet. In the background is a DUKW about to reenter the water, and the landing craft in the right distance is LCT-33. (Naval History and Heritage Command)

DUKWs with U.S. markings and drivers bring British troops and equipment ashore at Anzio. Loaded in the cargo compartment of the closest vehicle is an Ordnance QF 25-pounder gun/howitzer, which was comparable to the U.S. 105mm howitzer M2/M2A1. (Imperial War Museum)

During the long, drawn-out struggle for the Anzio beachhead, a German shell explodes just offshore as DUKWs laden with supplies attempt to land. The DUKWs were absolutely essential to the Allies in the four-month-long operation, and the Germans made of them a special target. (National Archives)

A DUKW rests in the water along the dock as a British Albion lorry and an M7 Priest disembark from an LST at Anzio in late January 1944. Partially hidden by the DUKW is what appears to be another DUKW holding British troops. (Imperial War Museum)

In a 10 January 1944 photo that the Signal Corps marked as being "reenacted," "wounded" men are helped out of the cargo compartment of a DUKW that has struck a Teller mine while landing near Pozzuoli, Italy. Another "injured" man lies on the beach. The DUKW's tandem wheels and the adjacent hull have sustained severe damage. (National Archives)

Left: A wounded man on a litter, his leg in a splint, is removed from the DUKW seen in the preceding photo. The casualties were given first aid on the spot. Several of the G.I.s rendering assistance have the insignia of the 3rd Infantry Division on their helmets. (National Archives)

Opposite page: This GMC magazine advertisement highlights a heroic deed performed by a DUKW crew at Salerno. During World War II, military contractors took advantage of every opportunity to emphasize the contributions they, their workers, and their products were making to the war effort.

Based on the actual experience of a Navy Seabee and his GMC "Duck" during the attack at Salerno.

Out of the Fire
Into the Firing Line

An LCT bringing ammunition to the British beachhead at Salerno was set afire by an exploding German shell. The ammunition was urgently needed on the battle line and the fire was spreading rapidly. A GMC "Duck" piloted by a Navy Seabee swam out to the LCT, salvaged five hundred rounds of 75 mm ammunition, made it back to shore, and rushed it inland to a corps of battling British tanks . . . The "Service Record" of the GMC "Duck" contains many such examples of distinguished service under fire. And Allied soldiers in Sicily, Italy and throughout the South Pacific have given high praise to its performance. One of the war's most unusual developments . . . a 2½-ton, six wheel truck mated with a 31-foot landing boat . . . it has performed some of the war's most unusual feats of land and water transport!

INVEST IN VICTORY . . .
BUY MORE WAR BONDS

GMC TRUCK & COACH DIVISION · GENERAL MOTORS
Home of Commercial GMC Trucks and GM Coaches . . . Volume Producer of GMC Army Trucks and Amphibian "Ducks"

On X-ray Beach in the Nettuno Area, Italy, on 5 February 1944, men of the 540th Amphibious Engineer Group (Amphibious) are employing a Quickway Coleman crane and a sling (a cargo net with lifting straps) to unload ammunition crates from a DUKW named "America." In the right foreground is a D-7 bulldozer. top (U.S. Army Engineer School History Office)

A DUKW with a cargo of drums of aviation gas fuels an American Spitfire Mark VIII fighter plane at a recently captured Sicilian airfield. Later assessment of DUKW operations in Italy noted that the long road haul required for such operations contributed to DUKWs achieving only 25% utility in the Theater. The soldier manning the .50-caliber machine gun on the DUKW's ring mount, is indicative of the volatility of the early operations in the area. (General Motors)

Two G.I.s observe a DUKW aflame in a British motor pool in the Nettuno area of Italy on 27 March 1944. A German shell caused the destruction, in which one member of the DUKW crew was killed. Another DUKW is faintly visible to the far left. (General Motors)

DUKW Aircraft Ferry

In an effort to provide a means of moving aircraft directly from transport ships to the front lines, Wright Field in September 1943 asked GMC to develop an aircraft ferry apparatus for use with the DUKW. A catamaran apparatus was devised, similar to rigging previously used to wet-ferry tanks, with the aircraft supported by troughs attached to the sides of a pair of DUKWs. These troughs would also serve as treadways upon which to roll the aircraft to the stern of the DUKWs, where specially designed ramps would allow the aircraft to be moved to the ground. Between 9 September and 8 October the ferry was designed, built, and shipped to Charleston.

A freighter was positioned in Charleston Harbor for trials, and by 28 October, testing using a P-38 with its outer wing panels removed had been completed. The initial premise for loading the aircraft during these trials was that the DUKWs would be moored parallel to the freighter. Ultimately, removal of the outer wing panels was felt unnecessary, and the tests were repeated with the aircraft fully assembled. In order to achieve this, the DUKWs were moored with their sterns secured to the side of the freighter This later battery of tests was completed by 16 November 1943.

In both cases the tests were successful. Based on this result, design studies were made toward creating ferry configurations suitable for use with other types of aircraft, including the Curtiss P-40, Republic P-47, North American P-51, and Bell P-63.

Despite the considerable engineering effort that was devoted to these studies, and the successful trials of the airplane ferry, even at night and in the open sea, no operational use of the apparatus was made. The war had quickly advanced, and longer-ranger aircraft were in production, negating the need to ferry aircraft ashore to expedient airfields.

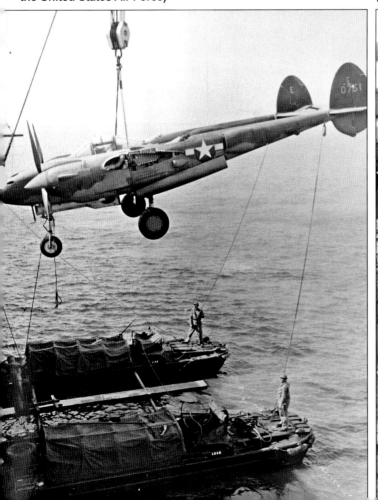

Between 9 September and 8 October 1943, in order to devise means to deliver short-range fighter planes to invasion beachheads so they could begin conducting combat missions as soon as airfields were captured or constructed, a DUKW ferry rig for transporting aircraft from ship to shore was quickly designed, built, and tested. The dry-ferry rig was very fundamental, with two DUKWs linked together side-by side with spreader bars, upon the center of which rested a plank, seen here, to support the nose landing gear. Resting on the spreader bars along the inboard side of each DUKW was a length of steel channel, to form a platform to support the main landing gear. Tests of the rig were conducted at Charleston, South Carolina, in October and November 1943. Initially, the DUKWs were moored at right angles to the ship, with the DUKWs's sterns toward the ship's hull. (National Museum of the United States Air Force)

A Lockheed P-38 Lightning twin-engine fighter, shorn of its outer wing panels and with its four nose-mounted .50-caliber machine guns and its nose-mounted 20mm gun removed, is being positioned on a DUKW dry-ferry rig off Charleston, South Carolina, in late 1943. Neither DUKW has a tarpaulin installed over its cargo compartment. The plywood closures are folded to the rear in their stowed positions. The positioning of the three tubular spreader bars is visible from this angle. The P-38 nose wheel is secured by a chock fashioned from crossed pieces of lumber fastened to the long plank at the center of the ferry rig, and a line is lashed around the nose gear and the plank to hold it securely in place. The main landing gear also was held taut by lashings; lines are visible from the wheel-strut joints running forward along the channel platforms, and other lines run aft from the main gear. (General Motors)

Right: Initially, in tests of the aircraft ferry rig in Charleston Harbor, the outer wing sections of the test aircraft, a P-38, were removed for clearance, because of the closeness of the DUKWs to the cargo ship it was moored to in parallel fashion. The main landing gear rested on platforms on the DUKW hulls, while the nose gear was on a plank. (National Museum of the United States Air Force)

Below: The DUKW dry-ferry rig delivers a de-winged P-38 to a beach off Charleston, South Carolina, during demonstrations in October 1943. To the far right, a man is exerting tension on the plane using a block and tackle, while men at the front of the plane pull it down the ramp. (National Museum of the United States Air Force)

After the P-38 was successfully lowered from the cargo ship and secured to the dry-ferry rig, the DUKWs proceeded from Charleston Harbor out to the Atlantic. During one demonstration, the DUKWs took the P-38 out into the Atlantic Ocean at night and made a successful landing on a beach. (National Museum of the United States Air Force)

During a second series of trials in Charleston Harbor, the DUKW ferry rig was moored at a right angle to the cargo ship, eliminating the need to remove the outer wing sections of the P-38 in order to clear the side of the ship. The plank upon which the nose landing gear will rest is secured to the struts between the two DUKWs. (National Museum of the United States Air Force)

The DUKWs motor away from the cargo ship bearing the P-38 with outer wings intact during one of the later demonstrations of this dry-ferry rig off Charleston in early November 1943. The C-shaped sections of the platforms the plane's main wheels are resting on are visible along the top of the DUKW hulls. (National Museum of the United States Air Force)

Moments after the preceding photograph was taken, the DUKWs begin to motor away from the cargo ship from which the vehicles received the P-38. Although the concept of DUKWs dry-ferring fighter planes from a transport ship to a landing beach were proven in late 1943, apparently the method was not pursued operationally. (Military History Institute via Jim Gilmore)

European Theater - Normandy Coast

The ability of the DUKW to move stores across stormy beaches was deliberately exploited for the first time by the planners of the Normandy invasion. The German General Staff, according to later reports by the Commander-in-Chief, Allied Expeditionary Forces, felt that the storm-lashed Normandy beaches provided no means adequate to support an offensive by several million men. Their judgment coincided with that expressed to Division 12 in 1942 by representatives of the Allied High Command, who concluded that the Allied forces would have to use captured ports. It appeared logical, therefore, that the Germans should base their strategy on a stubborn defense and subsequent demolition of Cherbourg and the other ports. The DUKW fleet was an essential element in the strategic surprise of the enemy and continued to support the advance to the Rhine in all weather. Representatives of Supreme Headquarters, Allied Expeditionary Forces, later advised the Chief of Division 12 of NDRC that between 6 June and 1 September the Allied DUKW fleet had carried across the beaches approximately 40 percent of the total stores landed.

The U.S. mustered 30 DUKW companies for the invasion, with additional companies under British command. During the invasion, the first DUKWs landed on D-Day and by D + 60 approximately 2,000 DUKWs were operating on the Normandy coast. Of these, about 800 were operated by the British, serving under the British 2nd Army on its sector of the coast. The others were operated by

amphibian truck companies of the U.S. Army Transportation Corps. Six of these companies, manned by white enlisted men, had been in England for more than six months before D-Day. They were attached to the 1st, 5th, and 6th ESB's and were trained under the cognizance of General Daniel Noce, whose EAC Command at Camp Edwards, Massachusetts, had supplied the detachment for the Provincetown demonstration in December 1943. Fully aware of DUKW problems, General Noce had met with OSRD personnel in London in January 1944 to review the various recent developments in other theaters, and arranged that these six companies, while stationed on the coasts of Devon and Wales, should be given ample time to incorporate these new developments in their training.

As mentioned earlier, black DUKW companies did not begin arriving until late in March 1944, and had been poorly trained. It was necessary to create facilities, retrain the men, and prepare their equipment. This was done under OSRD supervision. The 1st ESB landed on Utah Beach, the 5th and 6th on Omaha Beach. Their DUKWs were loaded with high-priority engineer equipment and ammunition. Routes through the underwater obstacles and the beach mine fields were being cleared and marked to a limited extent, but the beaches were under heavy enemy fire and a number of DUKWs were hit by mortar fire. Some were damaged by land mines, but it was noted that in such cases a DUKW driver is rarely hurt, perhaps the large flat bottom of the DUKW deflected the blast pressure to the sides, rather than channeling it upward as in the case of conventional

Scores upon scores of DUKWs are lined up at a vehicle park in England on 20 March 1944, being readied for the forthcoming invasion of Normandy. Bows can be seen stowed at the fronts of the cargo compartments. On the driver's compartment of the second vehicle, next to the driver's seat, is a stencil with tire-pressure recommendations for various conditions. (National Archives)

In February 1944 in preparation for the invasion of Normandy, a DUKW has been fitted with a large reel of communications wire for a test of running the wire across the river: in this case, the Severn River in England. The view is over the rear of the vehicle, looking forward. (National Archives)

vehicle design.

The first of the black companies arrived on the Normandy beaches in LSTs and LCTs on D + 3; others arrived later and were attached to port commands.

In order to minimize the DUKW land runs, transfer points were set up in the dunes close to the beaches. While the firm sand of the beaches was ideal for the DUKWS, other operating conditions were not so favorable. Notably, the ships widely used in the early phases were the relatively expendable North Sea two- or three-hatch coasters with an average 700-ton capacity. These ships were important because their small size made them difficult targets and because their shoal draft enabled them to anchor close to shore, though they had a very violent roll in the generally rough English Channel waters. In comparison with the usual large freighters, these coasters were not suited to efficient DUKW operations. Many of them had heavy guardrails along each side, and these caused much damage to DUKW hulls and headlights.

Another source of difficulty in the first few days was the great amount of tactical smoke that was generated among the ships. This made it so difficult for DUKWs and other landing craft to find their way between ships and beaches that the smoke screens were discontinued.

The condition of the sea was bad for much of the time. The prevailing wind was from the northwest, making it particularly bad at Omaha Beach, which was open to the north, The surf ran high at times, and tides occasionally ran as fast as 3 knots. Further trouble was caused by the great amount of wreckage and spilled cargo close to the shore. There was a high mortality in DUKW propellers and rudders until drivers were instructed to disengage their propellers and coast through the most congested water areas. The installation of the offshore breakwater at Arromanches, in the British sector, was of great value to British DUKW operations.

From then on, these DUKWs were able to operate in relatively smooth water, and their maintenance troubles were considerably lessened. A similar breakwater off the American beaches was almost completely destroyed on 23 June in the worst summer storm for 20 years. This meant that the U.S. Army DUKWs were obliged to continue operations in open sea conditions, which caused higher deadline rates.

Also, since the captured ports did not become usable as soon as had been planned, the additional load on the DUKW fleet was prolonged. Every available DUKW had to be used day and night, and first-and second-echelon maintenance was largely neglected. By the middle of September, most of the DUKWs operating in the United States sector were in very poor condition, this through no fault of the drivers. To aggravate the situation, spare parts were not available except in extremely limited quantities. The reason for this was baffling: a large supply of spare parts had been accumulated in England in preparation for the Normandy operation, but if they did arrive in France, they did not find their way into the hands of the hard-pressed DUKW companies. Field improvisation of spare parts and cannibalization of vehicles unquestionably used up many DUKW hours that could have been better spent on operations.

In spite of all the difficulties, the flow of supplies continued to pour ashore – 40 per cent by DUKW. The beaches continued to act the part of major ports into the late fall. The 2,000 DUKWs are reported

A DUKW (registration number 7017338-S) with an HO-17A shelter containing SCR-399 radio equipment undergoes preliminary trials near Bristol, England, on 4 March 1944. The SCR-399 was a high-frequency mobile unit equipped with one transmitting antenna and two receiving antennas. (National Archives)

The SCR-299/399 Radio System

The SCR-299 was a radio system originally designed to be mounted in a 1½-ton 4x4 Chevrolet tactical truck, towing a trailer with mounted generator. The entire vehicle/radio system was given Signal Corps Designation K51, while the associated generator trailer was designated K52. For increased mobility, a shelter was developed that would allow the radio system, with its operators, to be carried in the rear of a CCKW cargo truck. This shelter was the HO17 hut. Entrance into the hut was through an end-mounted door. When mounted in this shelter, the radio system was given the Signal Corps designation of SCR-399.

Assembled by Hallicrafters of Chicago, a large manufacturer of amateur radio equipment at the time, the SCR-399 was a mobile High Frequency station capable of Continuous Wave (telegraph) or voice communication (AM). The BC-610 transmitter was a military version of the Hallicrafters Model HT-4 and produced 400 watts output CW telegraph and 300 watts voice, operated on 2-20 MHz, and had a range of about 100 miles.

Two BC342 military receivers were installed, along with a BC-614 speech amplifier, BC-939 antenna tuner, BC-1052 multimeter, and RA-63 rectifier. Many spare parts and tools were stored in the CH-88 chest and CH-89 bench within the shelter. The entire radio system could be operated remotely from EE8 field phones from up to a mile away. The shelter was equipped with a fan, lights, heater, and a bench for sitting on or sleeping on.

Power for the system was supplied either by connecting to an external power supply, or via the PE-95 generator, which when used with a truck, was carried in the K52 trailer. Multiple versions of the PE-95 were built, with the -A, -B, and -C models powered by a Ford engine, and the -E, -F, and -G being powered by Willys engines.

Not surprisingly, a powerful, highly mobile radio system such as the SCR-399 was very desirable during amphibious operations. It was found that the HO17 hut could be placed in the cargo compartment of the DUKW, so long as either the door was cut, making only the top portion usable, or an access hatch was cut in the shelter roof. There then remained the problem of the generator, as the 1-ton K52 trailer was by no means amphibious. In some instances, the 10 KW PE-95 was mounted on the rear deck of the DUKW, and in other instances one or more smaller PE-75 2500-watt generators were carried instead.

The same DUKW with SCR-399 is viewed from the rear. The power unit for the SCR-399 has been mounted in wooden boxes raised above the aft deck; the door of the aft box is open. The HO-17A shelter was supplied with heat in the winter and was ventilated during warm weather. (National Archives)

Prior to the invasion of Normandy, training exercises were conducted in which DUKWs received supplies from cargo ships and transported them to land. In this photo, a DUKW departs from a cargo ship in rough seas, carrying piles of rations boxes.

A DUKW, apparently the same one shown in the preceding photograph, hauls a load of rations boxes during exercises prior to the Normandy landings. The boxes are secured together with steel bands so they could be loaded and unloaded as a unit.

Sailors watch from the forecastle as a DUKW embarks on LST-376 at a port in England in advance of the D-day invasion of Normandy. An A-frame is installed on the vehicle. Painted on the side of the hull by the driver's compartment is "Hitler" and an illegible word. (General Motors)

Sailors on the forecastle of LST-357 enjoy the show as a DUKW with a tarpaulin over what appears to be a 105mm howitzer in its cargo compartment waits its turn to board. Reportedly the location was a British port prior to the Normandy invasion. (National Archives)

176

to have averaged 21 tons per DUKW per day, an impressive record in the circumstances.

Channel Ports

Cherbourg was captured on 27 June but for several months its value as a port could not be exploited fully because of the heavy damage suffered by its facilities; nevertheless, it at least afforded a smooth water anchorage and it was an important railhead. Logically, one of the first projects at Cherbourg was the construction of a concrete ramp for DUKWs. Several DUKW companies were moved in as soon as possible and the first ships were discharged by them. The DUKWs brought supplies directly from ship to railroad freight car, where cranes transferred the loads. Later, this same system was used at Le Havre and other Channel ports which, because of damaged facilities, could not discharge ships at dockside.

River Crossings

When port facilities were repaired and the fighting fronts moved farther away, some of the DUKW companies were converted into truck companies. Others retained their DUKWs but were used to provide land transportation along the highways of France and the Autobahn of Germany. But even in the heart of Europe, the amphibious qualities of the DUKWs were still needed in the crossing of such great rivers as the Rhine and the Danube. Several DUKW companies were used to transport troops and supplies across the Rhine; with the use of the correct river-crossing technique (operations in swift coastal currents had been stressed at the school at Mumbles), no serious troubles were encountered in spite of the swift current. In some cases, Army divisions used DUKWs as part of their standard transportation across lower Germany.

Their technique consisted of bringing the assault troops up to a town by DUKW, deploying on foot to capture the town, and remounting on the far side to proceed to the next town. By this means, the difficulties presented by demolished bridges were greatly reduced. Crossing a river by DUKW was found to be an unquestionably better method than using Navy landing craft which had to be transported from many miles away along the narrow and already traffic-crowded European roads.

Four days before the commencement of the Normandy Invasion, DUKWs pass Sherman tanks of 13th/18th Royal Hussars at Gosport, England, on 2 June 1944. By this time, the British had adopted the U.S.-style star-in-a-circle, as seen on these DUKWs, as a recognition symbol.

A British DUKW, spare tire stowed on the forward deck, and a Sherman tank wait in line en route to their embarkation points to join the invasion of Normandy on D-day, 6 June 1944. On the side of the DUKW's hull is a five-pointed recognition star, pointed upside down.

Left: A DUKW waits its turn to embark on LST-294 as troops file up the ramp and others stand by in the foreground. The bundles on the rear deck of the DUKW appear to be chespaling matting, rolls of sticks bound together with wire, which were rolled out on beaches to provide a firmer surface for trucks to drive over. (U.S. Army Engineer School History Office)

Below: On D+1, 7 June 1944, G.I.s on a landing craft at Normandy observe vehicles gathering on the beachhead. Toward the center, a DUKW with a tarpaulin over the cargo compartment makes for shore. On the beach is at least one DUKW, to the left of center, with a star insignia on the side. (General Motors)

American infantrymen discharge from a Higgins boat at one of the beaches in Normandy on D+1. At the center, a DUKW has just landed on shore. To the far right, another DUKW is headed up the slope of the beach to proceed inland. (National Archives)

At one of the beachheads in Normandy on D+3, 9 June 1944, several DUKWs sit on a sandy road, waiting to move forward. Markings on the rear of the closest DUKW identify it as assigned to the 6th Engineer Special Battalion. Off the road to the left are three more DUKWs facing the photographer. (General Motors)

Before D-day, several DUKWs were fitted with 100-foot Merryweather fire-truck extension ladders provided by the London Fire Department for use by U.S. Army Rangers in scaling the cliffs at Pointe-du-Hoc, Normandy. On D-day, the Rangers were only able to make use of one extension-ladder DUKW. A ladder rig is shown during a pre-D-day training exercise. (National Archives)

Merryweather engineers dismissed the idea of fitting a DUKW with a ladder on a rotating turntable; it would add significant weight and risk tipping the craft. Instead they proposed a ladder that rose but did not rotate. The DUKW's winch would raise the ladder. Stabilizer legs mounted about midway along each side of the DUKW prevented tipping. (Steve Zaloga collection)

Swans

As the Allies drew up plans for the forthcoming invasion of France, they were seriously concerned, among other things, with the German batteries at Pointe Du Hoc. Seeking a solution, a Captain Holmes of the British Army approached R.E. Stubington, managing director of the Merryweather Company, a British manufacturer of fire apparatus, to ask whether it might be possible to fit a DUKW with one of the firm's 100-foot turntable ladders, allowing assault troops riding in such special vehicles to quickly take to the beach and scale the cliffs

Merryweather rejected the idea of rotating ladders, proposing instead an extension ladder that could by raised by the DUKW's winch. With a design established, five such ladders were ordered with the highest priority, and Merryweather delivered in just six weeks. The specially-equipped DUKWs were to be used by the U.S. 2nd Ranger Battalion, under the command of Lt. Col. James E. Rudder. Rudder had detailed two of his men, Staff Sgt. Jack Kuhn and PFC Peter

Karpalo, to the Merryweather factory to assist with the project.

Once the unique vehicles were completed, the Rangers trained with the machines on the beaches at Devon Cliffs until competent. The plan for 6 June 1944 was that the specially equipped DUKWs – by then nicknamed "Swans" – were to go into action at 0705 hours – a mere five minutes after the start of H-Hour. The crews were to begin raising the ladders as soon as their wheels contacted the beach, and then rapidly advance to the base of the cliffs on Omaha Beach.

Plans were one thing, however; reality was something else. The DUKWs reached shore 40 minutes late, with one sunk *en route.* Once on shore, the vehicles were hampered by slippery shale beach, and the Allied bombardment had littered the base of the cliff with so much debris that the ladders could not get close enough to serve as intended. The only actual use of a "Swan" occurred when Sgt William Stivison, his DUKW still bobbing in the surf, grabbed his submachine gun, climbed the partially-erect, swaying ladder, and fired a few bursts at the defending positions at the top of the cliff.

British tanks and vehicles are coming ashore on a beachhead in Normandy. To the left are parked several DUKWs. Among the landing ships in the background are LCT 503 and LCT 7096. In the foreground, a soldier gives directions to the driver of a Sherman tank with deep-water fording kit installed.

Riding in this DUKW during a tour of a Normandy beachhead on 12 June 1944 were some of the top brass of the United States. At the front of the cargo compartment are, left to right, Chief of Staff Gen. George C. Marshall; Supreme Commander of Allied Forces in Europe Gen. Dwight D. Eisenhower, and Commander in Chief, U. S. Fleet and Chief of Naval Operations Ernest J. King.

A British DUKW moored on the lee side of a cargo ship is taking on supplies lowered in cargo nets at Mulberry B Harbor, Arromanches, France. This was one of several artificial harbors constructed in Normandy after the invasion to create more port facilities. (Imperial War Museum)

A DUKW transports ammunition ashore at Arromanches on 22 June 1944, a little over two weeks after D-day. On the front deck is a white Allied recognition star. On the front left of the cowl is the insignia of General Headquarters and Lines of Communications Troops, 21st Army Group. The number 1392 is painted on the right side of the cowl. (Imperial War Museum)

Two DUKWs, including registration number 7017580-S to the right, pause at Red Beach Headquarters, Les Dunes de Madeleine, Utah Beach, Normandy, on 12 June 1944. The DUKWs were bringing in supplies to shore and returning to the ships with wounded G.I.s. (National Archives)

The harbor facilities of Cherbourg, a strategically important port on the coast of Normandy, were severely damaged by the time U.S. forces captured the harbor on 29 June 1944. Until the harbor facilities were repaired, DUKWs were used to bring in supplies from ships, such as these ones preparing to unload engineer equipment from Liberty ships on 18 July. (U.S. Army Engineer School History Office)

A DUKW is being prepped for shipment overseas at the Virginia Port of Embarkation on 1 August 1944. A temporary structure has been installed over the driver's compartment and the cargo compartment to keep out the elements during transit. (Library of Virginia)

DUKW registration number 7025119, with a temporary shelter for shipment overseas, is viewed from aft. This vehicle was produced in Pontiac, Michigan during June 1944. On the left stern are three non-lustrous yellow lines in three-inch intervals. The lowest is the DUKW's water line when operating at the DUKW's rated capacity, the center line is acceptable, and the upper line, five-inches below the rear deck and marked "Danger," is the least freeboard that was safe. These markings were subject to wear, and additionally where hard to see at night, hence ultimately many DUKWs had 3/16-inch holes drilled in the reinforcing ribs (not hull proper) at these levels to aid in locating the level. (Library of Virginia)

A DUKW of the 45th Infantry Division of the Seventh Army has just come ashore at Ste.-Maxime in southern France on 15 August 1944, and another DUKW is approaching the beach. Both vehicles have tarpaulins over the cargo compartments and star-in-circle national insignia. The lead vehicle has a canvas cover over the windshield. (National Archives)

Along the harbor at Cherbourg, France, on 13 August 1944, cranes, trucks, and DUKWs carry on the work of bringing in the massive amount of supplies necessary to support the Allied armies during their push deep into France. DUKWs are parked along the shore, and two are to the right of the crane at the center. (National Archives)

Seventh Army vehicles near a beachhead in the vicinity of St.-Raphaël in southern France on 16 August 1944 stir up considerable dust, while along the road to the left is parked a DUKW. In the background are barrage balloons, part of the beachhead defenses. (National Archives)

Above: A DUKW comes ashore at Alpha Red Beach, near Cavalaire-sur-Mer in southern France on 18 August 1944, while a string of other DUKWs makes its way to the beach from the transport ships in the background. The vehicle in the foreground has an unidentified frame-type device with braces at the rear of the cargo compartment. (Naval History and Heritage Command)

Left: At Alpha Red Beach, Cavalaire-sur-Mer on 18 August 1944, a DUKW comes ashore with supplies in cargo nets. On the side of the hull are the vehicle's identification code, 1-1, its nickname, Bermuda, and what appears to be a temporary placard with two horizontal red bars and one horizontal black bar. LCI-234 is docked to the right. (Naval History and Heritage Command)

A military policeman stands by as a DUKW makes landfall at Alpha Red Beach, Cavalaire-sur-Mer, on 18 August 1944. More DUKWs are heading in to shore. In the background is an impressive display of Liberty ships and other vessels of the invasion fleet. (Naval History and Heritage Command)

A DUKW nicknamed "Beaufighter" pauses on Alpha Red Beach, Cavalaire-sur-Mer, 18 August 1944. All of the DUKWs in the invasion of southern France were assigned to three battalions, with each battalion having 100 brand-new DUKWs with the central tire-inflation system and 100 early-production DUKWs. (Naval History and Heritage Command)

A cargo net full of ammunition is being lowered from a Liberty ship to a DUKW, U.S. Army registration number 7017809-S and vehicle number 137, off the coast of southern France for transport to the shore in August 1944. (National Archives)

A DUKW assigned to a port battalion transports supplies from a ship to the port of Cherbourg, France, on 18 August 1944. The worn and faded U.S. Army registration number on the side of the hull appears to be 7021765-S. (National Archives)

Sergeant Albert Jenkins, 1st Lt. Loren Pryor, and Sergeant Junius Meade use a specially fabricated machine to straighten a DUKW propeller shaft, an expedient undertaken at a time when there was a shortage of new propeller shafts in the European Theater of Operations. (National Archives)

Corporals Oscar Adams, a welder, and Floyd Carrio, a mechanic, designed an improvised rudder for DUKWs when replacement rudders became unavailable in Normandy for a period following D-day. Here, they are installing one of their rudders in early August 1944. (National Archives)

DUKWs carry supplies across the Seine River at Vernon, France, on 27 August 1944, two days after the British 43rd (Wessex) Division had forced the first crossing of that strategically important river at Vernon. DUKWs also had been used in that assault crossing. (Imperial War Museum)

187

A DUKW full of troops and two Universal Carriers of 5th Battalion, Duke of Cornwall's Light Infantry, 43rd Division, pause during campaigning in Holland on 18 September 1944. These troops were part of Gen. Brian Horrocks's XXX Corps during the ill-fated Operation Market-Garden, which had kicked off the preceding day. (Imperial War Museum)

A British DUKW ferries supplies and American paratroopers across the Waal River at Nijmegen, Holland, on 30 September 1944. In the background is the famed highway bridge, which the 82nd Airborne Division had attempted but failed to capture on the first day of Market-Garden. (Imperial War Museum)

A Liberty ship supplies DUKWs of the 470th and 819th Amphibian Truck Companies with filled gasoline drums at Bassin Darse Nord, Le Havre, France. Port facilities at Le Havre had been severely damaged, so DUKWs stepped in to help move supplies to land. (National Archives)

Allied engineers built this ramp through the wreckage of a dock warehouse at Le Havre to provide DUKWs with access to the harbor. On the right, several empty DUKWs enter the water to make a pickup run to a ship, while the DUKWs on the left are returning to shore with supplies. (National Archives)

Left: At Le Havre, dozens of DUKWs are parked next to railroad cars. The supplies on the DUKWs, just brought in from ships in the harbor, will be directly transferred to the freight cars, following which the badly needed materials will be transported where needed. (National Archives)

Below: At the railroad yards at the cotton warehouse in Le Havre, France, on 18 November 1944, bombs are being unloaded from DUKWs by a crawler crane. The bombs are being loaded in the freight cars to the left for shipment to forward air bases in France. (National Archives)

Loaded on this DUKW at Ninth Army Headquarters in early November 1944 are a 57mm antitank gun M1, in the foreground, and a 105mm howitzer M3 toward the front of the cargo compartment. It was a tight fit, but it could be done. (National Archives)

DUKWs of the 453rd Amphibian Truck Company are lined up in a sheltered position along a road near Hammersorf, Germany, on 6 December 1944. The force was awaiting a call to assist the 90th Infantry Division in its crossing of the Saar River. (National Archives)

Throughout its long history, time and again the DUKW would prove its usefulness as a lifesaving vehicle. Such was the case when this British DUKW evacuated civilians from Ostkepelle, Holland, during a flood on 21 December 1944. (Imperial War Museum)

A British Weasel tracked cargo carrier precedes a DUKW along a flooded road near Kranenburg, Germany, on 15 February 1945 after the Germans had blown-up dams and dykes along the Rhine to hinder the Allied advance. Both types of vehicles kept men and supplies moving during the floods. (Imperial War Museum)

Above: A column of DUKWs assigned to one of the amphibious truck companies of the 1st Division, U.S. Army, in an unidentified German village awaits orders to cross the Roer River on 24 February 1945. The lead vehicle has a machine gun ring mount, and tow chains are at the ready in case the vehicle has to be recovered. (National Archives)

Right: In preparation for the crossing of the Roer River in February 1945, Cpl. R. L. McDonald and Technician 3rd Class Seigel Stirewalt perform repairs on a DUKW of the 460th Amphibian Truck Company, assigned to the 299th Engineer Battalion, 1st Division. At least three other DUKWs are parked in the background, tarpaulins erected. (National Archives)

Technician 5th Class Earl W. Dyer enjoys a brief cigarette break next to a DUKW decorated with a shark's mouth, prior to the crossing of the Roer River in late February 1945. Tires were lashed to the bows of these DUKWs to act as fenders, in addition to the rope fenders fitted to the vehicles. (National Archives)

Private Eugene E. Kriebel uses a paint brush to clean debris off the forward deck of a DUKW of the 460th Amphibian Truck Company during a pause before the 1st Division's crossing of the Roer River. A close-up view is offered of the right headlight and brush guard and the right side of the surfboard. (National Archives)

Left: Left to right, Pfc. Elbert King, Technician 5th Class Earl W. Cooper, and Pvt. Grover Eastin warm their hands around a fire as they await the signal to begin crossing the Roer River. The nearest DUKW, sporting a shark's mouth, appeared in one of the preceding photographs. (National Archives)

Below: A DUKW full of troops of the 157th Infantry Regiment, 45th Infantry Division, along with a 57mm antitank gun crosses a river in France during training exercises in March 1945. The number 233 is marked on a light-colored rectangle on the hull, as is the nickname "The Texan." (National Archives)

Medics of the 79th Infantry Division, Ninth Army, load soldiers wounded on the east bank of the Rhine River into a DUKW near Rheinberg, Germany, on 25 March 1945. Two notched wooden beams have been placed across the coamings to support an upper tier of litters. This DUKW, registration number 7070727, was manufactured in 1945. (National Archives)

Left: Combat photographer Arthur H. Herz took this image, one of the iconic photographs of World War II, of troops of the 88th Infantry Division, Third Army, crouching down in a DUKW as they cross the Rhine River under fire near Oberwesel, Germany, on 26 March 1943. (General Motors)

Below: In the Bobenheim area of Germany on 26 March 1945, Seventh Army infantrymen are struggling to keep their DUKW from swamping while attempting to cross the Rhine River. The mishap may have been due to a combination of driver inexperience, a swift current, and an overloaded cargo compartment. (National Archives)

A DUKW, U.S. Army registration number 7026601-S and vehicle number 27 on the side, emerges from the Danube River with a blown bridge in the background near Donaustauf, Germany, on 26 April 1945. "3rd Bn" marked in chalk on two places on the side of the hull refers to the 3rd Battalion. (National Archives)

A DUKW, heavily laden with supply crates, is parked along a trail, waiting for a column of Sherman medium tanks to pass. To the front of the cargo compartment is a .50-caliber machine gun, fitted with a canvas cover. Four 5-gallon liquid containers are on the aft deck. (Imperial War Museum)

A British DUKW comes ashore and several more are approaching during a supply-ferrying operation across the Rhine River on 25 March 1945. Engineers have prepared a steel ramp at the shoreline to provide better traction for the vehicles as the exit the water, and striped posts provide a visual guide to the location of the ramp. (Imperial War Museum)

Plotting The Course

An odograph is a device for automatically plotting the course of a moving vehicle. This can be used in map-making, or for plotting the positions of military objectives. While an odograph mounted in a DUKW was used during the infra-red lighting tests in February 1943, specific testing of a DUKW-mounted odograph did not begin until March 1944, when the Engineer Board began testing an IBM M-1 odograph in one of the amphibians.

The M-1 is a land odograph, so to provide input data while afloat, a Bendix Marine Water Log, which was standard for the Navy, was also installed. This device uses a submerged impeller to provide an input for the log pickup mechanism. When operating on land, the M-1 provides an attachment for the speedometer drive which closes an electrical circuit with each revolution of the drive gear. A plotting pencil is driven by these inputs, drawing the course taken onto a map placed on the map table.

Testing of the odograph-equipped DUKW was conducted at the U.S. Navy Amphibious Training Base, Fort Pierce, Florida, from 18 March 1944 through 7 April 1944. While when operating on ground the odograph in the DUKW produced results comparable to those achieved in its normal jeep installation (error of 1% to 3%), in the water there were gross inaccuracies. This was attributed to the effect of tides and currents. While the pitching motion of the vehicle was felt by the odograph's compass, it was believed that this resulted in only about a 2% error. However, the tide, current, and drift encountered in water operations made the odorgraph readings completely meaningless. For faster moving craft, the effect of these forces is less noticeable, but in the case of the DUKW these forces can equal a sizeable percentage of the amphibian's own propulsive force.

Hence, the 12 June 1944 summary of these tests declared the odograph unsuitable for use in the DUKW.

Above: This DUKW was employed in the odograph tests at Fort Pierce. The top of the compass of the odograph is visible between the cargo-compartment bows. (US Army Engineer School History Office)

Left: Looking forward in the front of the cargo compartment, the components are, 1) the compass, 2) the power pack, 3) the plotting unit, 4) the log pick-up unit, and 5) the impeller-type log. The Impeller-type log was hung over the side of the hull when the odograph was in operation. (US Army Engineer School History Office)

The lid of the log pick-up unit is raised, exposing the inner mechanisms. This unit received data on revolutions per minute from the submerged impeller-type log. (US Army Engineer School History Office)

The Bendix impeller-type log is deployed on the forward starboard side of the cargo compartment of the DUKW. At the bottom of the shaft was the impeller itself. (US Army Engineer School History Office)

The DUKW proceeds with odograph tests off Fort Pierce, Florida. The impeller-type log is submerged, and a man is standing by in the cargo compartment to monitor the instruments and pull the log out of the water when the vehicle is prepared to come ashore. (US Army Engineer School History Office)

Pacific Theater - The Solomons

The 451st TC Amphibian Truck Company, the first to be activated and trained at Fort Story, was also the first to arrive overseas. It reached New Caledonia in March 1943 and was ordered by headquarters there to demonstrate the possibilities of DUKWs for ship unloading.

The performance was impressive. A Liberty ship lying a mile offshore in Nouméa Harbor was discharged at a rate of 22 tons per hatch per hour as compared to the usual 6 or 7 tons per hatch per hour when barges were used. The company was sent on to Guadalcanal and for many months unloaded approximately 90 percent of the rations for more than 100,000 troops on the island.

In spite of these early excellent results, however, the company's efficiency deteriorated rapidly, partly because of a complete lack of DUKW spare parts but also because of the failure of higher headquarters to appreciate the folly of reallocating trained drivers to other jobs, overloading the vehicles, failing to provide sufficient time for proper maintenance, and fever. In September and October 1943, following visits by OSRD personnel to Nouméa and to the Solomons, the non-medical conditions were alleviated to a certain extent, but it was many months later before an effective quantity of spare parts arrived in this area.

In the meantime, other companies arrived, one from Espiritu Santo in the New Hebrides, where it had been engaged in ship discharging, and several from the mainland. These companies went to the Russell Islands and to the New Georgia group, where they served to unload offshore shipping. In November 1943, after they had been reorganized on Guadalcanal following visits by the OSRD group, these Solomons-based DUKW companies were given their first opportunity to participate in an assault operation, the landings at Bougainville Island. These landings were made in Empress Augusta Bay, on beaches swept by a heavy surf. No serious difficulties were encountered, however, even though many landing boats were swamped. The DUKWs were largely responsible for supplying the assault forces with ammunition and rations.

New Guinea

The first appearance of DUKWs in New Guinea provides a good example of the risk involved in issuing a new weapon to untrained troops with orders to test it and report on it. In July 1943, 25 DUKWs were delivered at Milne Bay and issued for trial to the forces discharging ships there.

Dennis Puleston recounts in *The Gull's Way:* "From the Solomons I was sent to Douglas MacArthur's headquarters at Brisbane, Australia. Here I was shocked to find that an adverse report of DUKWs had come from New Guinea and that the DUKW companies were being used entirely for land transportation. Something must be seriously wrong. I requested authorization to go to Milne Bay and Finschaven, where these DUKWs had been grounded, to find out what had happened. The report indicated they were unseaworthy, which was of course utterly ridiculous."

"When I reached Milne Bay I found that several of our trained companies from the Charleston school were already there. They were in a great state of frustration, having to be used only for land operations. In making inquiries, I found the root of this situation. It appeared that before the arrival of the trained companies several DUKWs without trained crews had been sent to the New Guinea theater and put in the hands of a most unimaginative port officer, with the request that they be tested out for water operations. Without reading any of the directions about operation and maintenance of DUKWs, he simply ordered some of his men to drive them into the water, to see how they performed. These DUKWs had been shipped on the deck of a Liberty ship and, as was often the case, their bilge plugs had been left open in order to get rid of any rain and sea that had collected in the hulls."

"When the DUKWs were offloaded on land and then driven into the water, naturally the water poured through the bilge drains and they very quickly submerged. Without trying to find the reason for this, the officer responsible sent back a report: the DUKWs were "unseaworthy" and should not be used for water transportation. Thus the problem had arisen. I, of course, was obliged to go over the head of the port officer and contact his superior. When I explained the situation, he readily agreed that we should stage a demonstration by having our trained DUKW companies discharge some of the many vessels waiting to be unloaded. The result was spectacular; the companies were able to discharge the ships at rates that had been

A DUKW enters the water at Nouméa Harbor, New Caledonia, to make a run to a transport ship to bring supplies ashore on 25 April 1943. This was one of a series of photos documenting how DUKWs received cargo loads lowered by slings from a transport ship. The cargo slings would then be removed from the DUKWs by cranes at the supply yard on land. (General Motors)

Two DUKWs proceed to receive cargos from transport ships at Nouméa Harbor on 25 April 1943. Nouméa was an important U.S. military base during the Solomon Islands Campaign and was Admiral William "Bull" Halsey's headquarters. (National Archives)

unheard of in New Guinea up to that time."

Headquarters requested Puleston's team to analyze the amphibious logistics of northern New Guinea and to recommend steps for the full exploitation of the DUKW fleet. Such recommendations were made early in November to Commander-in-Chief, SOWESPAC, G-3, and were immediately acted upon. Nevertheless, neither this vigorous action nor the numerous demonstrations staged by the OSRD mission succeeded in fully overcoming the setback received at Milne Bay, as was determined later when OSRD personnel next saw this DUKW fleet in action, on Leyte in 1944.

With the arrival of trained amphibian truck companies from the mainland, however, the potentialities of DUKWs began to be realized to some extent and from that time on they participated in amphibious operations whenever available. They started with the 466th at Milne Bay and 464th and 465th Oro Bay, which were being built up as bases for future operations against Japanese-held New Guinea and New Britain. Next, with the capture of Lae, the 5204th provisional company were moved there to supply the new airfields at Lae and

Nadzab with aviation gasoline. All gasoline destined for forward areas was brought in by Liberty ships in 55-gallon drums. Eighteen of these drums, totaling about 7,500 pounds, made an ideal load for a DUKW, and with the usual shortage of cranes, DUKW A-frames were used at the dumps for unloading.

As in the Solomons, many hours of DUKW operation were lost because of spare parts shortages. So critical did this situation become that DUKW officers went as far as Brisbane in an effort to locate these missing items. There were no spare parts at Brisbane, either. After more strong recommendations were sent back to the United States, some parts eventually did arrive, but in the meantime many DUKWs had been cannibalized in order to keep others operating. DUKWs were also issued to the Australian Army in New Guinea, and the 165th transport company used DUKWs to supply forces at Buna while the 151st worked Lae. The men in these units were entirely self-taught. Later it was possible for OSRD to work with these companies and correct some of their operational faults in a relatively short time, since both officers and enlisted personnel were of exceptionally high caliber

At the center of the photograph, a column of five empty DUKWs motors out to a transport ship anchored in Nouméa Harbor. The DUKWs were assigned to the 451st Amphibian Truck Company, the first such company to be deployed to the Pacific. The 451st arrived in New Caledonia in March 1943. (National Archives)

A crane on a transport ship in Nouméa Harbor is lowering a cargo net full of supplies to an awaiting DUKW. Crews of DUKWs of the 451st Amphibian Truck Company were able to discharge cargo from a Liberty ship at a rate of 22 tons per hatch hour, compared to the much slower rate of 6 or 7 tons when barges were employed. (Military History Institute)

The net full of supply boxes safely ensconced in the cargo compartment of a DUKW, the amphibian vehicle departs from the transport ship and begins the trip back to shore. Leaving the cargo in the nets rather than unpacking the items from the nets and stacking them in the DUKWs facilitated a much faster turnaround of the payloads. (National Archives)

One of the DUKWs seen in the preceding series of photos discharges its slung cargo ashore at Nouméa with the aid of a crane. The crane would lower the cargo into a truck, which would take the load to a supply depot. (U.S. Army Engineer School History Office)

Above: A DUKW slowly navigates Australian waters on 10 June 1943. This DUKW was assigned to the Australian Transportation Corps. The Australians acquired 535 DUKWs from the United States, using many of them in the New Guinea Campaign. (National Archives)

Left: An Australian DUKW, most likely the same one seen in the preceding photo, comes ashore in Australia on 10 June 1943. The DUKW was a good fit with the Australians in their operations in the Southwest Pacific, which entailed far-flung maritime supply lines. (National Archives)

The same Australian DUKW has emerged from the water and is proceeding onto the beach over Marston matting, perforated steel sections that were joined together to form surfaces for a variety of uses, from aircraft runways to beach ramps such as this. (National Archives)

No wonder they call it *The "Duck"*

Amphibious action is playing an ever increasing part in World War II. And the 2½-ton Amphibian truck, now in volume production at GMC Truck & Coach Division factories, is giving American Armies an ever increasing advantage over the Axis. In the water, it has all the qualities of a large landing boat, *plus* the ability to keep going when it reaches shoals and shore line. On land, it provides performance comparable to a GMC "six by six" army truck, *plus* the ability to swim lakes and streams. Carrying cargoes from ocean freighter to inland supply depot ... establishing beach heads and bridge heads ... unloading ships where no harbor facilities are available...aiding in reconnaissance work where no roads or bridges exist ... carrying or pulling cannon and howitzers ... transporting scores of troops or tons of equipment ... are all in a day's work for this sturdy, seagoing truck. No wonder the GMC workers helping to build it, and the soldiers using it, both call it the "Duck." It's one of America's most vital and versatile military vehicles!

Above: General Motors Corporation's Truck and Coach Division took great pride in its military vehicles and singled out the DUKW for advertising purposes. This magazine ad stresses the newness of mechanized amphibious warfare, and boasts of the ability of the DUKW to proceed from ships offshore to depots and bases inland.

and had previously obtained moderately good results under easy operating conditions. Subsequently, after the Military had been advised on the basis of a preliminary reconnaissance that the conditions were suitable for DUKW operation, these men used DUKWs successfully in the Finschhafen landing.

At the invasion of Arawe, New Britain, on 15 December, DUKWs were used not only for supply work but to give supporting fire. Several DUKWs from the 2nd ESB were equipped with launchers for the 4.5-inch beach barrage rockets and although this firepower could have been afforded in part by other landing craft, the rocket DUKW could fire either on land or at sea and the results on the Japanese beach defenses were extremely effective.

A request from Headquarters, SOWESPAC, for a total of 1,150 DUKWs would bring more amphibian truck companies from the mainland, and they were playing an increasingly important part in amphibious logistics. At Manus, Biak, Hollandia, and many other landings they served to supply the assault forces. In the attack on the Mapia Islands in November 1944, a battery of 105mm howitzers was landed in DUKWs and unloaded by A-frames. The guns were in action within 15 minutes from the time they were landed.

Even after assault missions, DUKWs were still needed at important points along the New Guinea coast for transportation duties until pier facilities could be constructed. When Headquarters, SOWESPAC, moved to Hollandia, the continued service of several DUKW companies was necessary to build it up into a base for future assaults on Morotai and other islands to the northward and, eventually, on the Philippines.

Ellice Islands

The first Marine Corps DUKW operations took place in the Ellice Islands in September 1943. After the men were trained, a group of 21 DUKWs served to unload shipping in the lagoon at Funafuti atoll, which was being prepared as a base for coming assaults against the Gilberts and Marshalls. Here, for the first time, DUKWs operated over bad coral and proved that the findings made in the tests on the Florida Keys the previous February were correct: with skillful operation, DUKWs could be driven over bad coral reefs without appreciable damage or additional tire wear attributable to coral.

From Funafuti, these DUKWs were sent on northward to Nanomea, which was occupied without Japanese opposition except for bombing attacks. This small atoll has no passage into its lagoon, and its seaward reef is considered to be one of the worst in the Pacific. Yet, because of its proximity to the Japanese-held Gilberts, it was imperative that an air base be established there. LSTs were brought in as close as possible to the edge of the reef, and the DUKWs discharged them by driving up their ramps on to the tank deck, where they were hand-loaded and driven ashore over the reefs.

Unfortunately, DUKWs were not used at Tarawa and in the other Gilbert Islands operations. Their use was rejected in spite of the DUKW operation at Nanomea, which was reported favorably to CINCPAC, Pearl Harbor, by the concurring Navy captain who had witnessed these tests and who recommended that the Navy include DUKWs in the plans for forthcoming landings. Many discerning Marine Corps officers, however, had become convinced of the future importance of the vehicles, and in early 1944, Marine Corps DUKW companies were organized and first used in the Marianas operations.

Marshall Islands

At Oahu, while preparing for the assault on Kawjalein atoll, the U.S. Army 7th Division took advantage of the lessons of Tarawa and decided to capitalize on the valuable tactical use that could be made of DUKWs in landing 105mm howitzers. Accordingly, four provisional DUKW platoons were organized from division artillery personnel, and one platoon with its 15 vehicles and 3 A-frames was attached to each artillery battalion. The men in these platoons had been given no adequate training in DUKW operation and maintenance – an omission that was later reflected in the condition of their vehicles after a few days of use. Nevertheless, the units landed their artillery at Kwajalein very effectively, having been discharged from LSTs which remained afloat. Although it was not necessary as was shown in many subsequent operations, each DUKW had its side coamings recessed and its floor supports changed to accommodate the howitzer wheels. No modification is needed if the wheels are correctly chocked.

After completion of their primary mission, the DUKWs were used to unload seven LSTs which served as floating supply depots. The operations at Tarawa had already demonstrated that in atoll warfare a more flexible system than the normal ship-to-shore operation is necessary. As in the Ellice Island operations, the DUKWs drove directly into the LSTs, and again the system proved very satisfactory. At Burton Island, one of the islets in the Kwajalein atoll, the beaches were under enemy fire for 36 hours and the shore party did not function until the island was secured. During that time, DUKWs carried combat supplies to forward dumps without casualties. DUKWs would have been even more useful in the Kwajalein operation, however, if they had belonged to a regular amphibian truck company attached to the division. In this way, they could have continued discharging ships after their primary missions were completed. As it was, the DUKWs were wasted to a great extent once the LST's had been unloaded, for most of the ship unloading was done by a combined team of landing craft and tractors – a combination far less efficient than DUKWs.

Marianas Islands

The Marianas campaign affords another example of successful DUKW performance on very rough coral reefs. Except for Tanapag Harbor, a few unimportant sections of coastline on Saipan, and two very small beaches on Tinian, the islands are surrounded by barrier reefs.

In these operations were the First and Second Marine DUKW Companies and one black Army company, the 477th, which later gained additional distinction in the assault on the Kerarna Islands. The Marine drivers had had no previous experience with DUKWs and only a minimum of training, but the Army unit, which was attached to the 5th Amphibious Corps Artillery, had received extensive training on Oahu and was in excellent operating condition.

The DUKWs were transported in LSTs to their lines of departure and on 15 June 1944, went ashore behind the assault waves of Amtanks and Amtracs. The first DUKW waves were used to bring in troops, then ammunition, and eventually rations and medical supplies. The depths were too great to permit the shipping to anchor offshore, and DUKWs were often obliged to search for their ship as it was shifted by the currents. This made mooring alongside very difficult, especially since the ground swells were heavy.

A great many casualties were brought out from shore by DUKWs. Their land ability was found to be good and another mission was found for them is prime movers for 155mm howitzers over steep and difficult terrain. Eventually, when the island was secured, DUKWs were used to discharge some of the shipping in the relatively smooth waters of Tanapag Harbor. In the meantime, Marine Corps DUKWs under the 3rd Division participated in the landings on Guam on 21

Walking-wounded patients being evacuated from the island of Espiritu Santo, New Hebrides, are passing through the gate at Pier 1 on 26 June 1943. In the background is a DUKW filled with more patients. (National Archives)

DUKWs are lined up in convoy formation in a tropical locale, probably in the Southwest Pacific. The troops on board the vehicles appear to be G.I.s with a smattering of African-American troops in the mix. On the coamings are round insignia with a walking duck. (National Archives)

July 1944.

Thirty-nine days after the beginning of the assault on Saipan, the same DUKWs were used at Tinian. The night before the landings, they crossed the seven-mile channel from Saipan under their own power, some loaded with 105mm howitzers and 75mm pack howitzers and some with ammunition.

They anchored that night in the channel and awaited the dawn, which was heralded by an extensive artillery barrage from Saipan. The landing points were two very small beaches that indented the lava coast, one of them 65 yards wide, the other 130 yards. They were so narrow that to have used them for unloading landing craft to any great extent would have been dangerous, for a few broached boats could have blocked the beach. On the fourth day a distant typhoon caused heavy ground swells and nothing could operate in the heavy surf except DUKWs, which continued to discharge ships and support the offensive without trouble. For several days, DUKWs and transport planes were the only supply lines open. This was the first occasion on which official Navy recognition was accorded to the DUKW's surf ability.

Shortly after the cessation of hostilities in the Marianas, another outstanding example of the seaworthiness of the DUKW was afforded. A passing typhoon had built up a tremendous sea and a small freighter had been swept on to the offshore reef at Saipan. It hung there with not only spray but solid seas breaking over its decks and washing men into the sea. Some LCVPs were sent out but all returned immediately, except one which was swamped and another which was drifting out to sea with a drowned out engine. Two LVTs that attempted to put out were also swamped. A call was sent through to the 477th Amphibian Truck Company for some DUKWs. There were so many volunteers from the company that the commanding officer was obliged to order many of his men to remain on shore. Besides the men from the LCVP, approximately 70 men from the wreck were picked up alive out of the water. One DUKW was swamped when it was caught in the cross-seas close to the stem of the ship, but all its men, too, were saved.

As in many other operations, spare parts were not available during the Marianas campaign in sufficient quantities to keep pace with the demand, and therefore a number of vehicles were cannibalized in consequence.

Right: U.S. DUKWs assigned to the 5204th Provisional Truck Company are parked between missions at Lae, New Guinea, on 27 October 1943. The vehicle in the center background has the late-type coaming around the top of the cargo compartment, higher toward the rear. (National Archives)

Below: On 28 October 1943 a DUKW of the 5204th Provisional Truck Company transports empty oil drums to a ship in the harbor at Lae, New Guinea. The ship will transport the drums to another port for refilling. What appears to be another DUKW, filled with oil drums, is lying alongside the ship. (National Archives)

One of the DUKWs of the 5204th Provisional Truck Company comes ashore at Lae after delivering a load of empty oil drums to a ship in the harbor. The name painted on the side of the hull to the front of the driver's compartment appears to be *USS Flint.* (National Archives)

A DUKW backs up the ramp and into an LST at Milne Bay in New Guinea on 15 November 1943. The number 23 is painted on the side of the hull to the front of the driver's compartment. Rather than use the rear-view mirror, which is folded down, the driver has his head turned to the rear. (National Archives)

Above: Toward the end of 1943, a DUKW with several G.I.s aboard rests in a supply area on Makin Atoll in the Gilbert Islands. DUKWs were instrumental in the logistical support of this invasion by the 26th Infantry Division. In the background beyond the bow of the DUKW is a pile of rations boxes. (National Archives)

Right: A DUKW backs into the cargo bay of a landing ship, tank (LST) at Goodenough Bay, in the Southwest Pacific, on 17 November 1943. Marked on the stern are the number 23 on each side, and a circle with a capital A on the port side. A good view is available of the propeller, rudder, and propeller tunnel. (National Archives)

During maneuvers at Goodenough Bay on 17 November 1943, a DUKW exits a landing craft, bow first. Whenever possible, the preferred method of exiting a landing craft by way of the ramp was stern first, to prevent damage to the propeller and the rudder when the DUKW rolled off the ramp. (National Archives)

A DUKW carrying armed G.I.s is viewed through the doors of the LST from which the vehicle has just emerged, at Goodenough Bay on 17 November 1943. An identification or unit marking, D11, is roughly painted on the forward deck of the vehicle. (National Archives)

Palau Islands

The landing at Peleliu Island in the Palaus was one of the most difficult encountered by DUKWs in Pacific island warfare. The island is surrounded an by extremely jagged coral reef several hundred yards wide and on 15 September 1944, when the assault was made, typhoon weather caused heavy swells. In addition, Japanese beach defenses were strong and carefully concealed in the coral outcroppings.

In anticipation of heavy enemy small-arms fire, the two Charleston-trained Army amphibian truck companies attached to the Marine Corps for the assault had piled sandbags around the front and sides of their drivers' cabs. This excellent precaution unquestionably saved lives, although nevertheless several DUKW men were killed and many wounded, primarily by machine gun and mortar fire. The reefs contributed to high casualty rates, as the DUKWs were forced to traverse the worst coral areas at extremely low speeds, and many times DUKWs were hung up completely until they received tow chain assistance from another DUKW. Besides bringing in the majority of the assault supplies, the DUKWs at Peleliu performed valuable work in evacuating many wounded from field dressing stations, carrying them across reefs almost impassable by any other means, and delivering them to hospital ships.

This effective use of DUKWs over jagged coral during the assault phase against positions appears to confirm the strongly defended assurances given to the Navy in August 1943 that DUKWs would prove satisfactory in supporting the assault on Tarawa.

The original units at Peleliu were eventually reinforced by another company which had participated in the landing at Angaur Island to rhe south on 17 September 1944. Much more favorable conditions had existed at Angaur and the landing there was far less eventful.

Top: Another in the series of photographs of DUKWs on maneuvers at Goodenough Bay shows one of the vehicles transporting marines inland. The DUKW sufficed to move men from sea to shore but was not well configured for protecting and disembarking them. (National Archives)

Center: A DUKW with the identification number 26 on the hull to the front of the driver's compartment proceeds through palm trees on its way inland at Goodenough Bay on 17 November 1943. On board are marine infantrymen with weapons and full packs. (National Archives)

Left: Two USMC DUKWs pause during a move inland in maneuvers at Goodenough Bay. The DUKW in the foreground mounts a 105mm howitzer with a canvas cover fitted over the barrel and recoil mechanism. Marked on the gun shield below the sighting slot is "H-5." (National Archives)

Another USMC DUKW with a 105mm howitzer photographed at Goodenough Bay sports pinup art of a scantily clad girl on the top of each side of the shield. In the background, a crewmember grasps an aiming stake, used as a point of reference during indirect fire. (National Archives)

The Philippines

In the initial landings at Leyte on 20 October 1944, DUKWs were used on a larger scale than in any previous Pacific operation. Thirteen Army amphibian truck companies participated in the landings near Tacloban and Dulag. Most DUKWs were transported in LSTs, but for the first time some were shipped in LSMs and LSVs, which afforded a very satisfactory means of transporting assault-loaded amphibians to the combat area.

While sea and beach conditions ranged from moderate to good in the Leyte landings, the shore conditions were very poor and heavy rain turned the roads to deep mud. This held down tonnage figures which otherwise might have been quite high, since in most cases the ships were able to anchor within a mile of the shore and there was no need to contend with coral. Enemy air action interfered to some extent, especially during the first two months; red alerts were frequent and of considerable duration, but DUKW losses were practically nil.

For the first time, DUKWs and Weasels, the NDRC's tracked amphibian, worked together in this operation as two links in the supply chain. To service the artillery batteries, which in many cases were located on steep, muddy hills, the DUKWs brought in the ammunition to a point at which mud halted them, and there their loads were transferred directly into Weasels, which completed the delivery.

As in most operations, there was a shortage of cranes and dumps became very congested. Once again, it was learned that DUKW operations are controlled by the speed at which they can be unloaded on shore. If the dumps are slow, there is nothing to be gained by continuing to add DUKWs to the ship unloading cycle; additional DUKWs will only add further to shore congestion without unloading the ships any faster.

DUKW maintenance at Leyte was quite satisfactory, since operating hours were keyed to the under-strength T/O and the DUKWs were worked on a basis of two 12-hour shifts of 20 DUKWs from each company, with 10 DUKWs held out for regular maintenance checks. This schedule was later moderated to three eight-hour shifts of 22 DUKWs per company – an unsatisfactory arrangement, which, resulting in a breakdown in driver assignment, was later abandoned.

Some of the Leyte companies and others newly arrived from other islands or from the United States were used in the subsequent major landings in the Philippines, including Mindoro, the Visayan Islands, and Palawan. On 9 January 1945, three companies took part in the Lingayen Gulf landings in northwestern Luzon. The ground swells

Marine Corps DUKWs with empty cargo compartments are in a holding pattern off Perry Island, Eniwetok Atoll, in the Marshall Islands just before the assault on that island on 22 February 1944. Painted on the hulls are identification codes, the letter X followed by a two-digit number. (U.S. Army Engineer School History Office)

Above: This beachhead in the Marshall Islands on 24 February 1944 appears to be a study in organized chaos. Among stacks of ammunition and supply crates, oil drums, and other supplies, and Jeeps and light tanks and self-propelled howitzers is a DUKW at the center. Marked on its side is the code Z18. (National Archives)

were quite heavy and the surf ran six to eight feet high at times, but little trouble was encountered; slow-ups resulted mainly from conditions at the dump, as usual.

When Manila Harbor was opened to United States shipping in early March, it was found that pier installations were so damaged and so congested by sunken Japanese shipping that it was again necessary to use DUKWs to unload shipping. DUKW operations continued there until the end of hostilities.

Iwo Jima

Three Army and two Marine Corps DUKW companies participated in the assault on Iwo Jima on 19 February 1945. Their primary mission was to land the 105mm artillery battalions and to keep them supplied with ammunition. The three Army companies were made up of black enlisted men specially trained at the DUKW school on Oahu for their mission and attached to Marine Corps artillery regiments for the assault phase of the operation, The Marine DUKW companies had no operational experience and almost no training, despite OSRD urging in Washington.

The DUKWs, loaded with guns, ammunition, and gun crews, were discharged into the sea from LSTs at the line of departure some four miles out. Most of them went in only a few hours behind the assault waves of LVTs and landing boats, and the beaches were still under heavy mortar and machine gun fire from Mt. Suribachi. Information obtained before the operation had indicated that all beaches would provide firm sand with easy traction for wheeled vehicles. This, however, was found to be completely inaccurate, for they were composed of a fine volcanic ash, so soft that it was extremely difficult to walk in it. Moreover, most of the beaches were so steep that the front wheels of the DUKW would bury before the rear wheels could obtain proper traction, whereupon the vehicle would be swung broadside on by the surf and swamped if it were not towed off without delay. Eventually, a few spots were located where, with tires deflated as low as five pounds, the DUKWs could climb out, and at other points tractors were assigned to pull each DUKW up the beach grade as it landed.

Howitzers were unloaded by A-frame DUKWs and set up in battery position, and DUKWs then plied between the batteries and the ammunition-loaded LSTs to bring in 105mm shells. The LSTs remained at sea for several days; because of the great depth of water, they could not anchor and hold their positions, which made it extremely difficult for the DUKWs to locate them each time they made a trip from shore. DUKWs bringing the ammunition directly to the batteries were under mortar and small arms fire most of the time while on shore, and consequently many of the hulls were punctured. Conditions were so critical and the shore so crowded, however, that in the early phases of the operation it was necessary to send every DUKW back out to sea, regardless of its seaworthiness. Several LSTs had been designated as DUKW repair ships; once aboard, the DUKW hulls could have been easily patched, but in many instances a badly leaking DUKW was not permitted to drive aboard at once and foundered while standing by. Of its 50 DUKWs, one company reported losing 15 that could have been saved if taken aboard the LSTs immediately.

The losses in DUKWs during the first five days – well over 50 per cent – were higher than in any other operation. Most of them were due to the causes described above, but other DUKWs were swamped in the heavy surf, damaged against LST ramps while attempting to enter a bad sea, or holed on sunken landing craft near the beach. Casualties among the DUKW drivers were surprisingly light; the companies averaged only three or four killed or missing and about 10 wounded.

Despite the combination of difficult operating conditions and high equipment losses, the DUKWs succeeded in bringing almost all of their howitzers to shore, unloading them with the utmost efficiency, and keeping them supplied with sufficient ammunition to be one of the major factors in reducing the enemy garrison.

The black DUKW drivers received high praise for their courage and ability from many Marine officers, including the Commanding General, Fleet Marine Forces. One driver ran out of fuel while searching for a bowser boat out at sea, but although landing craft offered several times to pick him off his vehicle, he refused to abandon his DUKW and cargo, and drifted many miles to sea for 13 hours before a destroyer brought him in with his DUKW. When ship unloading started, the Army companies introduced the single spring line mooring system, which proved so successful in the heavy swells that the Marines also adopted it.

Above: An Esso smoke generator is loaded on a DUKW as part of a demonstration for a chemical officer at Base A, Milne Bay, New Guinea, on 26 February 1944. The generator is suspended from a crane mounted on a 4-ton Diamond T truck. (U.S. Army Chemical Corps Museum)

Left: The DUKW at Base A, Milne Bay, now has the Esso smoke generator secured in the cargo compartment. This type of generator was used to screen troop movements on land or water, such as river crossings. Smoke generator companies existed for this purpose. (U.S. Army Chemical Corps Museum)

Below: The DUKW with the Esso smoke generator slowly chugs along, laying down a smokescreen on Milne Bay during the 26 February 1944 demonstration held for a Major Terrell, a chemical officer. (U.S. Army Chemical Corps Museum)

The same DUKW with the Esso smoke generator seen in the preceding photographs emerges from the water at Milne Bay, New Guinea, during the demonstration on 26 February 1944. Smoke can be seen emanating from the upper rear of the generator. (National Archives)

Maintenance standards were also kept at a level far higher than that in many other landings conducted under easier operating conditions. This was due partly to the superior efforts of the maintenance sections in the DUKW companies, but also to the fact that, before loading at Oahu, they had received from the DUKW school there valuable advice and assistance in procuring adequate supplies of spare parts. One result of the performance of the Army companies at Iwo Jima was an order from the Fleet Marine Forces to the 4th and 5th Marine Divisions to send their DUKW companies to the Army-OSRD DUKW school on Oahu.

At the opening of the garrison phase of the operation, an additional company reinforced the three Army units, and all four reverted to the control of an Army amphibian truck battalion headquarters. Thereafter they served to unload Air Corps supplies and rations from ofishore shipping.

The Ryukyus

The invasion of the Ryukyus opened on 26 March 1945, with landings by the 77th Division in the Kerama Retto group. The 477th Amphibian Truck Company, attached to this division for the landing and for supplying its artillery, was an African-American manned unit which had already seen action in Saipan, Tinian, and the Philippines.

The DUKWs went ashore on Geruma Shima two hours behind the assault waves and unloaded the artillery under enemy small arms, machine gun, and mortar fire, but without loss.

Subsequently, the 477th moved on with the division artillery to Menna Shima, then to Ie Shima, and finally to Okinawa. On Ie Shima, extensive mine fields were encountered, and although other units suffered severely from personnel and vehicle losses, the DUKWs were fortunate in getting through without serious damage.

On Okinawa, seven Army and three Marine Corps DUKW companies participated in the initial assaults on 1 April 1945. The units landed on the west coast near Yontan and Kadena airfields. Although there was no enemy opposition on the beaches, the coral conditions were extremely unfavorable, the outer edge of the reef being scored by deep fissures and its face pocked for several hundred yards with scour holes and pits. These potholed reefs, over which the DUKWs drove day and night and at all stages of the tide except at high water, when they swam over, caused high mortality in front spring leaves, intermediate axle housings, and other underbody parts. On some days, one company would have as many as seven broken front springs. Accordingly, a new technique was successfully developed for welding broken leaves. DUKWs in most of the companies were

A DUKW of the 1st Cavalry Division is equipped with a small reel of communications wire at the rear of the cargo compartment for setting up secure ship-to-shore communications at Los Negros Island in the Admiralty Group on 24 March 1944. Painted on the bow is 1S-86. (General Motors)

already fitted with the propeller guard developed earlier. The other companies, realizing the value of this modification in reducing damage to the propeller, propeller shaft, and strut bearing, installed it as soon as they could.

Further compounding the difficulties was the threat to the cargo ships posed by Japanese *kamikaze*. Crews hastened to unload the ships in order that the merchantmen could leave the area. Dennis Puleston recounts in his *Gull's Way:* "Quite frequently netloads of cargo would come down to them that would be too much for the capacity of the DUKW. There were several incidents where DUKWs were actually sunk by overloads. We called all the DUKW operators together and told them that if they saw a load coming down that was not a sensible size, they were to cast off immediately and refuse to accept it. In one instance a black driver saw this huge netload coming down and realized it was beyond the capacity of his craft, so he immediately released the spring line that was holding him against the side of the ship. At once an officer on the deck began screaming obscenities at him and ordering him to come back and accept the load. The black driver looked at him and said, "And who are you?" "I am the first officer on this ship," came the response, upon which the DUKW driver replied with great dignity, "Well, I am the captain of this here vessel and I don't take no orders from my inferiors." And he refused to take that load. This was the morale of our DUKW drivers right up to the end."

In order to cut down the DUKW land runs as much as possible, transfer points were set up close to the operating beaches, and trucks were used for land hauls of two miles or more. On Okinawa, DUKWs were used in a truly combat role only when they brought the ammunition directly to the batteries during the artillery assault on the main Shuri-Naha lines.

The original Army companies, together with the 3rd and 6th Marine DUKW companies, went under the control of two Army amphibian truck battalion headquarters on 1 May, together with six more companies that arrived afterwards. Two of these new companies were from Oahu, two more had come directly from training in the United States, and the other two had come from the European Theater by way of the United States. The two companies trained in Oahu operated in full within 24 hours of landing, but the other four needed a minimum of two weeks to prepare and modify their vehicles.

The need for DUKWs on Okinawa was vital. When the last organized Japanese resistance had been overcome in early July, the DUKW companies were required to work even harder, for the island was not only the site of 23 proposed airfields but was also being built up into a major base for the coming assault on the Japanese home islands. Naha Harbor, for which high hopes had been held as a port, was a disappointment, being too thickly filled with the wreckage of Japanese shipping to accommodate any thing more than a few LCTs until October at the earliest. All the beaches were fronted by coral that dried out at half tide – hence lighters could make only two round trips in 24 hours. Therefore, the services of DUKWs were essential to bring in the great majority of general cargo and Air Corps supplies. Each company was required to keep a minimum of 35 DUKWs operating around the clock without let up, week after week. This, together with the severe coral conditions and the fact that all but the units newly arrived from the mainland were under strength from the normal attrition of sickness, put such a strain on the companies that they were scarcely able to keep their maintenance up to an efficient level. At the end of June, the Engineers constructed ground coral causeways to the edge of the reefs. Deadline rates decreased promptly, though a shortage of mechanics remained apparent. Eleven mechanics, as prescribed in the T/O, are not enough, but by that time most companies were reduced to seven or eight.

To assist in operations, a system of "hoppers" was put into effect. This system, first developed by OSRD at Funafuti in September 1943, consisted of having only one DUKW company man on a DUKW at one time. At shipside, the DUKW picked up a "hopper" – an additional man detailed for this work from the Seabee or port unit operating the hatch-who assisted in mooring the DUKW and in placing the loads. After casting off the loaded DUKW from the mooring line; the hopper hopped to the next DUKW. In this way, even when a DUKW company was as much as 10 percent under strength, it could just manage round-the-clock operations.

All the DUKW companies at Okinawa and one at Ie Shima continued to operate on a full-time basis up to the end of August, after which the flow of supplies to the island rapidly dwindled. Five of the companies were reconditioned to operate in Korea and to unload supplies for the occupation troops there. Other companies continued to unload ships at various points in the Pacific after the end of the war, but on a very reduced scale.

A fully loaded DUKW of the 541st Amphibian Truck Company rolls ashore at Bougainville on 3 March 1944. The vehicle was transporting supplies from one of the AK (cargo) ships in the harbor. The bow to the rear of the driver has a large dent in it. (National Archives)

A DUKW of the 541st Amphibian Truck Company is receiving a load of cargo from an AK ship off Bougainville on 3 March 1944 while another DUKW waits its turn. One load of cargo in a sling is already in the cargo compartment, and another one will be loaded. (National Archives)

In another of the series of photos taken on Bougainville on 3 March 1944, African-American G.I.s are unloading rations boxes from a DUKW of the 541st Amphibian Truck Company at a rations dump. Roller conveyors facilitate the work of moving the cartons. Trucks in the background are receiving rations for further distribution. (National Archives)

During the U.S. landings at Aitape, New Guinea, on 22 April 1944, DUKWs that have deposited cargos on the beachhead are bound for supply ships offshore in order to bring in more materiel. The two nearest vehicles have unusual objects, apparently boards with two angled pieces joined to them, on their rear decks. (National Archives)

Two DUKWs enter the harbor at Finschafen, New Guinea, on 20 April 1944, to make the short passage to their mother ship, in preparation for an invasion landing farther up the coast. In the background is a landing ship, tank, whose hull number ends in 78. (National Archives)

A DUKW with the SCR-399 radio set housed in the HO-17A comes ashore in New Guinea around April 1944. The vehicle number, 37, was painted above the forward wheel house, and a small insignia or sign was painted aft of the number and also on front of the cowl. (National Archives)

A DUKW with SCR-399 rests on a beach after a successful offshore test of the radio system, 4 April 1944. The power unit here was the model PE-75; a spare PE power unit was aft of the driver's seat. The SCR-399 installation had been performed by the 16th Signal Operation Battalion and the 99th Signal Battalion at Finschhafen, New Guinea. (National Archives)

A DUKW with SCR-399 and the HO-17A shelter enters the water in New Guinea around April 1944. The power unit, on a rack above the aft deck with no protective enclosure, was the model PE-75, with a Briggs & Stratton gasoline engine powering a generator. One whip-type transmitting antenna is installed on the front of the roof of the shelter, and two receiving antennas are on the rear of the shelter roof. Inside the shelter is a tightly packed array of radio equipment and seats for two operators. On the left side of the compartment are two chests containing the BC-312 and BC-342 radio receivers. To the front of the compartment is the BC-939-A antenna tuning unit, below which is the BC-610-EM radio transmitter with a power output of approximately 400 watts for continuous-wave operation and 300 watts for voice transmissions, capable of a range of up to 250 miles. On the right side of the compartment are several equipment chests, a wire-antenna reel, and a ventilating blower. (National Archives)

Army personnel and a man in a bush hat who may have been an Australian pose on the aft deck of the same DUKW seen in the preceding photo. A clearer view is available of the PE-75 power unit mounted above the winch and the supporting frame. (National Archives)

Eight-tube rocket-launcher mounts have been installed on the rears of a DUKW and an LTV amphibious tractor. Rather than the 120-tube 4.5-inch barrage-rocket array mounted on some DUKWs, these are eight-tube, 4.5-inch mounts that could be used for direct fire. (National Archives)

The DUKW shown in the preceding photo is observed from aft, revealing further details of the 4.5-inch rocket-launcher mount, including the elevating hand wheel and the sight. This photo and the one above were taken on Guadalcanal on 8 May 1944. (National Archives)

Members of the 162nd Infantry Regiment ride DUKWs toward Biak Island in New Guinea on 13 June 1944. That regiment had been battling the Japanese for Biak since 27 May 1944. The DUKWs proved an expeditious means of transporting troops along the coasts of New Guinea as U.S. forces attacked one Japanese stronghold after another. (National Archives)

DUKWs splash into the surf at Lunga Point, Guadalcanal, on 23 June 1944. They were transporting 105mm shells from an ammunition dump on the island to a ship lying off shore. The vehicle in the water to the left has the number 162 on the side of the hull. The DUKW next to it has an illegible number and what appears to be "The Long Knives" or "The Long Rider" painted on the hull. (National Archives)

Left: Around February 1945, this shoulder patch was designed for GMC representatives at the Amphibious Training Center, Camp Gordon Johnston, Florida. The insignia symbolized the DUKW's main role as an amphibian cargo carrier that often served in combat zones. (General Motors via Michael Honings)

Below: Cal Beautty, GMC Art Department supervisor, looks on as Robert Harger, a GMC staff artist, puts the finishing touches on the design for the DUKW shoulder patch. (General Motors via Michael Honings)

Above: The side of the bow of this DUKW has been blown out and the front wheel-house cover has been jarred loose. The number 65 is on the front of the cowl and is faintly visible on the side of the hull. One of the bows of the cargo compartment is hanging over the machine-gun ring mount. (National Archives)

Left: A combat photographer captured this magnificent image of a DUKW driver at work. The scene apparently was not a combat area, judging from the driver's lack of a helmet. On the dashboard to his front are the Pioneer compass and several large informational placards. Below the right side of the dash the right is a first-aid kit. (National Archives)

The A-frame boom of a U.S. Marine Corps DUKW is being put to use lifting a large part from the front of a landing craft. In the foreground is a pallet full of 105mm howitzer ammunition. This configuration of packing tubes for 105mm rounds was referred to as a cloverleaf bundle. (National Archives)

As the U.S. armed forces continued their Pacific island-hopping campaign into the Marianas Islands in 1944, DUKWs were once again at the forefront, transporting men and materiel from ship to shore and even inland. This DUKW fitted with a ring mount is rolling down a road in the town of Garapan on the island of Saipan. (National Archives)

A DUKW laden with combat troops proceeds down a dusty road on Saipan as another DUKW follows in the distance. This vehicle was assigned the number 45. Two USMC DUKW companies and one U.S. Army DUKW company served in the Saipan campaign. The USMC drivers lacked previous experience on the vehicles, while the army drivers, African-Americans of the 477th Amphibian Truck Company, were well trained on the DUKWs. (National Archives)

DUKWs, including the 8th vehicle of the 1st Platoon, 2nd Amphibian Truck Company, 4th Marine Division in the foreground, with Cpl. Donald Shults at the wheel, carry men and supplies down the same stretch of road seen in the preceding photograph. These vehicles were used extensively as cargo haulers on land on Saipan, and some were even put to use as prime movers for 155mm howitzers. (National Archives)

Above: A DUKW, front wheels on the sand, emerges from the water as it brings in a slung load of crates to a port. The number 6 is on the front of the coaming, and 6/1 is on the side of the hull. A woman's name, Kay and an illegible second word, is painted on the side of the driver's compartment just below the driver's head. (National Archives)

Right: Seven days after the initial U.S. landings at Saipan, on 22 June 1944, a wounded soldier on a litter is being transferred over the side of a DUKW at a hospital captured from the Japanese. DUKWs served as ambulances, picking up wounded troops at the front lines. (National Archives)

This and the following two photographs document the use of DUKWs in transporting 105mm howitzer ammunition. Here, stacks of crated ammunition await transfer to DUKWs, while two men in the DUKW in the background load crates into the cargo compartment. (National Archives)

The loading operation is viewed from the front of the driver's compartment. Each of these wooden crates held three rounds of 105mm ammunition stored in cloverleaf bundles, which consisted of three fiber packing tubes held together by a cloverleaf-shaped cap on each end. A metal rod held the end caps in place on the fiber tubes. (National Archives)

Marines hoist a crate of three 105mm howitzer rounds up to the men in the cargo compartment. Markings on the crates identified the type of ammunition and fuse, the date it was packed, the weight, shipping information, and so forth. (National Archives)

Members of the U.S. Army's 41st Signal Company use a DUKW to string communications wire across Japen Strait to Owi Island, off Biak Island, New Guinea, on 20 June 1944. Tripods made of sticks support the wire above the water. (National Archives)

A crew of the 253rd Signal Construction Company, U.S. Army, lay a submerged communications cable off Wakde Island, New Guinea, on 20 June 1944. In the foreground are the front of the port side of the cowl and the vehicle's driver. (National Archives)

Two DUKWs mounting 105mm howitzers are parked in the water along a beach on Saipan prior to making the seven-mile crossing, under their own power, to assist in the assault on neighboring Tinian. Both 105mm mounts are fitted with canvas covers. The first vehicle has the number 5 on the fronts of the coamings and on one of the five-gallon liquid containers on the rear deck, and the marking 5/1 on the side of the hull. (National Archives)

On the first day of the assault on Japanese forces on Noemfoor Island, New Guinea, 2 July 1944, members of the 158th Regimental Combat Team struggle to unload a 37mm antitank gun from the cargo compartment of a DUKW. This was the first of several attempts to unload the gun. (National Archives)

Right: A DUKW burns after being hit by a Japanese mortar round on the beachhead at Noemfoor Island on 2 July 1944. Painted in rough figures on the side of the hull is 76A-543. To the right of the DUKW is what appears to be a 6x6 cargo dump truck, piled high with supplies. (National Archives)

Below: DUKWs conduct landing operations, possibly at Noemfoor Island on 2 July 1944. The nearest DUKW, marked D9D-8 on the side of the hull, has an A-frame boom assembly installed, ready to be put to use immediately upon landing. The next DUKW is marked 4-10. (National Archives)

Bottom: On D-day at Noemfoor Island, 2 July 1944, DUKWs of the 158th Regimental Combat Team make their run for the beachhead. To the right, with its loading doors open, is LST-397. Several DUKWs have just disembarked from another LST in the distance. (National Archives)

Left: One week after the assault landings on Noemfoor Island, New Guinea, a DUKW brings a sling full of supplies from a Liberty ship to the beach. As sometimes was the case, the bow to the rear of the driver's compartment is deformed, probably the victim of a collision with a sling of cargo. (National Archives)

Below: DUKWs are parked on the beach at Noemfoor Island. The two nearest ones are equipped with A-frames, and at least one of the DUKWs in the distance have an A-frame as well. To the far right, a DUKW is in the water, which only comes up to the centers of the wheels. (National Archives)

Off Noemfoor Island, DUKWs are swimming out to a Liberty ship to receive cargo on 8 July 1944. A little aft of amidships of the Liberty ship, a DUKW is moored alongside, and one of the booms of the ship is lowering a sling full of cargo to the DUKW. (National Archives)

Troops of the 558th Quartermaster Railhead Company unload rations boxes from a DUKW on Noemfoor Island on 8 July 1944. They are sliding the cartons down a conveyor track. Marked on the left rear of the hull is the number 121. (National Archives)

Marines hug the sand on an invasion beach on Guam in July 1944 while several DUKWs of the 3rd Marine Division operate in the background. The DUKW toward the right is heavily laden with cargo, while a partially hidden DUKW in a draw toward the left has a 37mm antitank gun on a field carriage on its front deck. (National Archives)

A DUKW uses its A-frame boom to offload a 75mm pack howitzer from another DUKW that has just landed on Guam. Most of the weapon is hidden by a canvas cover, but a wheel is visible. Pack howitzers offered a highly portable means of bringing significant firepower onto Japanese positions. (National Archives)

Amid a chaotic scene on a beachhead on Guam, wounded men are being loaded into a late-production DUKW for transfer to ships off shore for further treatment. The DUKW's ability to take a casualty directly from a battlefield to a hospital ship resulted in the survival of many gravely wounded men. (National Archives)

A procession of DUKWs comes ashore on the island of Tinian in the Mariana Islands on 25 July 1944, while two DUKWs to the right prepare to reenter the water to receive more supplies from the ships lying offshore. Also present on the beach are several LVTs and a bulldozer. (National Archives)

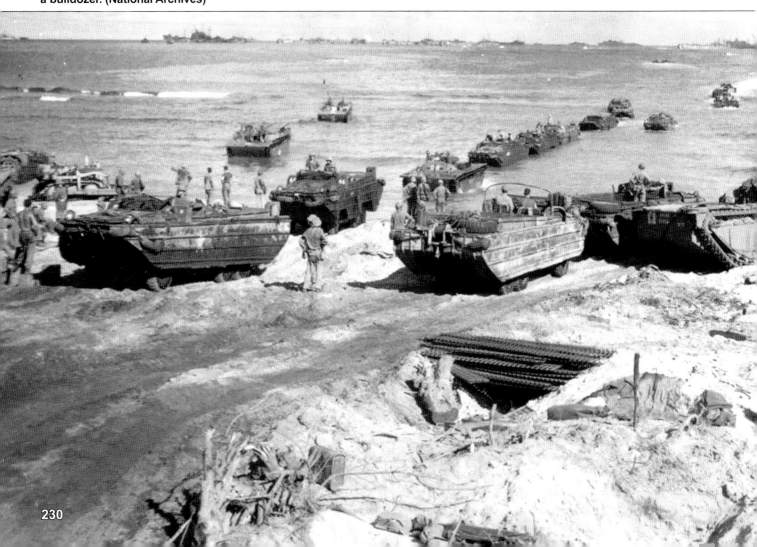

Right: A DUKW numbered 68, left, arrives at a beachhead on Tinian while another DUKW with a ring mount for a machine gun enters the water, probably to make a replenishment run. In the background are several landing craft, vehicle, personnel (LCVPs), including one that is listing badly. (National Archives)

Below: Two DUKWs of the 20th Marine Engineers, the second and fourth vehicles from the foreground, are interspersed with LVTs and a Jeep on a beach on Tinian. The DUKWs are heavily weathered and exhibit light-colored areas adjacent to the wheel houses and the rub rails that may represent spot priming. (National Archives)

During World War II, DUKWs were called on to transport many an unusual cargo. Here, a U.S. Marine Corps DUKW with the side number 76-1 has just brought a radio Jeep onto Tinian on 25 July 1944. The clearance is tight, and the marine kneeling on the side of the DUKW is carefully monitoring it. (U.S. Marine Corps)

On Tinian on 25 July 1944, a DUKW A-frame boom is being put to work hoisting a 75mm pack howitzer from the cargo body of another DUKW. These vehicles were assigned to the 2nd Marine Division. The howitzer has been disassembled and packed in its transport configuration; protruding from the canvas cover is a tow bar. (U.S. Marine Corps)

The 75mm pack howitzer shown being hoisted in the preceding photograph is now on the ground, the cover has been removed, and several marines are preparing to tow it away. To the right is the DUKW with the A-frame that hoisted the howitzer from the other DUKW. (National Archives)

The Cleaver-Brooks WTCT-6

Despite the failure of the General Motors trailer in 1943, due to impairment of water operations, there were those who still advocated a trailer for use with amphibians, both the DUKW and the new tracked landing vehicles, the LVT. The Cleaver-Brooks Company of Milwaukee, Wisconsin was tasked with creating such a trailer. The result was the Duckling, a steel-bodied trailer with a 3½ ton payload rating.

This trailer was tested first in Milwaukee Harbor in April, and production for the Marine Corps began the next month. The Marines used 60 of these trailers during Operation Stalemate, the attack on Peleliu, and 78 of them during Operation Detachment, the attack on Iwo Jima. The results were less than spectacular, with both the launching and operation of the trailers being difficult. Often the trailers were discarded after the initial landing.

An improved version of the amphibious trailer was created, the WTCT-6, rated at 2½ tons. The body of the trailer consisted of three compartments: the center cargo compartment, a bow compartment, and a false bottom pontoon compartment, through which the axle extended, each watertight and made of welded steel. On each end of the axle were dual 8.25-20 10-ply tires. A one-piece hatch, hinged on the right closed the top of the trailer. Hold down clamps secured with wingnuts were used to secure the hatch, making a watertight enclosure. Timbers attached to each side and the rear of the trailer acted as marine fenders.

A sophisticated drawbar, flexible in water but rigid on land, and equipped with an automatic release, was affixed to the front of the trailer. Retractable support legs, front and rear, stabilized the trailer when it was disconnected from a towing vehicle.

The Marines purchased about 500 of these trailers, and caught the attention of the Development Division, Office, Chief of Ordnance-Detroit, who borrowed one of the trailers and refitted it with 11.00-18 DUKW tires and wheels. Subsequently it was tested at Aberdeen Proving Ground, Maryland and Rehoboth Beach, Delaware. During testing it was observed that were the trailer loaded to its maximum capacity, each of the tires would be overloaded some 1,500 pounds each. Nevertheless testing proceeded, with road and water operations satisfactory. As was expected, there was some loss of water speed – about 1½ MPH – when the trailer was loaded.

Sand operations where hampered because the tread (distance between wheels) of the trailer and DUKW were different, so that the trailer wheels did not track in the path of the DUKW wheels. This meant a substantial increase in rolling resistance.

To address the overloading of the 11.00-18 tires it was recommended that larger, 14.00-20 12-ply tires be used. Such a conversion, using the hubs, wheel bearings, axle nuts, tires and wheels from the M21 4-ton ammunition trailer was made. At the conclusion of the testing on 17 September 1945 a memorandum was issued directing that the trailer be placed in the collection of the Aberdeen Proving Ground Museum.

Although experiments with a plywood trailer for the DUKW in February 1943 had gone nowhere, Cleaver-Brooks Co. of Milwaukee, Wisconsin, built a prototype amphibious trailer called the Duckling in 1944. It is seen here during trials in Milwaukee Harbor on 12 April 1944. (Cleaver-Brooks)

The Duckling had a capacity of 3.5 tons and were intended to increase the ability of DUKWs and LVTs to bring emergency and medical supplies to shore. It had two single tires and three watertight hatches on the top deck. Production of the Duckling began in May 1944. (Cleaver-Brooks)

WTCT-6 Specifications:

Empty weight	4,000 pounds
Payload	5,000 pounds
Length, overall	256½ inches
Length, cargo bay	156 inches
Width, overall	94 inches
Height, overall	72 inches
Height, cargo bay	41 inches
Ground clearance	15¼ inches
Track	69¼ inches
Tire size	8.25-20 inches

Above: A DUKW comes ashore along Lake Michigan near Milwaukee with a Duckling under tow during a test run with army officers and civilians on board on 12 April 1944. The trailer was hitched to the DUKW with a standard lunette and drawbar. (Cleaver-Brooks)

Below: The Marines acquired a large share of the Ducklings. A USMC amtrac tows two Duckling trailers in tandem during an exercise (or, judging from the swimsuits, a recreational jaunt) off Camp Lejeune, North Carolina. The aft trailer has a big numeral 1 painted on the bow. (Marine Corps Museum)

Four Ducklings are loaded on a railroad flatcar, stacked two high. Stenciled on the bow of the lower front trailer is "Lois Philippi / No. 1." Unlike the prototype, these Ducklings had D-shaped steps above the wheel houses to make it easier to climb to the top deck. (Marine Corps Museum)

On 8 September 1944, an experiment is underway to couple a Duckling trailer to an LVT(4) amtrac by means of a boat hook. It bears the markings of the Landing Vehicle Board, Test Operation, based at Fort Ord, California. The trailer had an overall length of 256.5 inches, an overall width of 84 inches, and an overall height of 72 inches. (National Archives via Jim Gilmore)

The Landing Vehicle Board's Duckling number 40 bears the registration number 98067 on the stern. The tires were 8.25-20 10-ply, and, unlike the prototype with its single tires, production Ducklings had dual tires. (National Archives via Jim Gilmore)

The same Duckling trailer in the preceding photo is observed on shore. The pole extending from the drawbar to the bow was called the hitch column. It had an adjustable coil spring at the top, and it served to make the drawbar flexible during operation on water or rigid on land. (National Archives via Jim Gilmore)

In a photo prepared for the Landing Vehicle Board, Fort Ord, California, a watertight cargo trailer for use with DUKWs and amtracs is viewed from overhead on 30 August 1944. The watertight cover for the cargo compartment is in the closed position. (National Archives via Jim Gilmore)

The cover, hinged on the starboard side, has been raised on the same watertight cargo trailer, showing the net inside. Dogs for securing the cover are on the port side of the compartment. The tops of the wheel houses were open, and the tops of the tires are visible. The axle features two tires on each side. (National Archives via Jim Gilmore)

A later version of the Cleaver-Brooks 2 ½-ton amphibian trailer, designated the WTCT-6, was delivered in 1945. Key differences between it and the Duckling included square wheel-house openings and a prominent wooden rub rail on each side. This example, with a wheel-house cover, was photographed at Aberdeen Proving Ground in 1949. (Ordnance Museum)

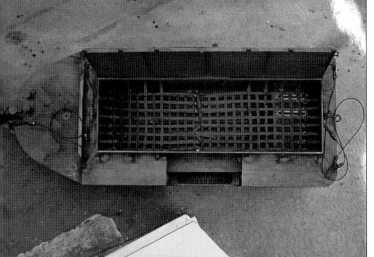

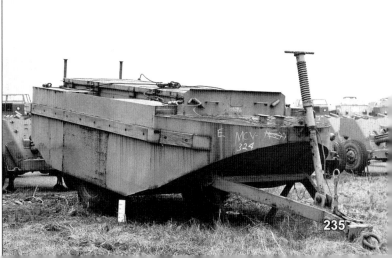

Above: A marine takes cover during the landings on Peleliu on 15 September 1944. In the right background is a DUKW that has been hit and is smoking. A 37mm antitank gun to the rear of the marine has been unloaded by ramps from the DUKW to the right. (National Archives)

Left: The same DUKW and 37mm antitank gun shown in the preceding photograph are viewed from another angle, showing more of them, among the detritus on a Peleliu beachhead, 15 September 1944. The ramps for offloading the 37mm gun are still leaning on the DUKW. (National Archives)

Below: A G.I. walks along a beachhead on Peleliu past two DUKWs with U.S. Army markings and an LVT. Although the Peleliu landings were a USMC operation, the DUKWs were assigned to the 454th and 456th Amphibian Truck Companies, on detached service to the Amphibian Transport Group, 1st Marine Division (Reinforced). (National Archives)

Destroyed and disabled DUKWs litter a beachhead on Peleliu. Losses of DUKWs were high on D-day on Peleliu, with more than 50 percent of the total force of them being destroyed. Some were knocked out by mines and others by artillery. (National Archives)

Left: This DUKW knocked out on a beach on Peleliu is viewed from its front. The vehicle is on its side, and the engine access hatch door is open, showing the U.S. Army registration number inside the door. Numerous punctures are on the lower part of the bow. (National Archives)

Below: Marines examine a knocked-out DUKW, numbered 443, on a beach at Peleliu. Damage includes a large hole in the side of the hull by the driver's compartment and numerous shrapnel and bullet holes. The tide apparently has partially buried the tires in sand. (General Motors)

Marines take a brief rest among supply crates near a DUKW on a beach on Peleliu. The vehicle number 435 is painted on the hull. This DUKW apparently was equipped with an A-frame, judging by the stays running aft from the lifting eyes. (National Archives)

Above: Marine infantrymen pass DUKWs at a vehicle park on Peleliu. To the rear of the DUKW at the center of the photo is a vehicle, probably a DUKW, with an A-frame boom. U.S. Army markings are on the sides of the hulls. (National Archives)

Right: On Peleliu, a DUKW advances across the captured Japanese airfield. Dark-colored sand bags are piled on the front deck of the vehicle to afford it some protection against frontal fire. To the left is the rear end of a marine LVT-4. (National Archives)

After the marines secured the beachheads and the airfield on Peleliu, their offensive stalled into a hard-fought contest with Japanese troops firmly dug-in on Bloody Nose Ridge. During this stage of the fighting, DUKWs such as these were employed as cargo trucks and personnel carriers. (National Archives)

Above: A bulldozer and a crawler crane move among knocked-out DUKWs and an LVT on a beach on Peleliu. The DUKWs had a hard time in this landing. First, they had to contend with jagged coral reefs and heavy swells during the approach, and then they faced deadly Japanese beach defenses. (National Archives)

Left: DUKWs, including several full of personnel, are stopped along a muddy trail on Peleliu. The nearest DUKW has the number 447 on the front of the cowl, and the vehicle behind it has the number 448 on the coaming. (National Archives)

DUKWs being used as troop carriers pass Japanese huts on Peleliu. In addition to transporting troops, DUKWs on Peleliu were put to work evacuating wounded personnel to ships offshore for further medical treatment. (National Archives)

A DUKW was photographed from overhead at a supply dump on Peleliu, with another DUKW partially visible to the right. The closer DUKW is equipped with radio sets in the cargo compartment, and an antenna mount is present on each side of that compartment. (National Archives)

Men are unloading artillery projectiles from a DUKW with army markings and an A-frame boom on Peleliu in September 1944. Because of DUKWs' ability to pass over the jagged coral reefs offshore of this island, these vehicles made a tremendous contribution to the logistical support of the invasion and battle of Peleliu. (National Archives)

At a camp on Peleliu, a wounded man on a litter is being hoisted up to a DUKW for transport to a ship off shore for further medical treatment. A cameraman standing on the aft deck of the DUKW is filming the incident. At least one other wounded G.I. is lying in the cargo compartment. (National Archives)

Another patient in a litter is being hoisted up to the same DUKW seen in the preceding photograph. Just as DUKWs facilitated moving inbound supplies across Pelelieu's coral reefs to shore, these vehicles saved many lives by their ability to move the wounded directly from the battlefield to hospital ships. (National Archives)

The **DUKW** at the camp in Peleliu is now full of litter patients and will soon be moving out. The litters are not the traditional type with two poles, which could be rested crosswise on the cargo compartment coamings, but were Stokes litters, a basket design that allowed the patient to be strapped safely to it. (National Archives)

Above: The 1st Marine Division was assigned 60 Duckling amphibian trailers for the use of its DUKWs and LVTs during the September 1944 invasion of Peleliu. An insignia or tactical sign, "3 ART" in a circle, is on the hull of this Duckling being towed over coral by a bulldozer on Peleliu. (USMC Museum)

Left: A crew of the Radio Detachment, 98th Signal Battalion, on Som Som Island in the Halmahera Group uses an SCR-399 radio set with a PE-35 power unit to communicate with General Headquarters in Hollandia, New Guinea, 16 September 1944. (National Archives)

Two DUKWs assigned to Marine Air Group 45 are parked at Falalop Airfield on Ulithi Atoll in the Caroline Islands during the final year of World War II. The vehicles undoubtedly were very handy for making supply runs to the ships in the lagoon. (National Archives)

Above: A procession of DUKWs carries troops past landing craft off Pavuvu in the central Solomon Islands. The closest DUKW has the number 443 on the front of the starboard side of the cowl and an insignia or placard with triangles on front of the port coaming. A small tire protects the winch chock or eye at the center of the bow. (National Archives)

Right: DUKWs bring troops ashore on Pavuvu during training exercises. The marines used Pavuvu as a rest area and also conducted training exercises there, including those in preparation for the 1944 invasion of Peleliu. (National Archives)

Marines gather around a 37mm antitank gun next to a DUKW with the name "The Lone Wolf" on the hull, on Pavuvu. The 37mm gun M3 has a type of shield with an extended top often used by the marines in the Pacific. The top of the shield was cut in a wavy pattern, for camouflage purposes. (National Archives)

DUKWs discharge troops during a training exercise on Pavuvu. To the left is a DUKW with the number 405 on the front of the starboard side of the cowl and a placard or insignia with three triangles, similar to one seen in a preceding photo, on the port coaming. (National Archives)

A DUKW crew are preparing the A-frame for use. The telescoping legs of the boom have been extended and secured, the cable and sheave have been installed, and two men are preparing to insert outrigger legs in sockets at the rear of the hull, for stability. (National Archives)

As DUKWs come ashore during an invasion of an island in the Schouten Island Group of New Guinea, a Japanese artillery shell explodes in the water. To the rear of the DUKW in the right foreground is a DUKW with a radio shelter over the cargo compartment. (National Archives)

A DUKW brings up reinforcements during fighting around San Pablo, Leyte, Philippine Islands, in late 1944. During the initial landings on Leyte on 20 October 1944, DUKWs were used in greater numbers than in any previous operation, with 13 army amphibian truck companies involved. (National Archives)

Right: On 22 October 1944, the second day after the U.S. landings on Leyte, a DUKW carrying cavalry troops approaches an overturned Japanese flatbed truck in the street of a village. At least one civilian is on board the DUKW: probably a Filipino acting as a guide. (General Motors)

Below: Troops of the 828th Amphibian Truck Company advance in a convoy of DUKWs toward the front lines near Julita, Leyte, on 28 October 1944. The G.I.s in the nearest DUKW are wary of enemy activity, and two of them stand ready with M1 carbines. (National Archives)

Filipino men in several DUKWs lined up outside of the Philippine Civil Affairs Unit at Tacloban, Leyte, are about to be driven to a U.S. signal depot, where they will work for pay. The date was 31 October 1944. (National Archives)

The same line of DUKWs filled with Philippine civilians at the Philippine Civil Affairs Unit headquarters at Tacloban is viewed from another angle. The coastal nature of the area of operations in Leyte lent itself well to the DUKW. (National Archives)

At Tacloban on 31 October 1944, volunteer Filipino laborers board a DUKW for transport to a signal depot. They were hired through the auspices of the Philippine Civil Affairs Unit, an agency created to provide rapid relief to the people of that country. (National Archives)

Troops of the 43rd Infantry Division brace themselves as the DUKW they are riding starts up the ramp of LST-22 at Aitape, New Guinea on 26 December 1944. This DUKW and landing ship were part of a force that was preparing to carry out another invasion. (National Archives)

A DUKW loaded with a 105mm howitzer backs down the ramp of a landing ship, tank, at Ormoc Bay, Leyte, on 7 December 1944. The aft deck is almost awash. The vehicle is marked H112 on the surf board and on the front of the port driver's compartment coaming. (National Archives)

Crewmen work on a DUKW armed with a 120-tube 4.5-inch barrage-rocket array at a village in the Southwest Pacific Area in 1944. For self-defense, this vehicle had two .30-caliber machine guns on pintle mounts, one on each side of the driver's compartment. A rations box is on top of the engine access hatch. (National Archives)

DUKWs deliver supplies, including crated ammunition in the foreground, to the Dagupan railhead along Lingayen Gulf on Luzon, for shipment to the battle fronts. Dagupan was the site of Blue Beach, where part of General MacArthur's invasion force landed on 8 and 9 January 1945. (U.S. Army Engineer School History Office)

Above: An inbound DUKW passes Landing Craft, Tank 735 (LCT-735) at Blue Beach at Lingayen Gulf, Luzon, Philippine Islands, in 1945. In the Luzon campaign, as in so many others, DUKWs performed in the amphibious role well as well as a land-transport vehicle. (National Archives)

Right: The San Francisco Port of Embarkation Ordnance Shop was one of the facilities that prepared DUKWs for shipment overseas. Here, in 1944 a woman employee of that shop steam-cleans a DUKW, after which it will be repainted to protect it during the coming sea voyage. (Military History Institute via Jim Gilmore)

It is 19 February 1945, D-day at Iwo Jima, and a DUKW has just backed off the ramp of an LST prior to making a run for shore. Five amphibian truck companies participated in the D-day landings on Iwo Jima. Participating in the landings were the USMC 4th and 5th Amphibian Truck Companies and, on detached service to the Marine Corps, the U.S. Army's 471st, 473rd, and 476th Amphibian Truck Companies. (National Archives)

A DUKW of the 5th Amphibian Truck Company that has just departed from a landing ship off Iwo Jima on D-day, 19 February, is viewed from above. It carries a cargo of members of the 13th Marines, the artillery unit of the 5th Marine Division, and several large crates. The principal task of the DUKWs in the landings on Iwo Jima was to transport ashore the Marines' 105mm howitzers and their crews. (National Archives)

In a general view of the invasion beach at Iwo Jima, numerous DUKWs are parked, including one at the center with a ring mount for a machine gun. The DUKWs began arriving ashore with artillery around mid-afternoon on D-day. U.S. Army multi-color camouflage paint schemes are visible on several of these DUKWs. (National Archives)

Above: DUKW crewmen take cover after their vehicle is hit by Japanese mortar fire on Iwo Jima. In the first five days of the battle, over 50 percent of the DUKWs were lost: some from artillery fire, and others from swamping. Fortunately, losses of DUKW crews were quite light. (National Archives)

Left: Disabled and destroyed vehicles litter Beach Yellow Two on Iwo Jima, including a USMC DUKW with the nickname Cherry painted on the cowl and numbers 115122 and 2-1-4 painted on the hull. To the left is a ship the Japanese beached before the U.S. landings to serve as a sniper nest. (National Archives)

At Iwo Jima, as in other campaigns the DUKW served in, these amphibious trucks often served as medevac vehicles, transporting the wounded directly from the battlefield to hospital ships waiting offshore. Here, several patients on litters are in the cargo compartment of a DUKW headed out to sea. (National Archives)

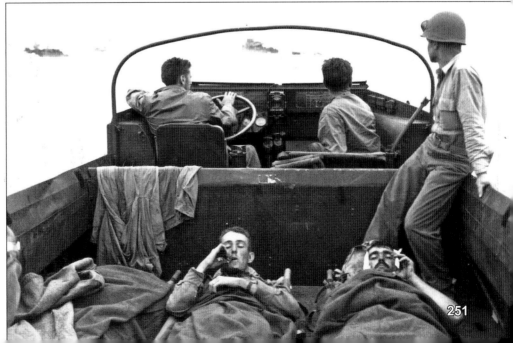

A DUKW rests in front of a Japanese bunker on Iwo Jima. The vehicle features a roughly applied, multicolor scheme of camouflage paint. On Iwo Jima, such schemes featuring three colors and four colors were observed, the colors comprising olive drab, brown, sand, and black. (National Archives)

A DUKW comes ashore directly from a landing craft to the beach at Iwo Jima. Although the initial waves of DUKWs had to circle offshore for hours before places could be cleared on the beaches for them to land, later waves were able to disembark at the shore. (National Archives)

Thick, black volcanic sand on the invasion beaches at Iwo Jima posed a problem for wheeled vehicles emerging from the water. That condition may have led to the swamping of the DUKW in the foreground. Cables have been rigged from the DUKW to a tractor in an effort to recover the vehicle. (National Archives)

Right: To aid the DUKWs in coming ashore and entering the water on Iwo Jima, engineers placed ramps made of Marston matting at key entry/exit points on the beaches. An overturned DUKW lies in the sand next to this ramp; an amtrac sits in the surf. (National Archives)

Below: A Seabee bulldozer clears a path for one of the U.S. Army DUKWs detached to the marines for the Iwo Jima invasion. This vehicle, numbered 162, has the full four-color camouflage scheme of olive drab, brown, sand, and black. (National Archives)

The DUKWs operating in support of the Marines on Iwo Jima were camouflaged, rather then the basic olive drab paint scheme found in most every other operation. The Iwo Jima DUKWs wore a scheme of olive drab, dark sand yellow and light sand yellow.

Marines on Iwo Jima hoist a wounded man on a litter up to a DUKW for medical evacuation. The vehicle is marked with the code DGF on front of the cowl and with the numeral 5 on the side of the hull. Another DUKW is to the rear of this one. (National Archives)

Above: On a beach on Iwo Jima after the initial landings, a crawler crane is unloading cargo nets full of supplies from DUKWs. The U.S. Army DUKW to the left has four-color camouflage and the number 111 on the side of the hull. The man to the right is walking on Marston matting. (National Archives)

Left: A marine unloads crated artillery ammunition from the cargo compartment of a DUKW on a beach on Iwo Jima. The name "Cannon Ball" is painted freehand on the side of the hull. The painter of the camouflage scheme took care to cut-in around the "sling here" stencil below the lifting eye to the left. (National Archives)

Right: Camouflaged USMC DUKWs are lined up on a beachhead identified in the original caption only as "Yellow Beach No. 1." Stenciled on the hull of the nearest DUKW is its registration number, 97244, to the front of which is a duck insignia with the number 3. The number 12 is on the side of the driver's compartment. (National Archives)

Below: Amidst the debris and wrecked landing craft and vehicles on Iwo Jima's Red Beach 2 on 27 February 1945 is a Duckling amphibian trailer, USMC registration number 98229. These vehicles lacked tail lights, but had two round reflectors on the stern. (USMC Museum)

DUKWs were present for the final U.S. invasion of World War II: Operation Iceberg, the assault on Okinawa. Two months after the initial landings, African-American G.I.s are supervising the unloading of a cargo net full of medical supplies from a U.S. Army DUKW on Orange Beach on Okinawa on 6 June 1945. The DUKW is marked M111 and has four small Japanese flags painted on the cab coaming. (U.S. Army Quartermaster Museum)

At an organizational dump at Orange Beach, Okinawa, on 6 June 1945, African-American troops are using an A-frame on a DUKW to hoist supply crates to an awaiting cargo truck. The thick mud certainly added to the misery quotient for these men. (National Archives)

A DUKW is backed into a trench at a supply dump in the Central Pacific Area where 50-gallon drums for diesel fuel are being stored, in 1945. A small crawler crane is being used to hoist the drums, three at a time, using slings. (U.S. Army Quartermaster Museum)

A crawler crane alongside a DUKW is handling a cargo net full of supplies somewhere in the Central Pacific Area in 1945. A net full of crates is on the ground to the left. Another DUKW is waiting close behind the one in the foreground. (National Archives)

Although by 1945, when this photo was taken, A-frames were being furnished at a rate of one A-frame set per five DUKWs, it was preferable to use cranes to unload DUKWs whenever they were available. The reason for this was simple – few vehicles possessed the amphibious capabilities of the DUKW, and utilizing one of the vehicles in a stationary, materials-handling role, was a waste of the valuable ship-to-shore asset – the purpose for which the DUKW was created. (National Archives)

Above: U.S. Marine Corps DUKWs containing rations make their way through Naha, Okinawa, in early June 1945. The rations boxes are very neatly stacked in the cargo compartments. On the side of the hull toward the bow on these vehicles is a small insignia of a duck with the number 3 superimposed. (USMC)

Right: A procession of DUKWs crosses a body of water somewhere in the Southwest Pacific around 1945. The drivers are African-Americans. The first DUKW, marked T-39 and registration number 7028555, is carrying a load of oil or gasoline drums. The second DUKW carries a group of white G.I.s. (National Archives)

A DUKW at a camp near a beach in the South Pacific was photographed from the front deck. A good view is offered of the lowered windshield, including the windshield-wiper motors and diagonal braces. Other DUKWs are parked in the background. (National Archives)

Armored DUKW

Almost from the time the Army was shown the prototype DUKW, there had been suggestions that the vehicle be fitted with some form of armor. By December 1943 there was sufficient pressure that a project was begun to see if it was practical to supply an armor kit. Due to weight considerations, it was suggested that this armor be styled along the lines of that used with aircraft, using as little armor as possible to achieve the maximum protection. A plywood mockup of a proposed armor arrangement, protecting the engine and driver's compartment of the DUKW, began at the GM plant that month. In time, this mockup was refined to a working model.

Rod Stephens went to Fort Ord in January 1944. He spent two days in the surf to ascertain the general effect of the weight which would be added by the proposed armor. Stephens sent his recommendations to GMC Director of Research Everett W. Allen as well as Hatley Rowe and Roger Warner of the OSRD on 1 February.

He recommended that the overall weight of the armor kit be limited to 700 pounds, centered not more than one foot forward of the forward edge of the windshield; that the gas tank be bullet-proofed, that the standard windshield be eliminated, with armor plate of a similar shape replacing it; and that the armor be carefully installed to allow satisfactory vision and easy access to the engine.

In February 1944 a mild steel version of the GM mockup armor was fabricated and installed on a DUKW. This DUKW was then tested for land and water operation at the General Motors Proving Ground. Operation in both instances was found to be satisfactory, however, an armor-equipped DUKW, without cargo, could not reverse in marine operations. This is because the weight of the armor depressed the bow of the DUKW, raising the stern, and causing propeller cavitation. This was corrected by installing a flap over the rear of the propeller tunnel, similar to the flap that had been used on the Marmon-Herrington QMC-4 prototype and early GPA. This flap prevents the propeller from sucking air into the tunnel.

Following these tests, two sets of face-hardened armor plate were then fabricated. The kit was then tested by the Landing Vehicle Board at Fort Ord, California. The kit consisted of 17 pieces of ¼ armor plate, with a total weight of 1,000 pounds.

GMC supplied two men to aid with the installation of the kit on the test vehicle, largely by bolting through holes drilled in the hull stiffener ribs. The armor-equipped DUKW was tested against a conventional DUKW over a three-mile triangular test course in Monterey Bay, with no practical difference in speed being observed. Interestingly, the Landing Vehicle Board found the rear propeller tunnel flap unnecessary.

Further comparison tests were conducted in an eight-foot surf. The armor-equipped DUKW actually performed marginally better in these conditions than the standard DUKW, with reduced yaw and less pitching when entering the water. Plus, the armor kit protected the windshield from damage. With tire pressure properly adjusted, the armored DUKW also equaled its unarmored sibling in soft sand and highway operation, although from the driver's standpoint, driving the armored DUKW was much like driving a half-track with the armored flaps closed.

Although no firing tests were conducted, it was suspected that here too the armored DUKW would be comparable to a half-track as far as armor protection. In its final report on the subject, 15 February 1945, the Landing Vehicle Board recommended that the armor kit be procured, and that it be installed in Depots or base shops, but only as directed by theater commander. However, no records of such kits being procured have surfaced.

To provide DUKW crews with better protection against frontal fire, experiments were conducted with armor. In December 1943, a plywood mockup of bow and windshield armor was produced. Two months later, a pilot model was made with soft-steel "armor," seen here. (TACOM LCMC History Office)

On front and sides of the bow, armor protection extended only to the waterline, and it followed the general contours of the bow. Driver's compartment protection included armor plates over the cowl and a three-panel hinged windshield guard with vision slots with sliding covers. (TACOM LCMC History Office)

Inside the engine compartment, a piece of armor was mounted laterally, aft of the engine. At the bottom is the air cleaner, and details of the inner side of the engine compartment hatch door are visible. In the background is the driver's compartment frontal armor. (General Motors)

As viewed from the starboard side of the driver's compartment, the armored coverage ended at the sides of the cowl. Operating handles for the sliding vision-slot covers protrude above the top of the windshield guard. The armor, if it had gone into production, would have offered protection primarily against splinters. (TACOM LCMC History Office)

In late 1944 and early 1945 the Landing Vehicle Board at Fort Ord, California, field-tested an armor kit for the DUKW. The plates that comprised the cab-armor part of the kit are displayed, and they offered protection from the front and the sides. The nearest plate is the upper part of the frontal windshield armor, with two vision ports with sliding covers. (National Archives)

The armor kit also included bow armor, and those plates are laid-out around the test DUKW at Fort Ord on 22 January 1945. The plates were made of ¼-inch face-hardened armor, and the kit had a total weight of 1,000 pounds. It took 30 man-hours to install the armor kit on the DUKW. (National Archives)

The armor kit is installed in this 18 January 1945 photo. The bow plates protected the front of the vehicle to the waterline. The top frontal and side plates of the cab armor were hinged and are in the lowered position with the top of the windshield showing. (National Archives)

A major concern of the tests of the armor kit at Fort Ord was that the 1,000-pound extra weight of the kit would diminish the vehicle's performance on water, but this proved not to be the case. In this 16 December 1945 photo, the vehicle displays proper trim in the water. The overall results of the water and land tests were satisfactory. (National Archives)

China-Burma-India Theater

At the Quebec Conference in August 1943, the British requested a future issue of 8,000 DUKWs. A large proportion of these were intended for coming operations in Southeast Asia, although it was subsequently realized that the great areas of mud and rice paddies on the Southeast Asia coasts made DUKWs unsuitable for large-scale use in amphibious work there. Eventually, only a few hundred were allocated to this theater.

In late 1943, an amphibious assault on the port of Akyab on the Arakan coast of Burma was being planned. Two RASC DUKW companies were in training in India and a small fleet of LSTs and other landing ships was being prepared for the assault. At the Teheran Conference, however, it was decided that other theaters must be given a higher priority and consequently much of the equipment and supplies intended for Burma operations was diverted to the NITO and SOWESPAC. The actual operation was therefore reduced in scale and had only the limited objective of establishing beachheads on sections of the Arakan coast above Akyab.

These were to command the mouths of several rivers up which the Japanese were established. For this operation, 25-pounder artillery was loaded into DUKWs, which in turn were loaded into landing ships. At the landing, the beaches were hard and unobstructed by coral, but inland the presence of rice paddies and swamps made the terrain unsuitable for the use of anything but tracked amphibians. After this section of the coast was secured, it was held for about a year, after which it was expanded by the landings at Akyab, Ramree Island, and Taungup. It was during these operations that at the Naf River Dennis Puleston was severely injured as a result of a Japanese shell landing nearby. Several vertebrae were damaged, and he also suffered a concussion. After a 10-day hospital stay, and over the objection of his doctors, he left the hospital and proceeded to the Mediterranean and then on to England in order to prepare for the Normandy invasion.

The dropping of the atomic bombs – another project that the NDRC had a hand in – and the subsequent surrender of Japan negated the need for a bloody amphibious assault on mainland Japan. While some DUKWs went to Japan for occupation duty, including the Second Marine Amphibian (DUKW) Company, many of the DUKWs in the Pacific theater were now surplus. The war-weary vehicles were scrapped or cannibalized, while the newer, better vehicles were returned to supply depots.

Some DUKWs found their way into the Indian Army during World War II, including these vehicles assigned to the 35th General Purpose Transport Company, lined up at a vehicle park at Cocanada, India, on 25 June 1944. (National Archives)

Above: Troops of the Indian 35th General Purpose Transport Company stand for inspection to the rears of their DUKWs at Cocanada, India, on 25 June 1944. Visible above the men are plywood closures or surfboards at the rears of the cargo compartments and the triangular braces that served to reinforce the closures. (National Archives)

Left: A close-up photo shows an insignia on front of the starboard side of the cowl of a DUKW of the 35th General Purpose Transport Company and Cocanda, India, on 25 June 1944. It depicts a duck with a propeller and propeller shaft protruding from its hindquarters. (National Archives)

The British employed DUKWs to good effect in the riverine environment of Burma in World War II. They were particularly useful in medevac operations but weren't plentiful enough in Burma to adequately carry out that role. Here, a column of DUKWs plies the Chindwin River in January 1945. (Imperial War Museum)

DUKWs often performed odd jobs. Here, a DUKW of the Indian 19th Division tows a Class 40 raft across the Irrawaddy River. This type of raft had a capacity of 40 tons and could carry three fully loaded 6x6 trucks, one jeep, and 75 men. (National Archives)

Japanese prisoners of war load a DUKW of 56 Water Transport Unit, Royal Army Service Corps (RASC), with Japanese ammunition that the British captured at dumps in Singapore. Subsequently, the ammunition will be disposed at sea. (Imperial War Museum)

A DUKW of 56 Water Transport Unit, Royal Army Service Corps, transports captured Japanese ammunition from dumps in Singapore toward a landing craft waiting offshore. The ammunition will be transferred to the landing craft before being dumped into the ocean. (Imperial War Museum)

Almost immediately after VJ Day, the III Amphibious Corps, USMC, was staged to China for occupation duty. Seen here is a USMC DUKW towing a WTCT-6 amphibian trailer down a street in Shanghai in 1945. The square wheel-house opening and the rub rail around the hull above the wheel house differentiated this trailer from the Duckling. (Imperial War Museum)

The same DUKW that appears in the preceding photo is viewed from the front. Curiously, the manual bilge pump, an essential accessory that almost always is seen in its stored location on the front deck of DUKWs, is missing, as are the pioneer tools. (Imperial War Museum)

Chapter 21
Post WWII Military Service

During WWII the DUKW proved to be a remarkably successful vehicle. Its successes as well as its relatively unique amphibious capabilities caught the eye of the public, fostering further publicity such as the four-page story "Three Men in a DUKW" by Milton Silverman appearing in the April 20, 1946 edition of the Saturday Evening Post. Neither was the value of the DUKW lost on the military. Also in 1946 amphibious training began at Fort Story, Virginia, with the 458th Amphibious Truck Company (formerly the 458th Amphibian Truck Company), which was soon joined by the 425th Amphibious Truck Company. By 1948, when the installation was transferred to Transportation Training Command, the 54th Transportation Truck Battalion was handling the training. Fort Story would remain the home for DUKW training until the vehicles were withdrawn from service decades later.

Overseas, a smattering of US Army units continued to operate the DUKW, as did the British, Australians and French. With the DUKW no longer in production, maintenance, always important, became doubly so.

Long a source of problem were the ribs running the length of the DUKW hull. This ribs trapped moisture, and invariably led to rust. Even as the DUKWs were being assembled, the NDRC raised concerns about this, GM tried applying Dolphin-brand marine coating to the inside of the rails.

Further, experiments were tried with the ribs being formed into the actual hull sides. These experiments pointed to two potential problem areas with this method of construction. First, strain produced stress cracks near the embossments. Secondly, in use the separately applied ribs serve as the wear point when working alongside ship (in the event that the rope fenders fail to protect the hull) or moving through brush. Should the welded-on ribs be damaged, as they often were, this did not impact the watertight integrity of the hull. Were the ribs formed into the hull, such damage would puncture the hull proper, so Sparkman and Stephens recommended against this.

A partial solution to the problem of hull rusting was implemented on 7 November 1949 when Modification Work Order G 501-W31 was issued. This Modification Work Order (MWO) called for the cutting of four-inch gaps in the outer face of the rub rails in specific locations along the vehicle, in order to promote drainage. Instructions were provided for cutting these notches with either air-chisels or grinding wheels.

Six months later another MWO, G 501-W32, was issued to address another recurring issue with the DUKW. As was discovered during WWII, the distance between coamings on the DUKW was insufficient to accommodate the 105mm howitzer when fitted with combat wheels. As a wartime expedient, this had been resolved with sledge hammers and pry bars. On 5 June 1950 a somewhat more elegant solution to this problem was promulgated by the aforementioned MWO. This MWO described the cutting of a 12-inch notch in the coamings 16 inches behind the front wall. The severed section of coaming was then moved 2½ inches outward, providing clearance for the gun carriage. These instructions were amended 10 January of 1951 to alter the 16-inch dimension to 15 inches.

At the end of World War II, DUKWs, like other U.S. military equipment, suddenly became surplus, such as these examples assembled at a base. Nonetheless, because of their utility even in peacetime, large quantities of them were preserved, and DUKWs went on to serve in subsequent wars as well in civilian capacities. (Jim Gilmore collection)

A small group of troopers of the 11th Airborne Division comes ashore in a DUKW on 27 September 1946. They were preparing for full-scale training maneuvers by the U.S. Eighth Army at Yokosuka, Japan. (National Archives)

DUKWs in an Army Day parade on 7 April 1947 roll past the reviewing stand on Constitution Avenue in Washington, D.C. Emblazoned on the vehicle to the left is the information that it was assigned to the 460th Amphibian Truck Company, 7th Regiment, Transportation Corps, U.S. Army, Fort Eustis, Virginia. Painted on the front of the cab are the names of the driver and assistant driver: T/5 W. E. Brightman and T/5 W. N. Hanson. (National Archives)

A civilian examines a DUKW with the side of its hull cut away for training use. The vehicle was part of an exhibit by the Transportation Corps in Washington, D.C. during the week of the inauguration of President Harry Truman in January 1949. (U.S. Army Transportation Museum)

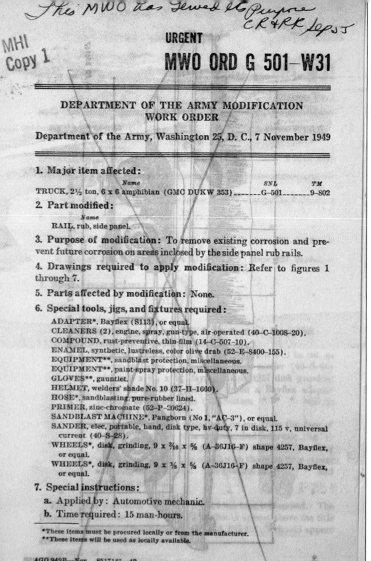

MWO ORD G 501-W31

DEPARTMENT OF THE ARMY MODIFICATION WORK ORDER

Department of the Army, Washington 25, D. C., 7 November 1949

---

1. Major item affected:

Name		SNL	TM
TRUCK, 2½ ton, 6 x 6 amphibian (GMC DUKW 353)		G–501	9–802

2. Part modified:

Name
RAIL, rub, side panel.

3. Purpose of modification: To remove existing corrosion and prevent future corrosion on areas inclosed by the side panel rub rails.

4. Drawings required to apply modification: Refer to figures 1 through 7.

5. Parts affected by modification: None.

6. Special tools, jigs, and fixtures required:

ADAPTER*, Bayflex (S113), or equal.
CLEANERS (2), engine, spray, gun-type, air-operated (40–C–1008–20).
COMPOUND, rust-preventive, thin-film (14–C–507–10).
ENAMEL, synthetic, lustreless, color olive drab (52–E–S400–155).
EQUIPMENT**, sandblast protection, miscellaneous.
EQUIPMENT**, paint-spray protection, miscellaneous.
GLOVES**, gauntlet.
HELMET, welders' shade No. 10 (37–H–1660).
HOSE*, sandblasting, pure-rubber lined.
PRIMER, zinc-chromate (52–P–20624).
SANDBLAST MACHINE*, Pangborn (No 1, "AC–3"), or equal.
SANDER, elec, portable, hand, disk type, hv-duty, 7 in disk, 115 v, universal current (40–S–28).
WHEELS*, disk, grinding, 9 x 3/16 x 5/8 (A–36J16–F) shape 4257, Bayflex, or equal.
WHEELS*, disk, grinding, 9 x 1/8 x 5/8 (A–36J16–F) shape 4257, Bayflex, or equal.

7. Special instructions:

a. Applied by: Automotive mechanic.
b. Time required: 15 man-hours.

*These items must be procured locally or from the manufacturer.
**These items will be used as locally available.

AGO 949B—Nov. 851718°—49

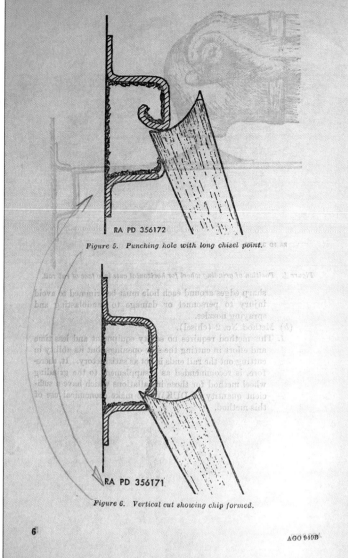

RA PD 356172

Figure 5. Punching hole with long chisel point.

RA PD 356171

Figure 6. Vertical cut showing chip formed.

6

AGO 949B

A perennial problem with DUKWs as manufactured was the tendency of water to collect in the rub rails, which were spot-welded to the hull, leading to rusting. To correct this problem, Department of the Army Modification Work Order G 501-W31 was issued 7 November 1949. This document contained detailed instructions for cutting away sections of the rub rails so water could drain out of them. (National Archives via Jim Gilmore)

The interiors of the rub rails were treated with a petroleum-based preservative, so it was forbidden to use a cutting torch to cut the openings. A grinding wheel or air-powered chisel, as seen here, was to be used instead. The drawing captions were reversed, but in the lower drawing the longer point of the chisel makes the initial vertical cut, and in the upper drawing the shorter point of the chisel continues the cut. (National Archives via Jim Gilmore)

This diagram from Army Modification Work Order G 501-W31 indicated the intervals at which sections of the hat-channel rub rails were to be cut off. This document gave instructions for multiple techniques for cutting away sections of the rails. (National Archives via Jim Gilmore)

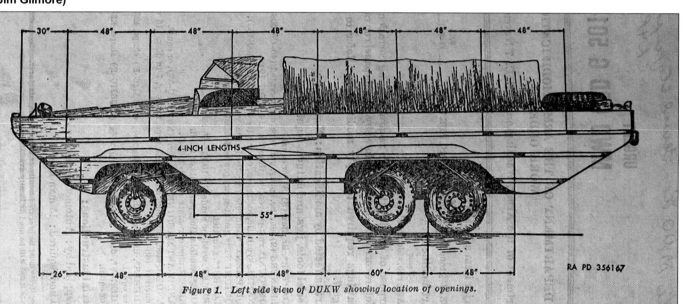

4-INCH LENGTHS

RA PD 356167

Figure 1. Left side view of DUKW showing location of openings.

MWO ORD G501-W32

NORMAL

DEPARTMENT OF THE ARMY MODIFICATION WORK ORDER

Department of the Army, Washington 25, D. C.　5 June 1950

1. **Major item affected:**

Name	SNL	TM
TRUCK, 2½-ton, 6 x 6, amphibian (GMC DUKW-353)	G-501	9-802.

2. **Part modified:**

　　　　Name
　COAMING, deck, left and right sides.

3. **Purpose of modification:** To permit the transportation of 105-mm howitzer equipped with combat tires.

4. **Drawings required to apply modification:** Refer to figures 1 through 6.

5. **Parts affected by modification:** None.

6. **Special tools, jigs, and fixtures required:** None.

7. **Special Instructions:**

　a. Applied by: Ordnance welder.

　b. Time required: 8 man-hours.

　c. Procedure of operations:

　　(1) Using a cutting torch with the smallest tip available, make two vertical cuts in each side of the cargo-compartment inside walls, one cut 16 inches to the rear of the front cargo bulkhead, and the other cut 12 inches behind the previous one. These cuts will be started at the top of the deck coaming and extend downward to approximately one-half inch beyond the bottom bend in the wall where it turns outward to the hull (fig. 1). Continue these cuts around the outside of the coaming until the one-foot length of sections is severed from the deck coaming on each side.

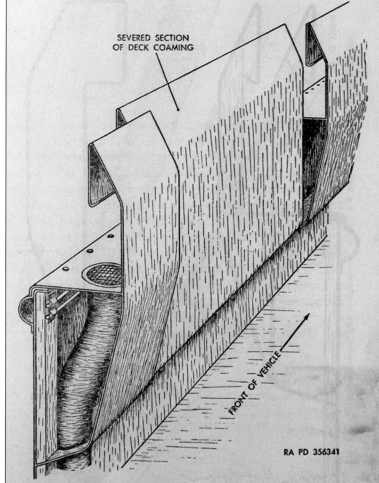

SEVERED SECTION
OF DECK COAMING

FRONT OF VEHICLE

RA PD 356341

Figure 4. Severed section bent to new position (view from inside cargo compartment).

Army Modification Work Order G 501-W32, dated 5 June 1950, gave instructions on modifying the right and left coamings of the cargo compartment of the DUKW so a 105mm howitzer with combat wheels could fit. (National Archives via Jim Gilmore)

In that modification, a torch with a small cutting tip was used to cut away a one-foot-wide section of coaming and exterior deck, the forward end of which was 16 inches from the forward bulkhead of the cargo compartment. (National Archives via Jim Gilmore)

The cut-away sections were then welded outboard of the coaming, and the gaps were filled with sheet-steel pieces welded in place. The results were two pocket-shaped extensions on the sides of the coamings that provided clearance for the howitzer axle and wheels. (National Archives via Jim Gilmore)

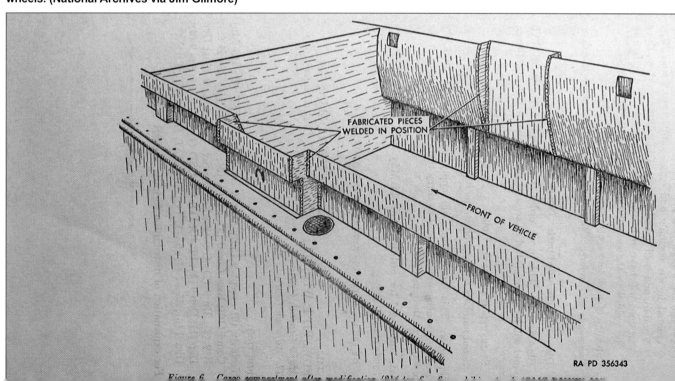

FABRICATED PIECES
WELDED IN POSITION

FRONT OF VEHICLE

269

RA PD 356343

Figure 6. Cargo compartment after modification

Chapter 22
War Again

When war broke out on the Korean Peninsula on 25 June, 1950, the United States, whose troops represented 88 percent of the United Nations forces, moved quickly to push the Communists back across the 38th parallel. DUKWs saw extensive use during the Battle of Pusan Perimeter as well as taking part in the amphibious landings at Inchon.

Not surprisingly, DUKWs were involved in this counteroffensive, including the 1st Marine Amphibious Truck Company, as well as the army 3rd and 558th Amphibious Truck Companies and the 532nd Engineer Boat and Shore Regiment of the 2nd Engineer Special Brigade. To supply these army troops, the 1st Training Replacement Training Group was activated at Fort Story.

The first DUKWs to arrive were 66 DUKWs of the 8062nd Amphibious Truck Company (later redesignated as the 3rd Transportation Amphibian Truck Company), embarked 11 July 1950 at Yokohama in preparation of moving ashore with the 1st Cavalry Division. The primary mission of the DUKWs was to transport 105mm howitzers, both in the water and ashore. LSTs landed the vehicles directly to shore on 18 July. From 1 August through 26 August the men of this unit moved 26,500 tons on ammunition into Suyong. Following the recommendations developed during WWII that DUKWs only be operated by dedicated units, several detachments of the 3rd Transportation Amphibian Truck Company supported other operations, including an 8 August 1950 detachment operating with the 1st Marine Brigade operating at Masan; an 11 August detachment unloading ammo and transporting wounded at Yongdok; and a 16 August detacment unloading supplies in Pohang-dong.

Two platoons of DUKWs aided the 2nd Infantry Division in crossing the Naktong River on 19 September 1950. This operation brought about a revival of the WWII-tank ferry concept, when two DUKWs were used to individually move 138 tanks across the river, with the tanks riding on a section of pontoon bridge lashed between the two DUKWs.

Also during the 32nd Infantry Regiment's assault on Seoul in September 1950 across the Han River, considerable assistance to the attack was provided by DUKWs of Company B, 532nd Engineer Boat and Shore Regiment. At Inchon, the shoreline would not permit DUKW operations, so the 50th Engineer Port Construction Company blasted DUKW ramps into the harbor. During October operations three DUKWs sank while transporting material from ship to a shore-based railhead. It was believe that the three DUKWs were lost due to rust weakening the watertight integrity of their hulls.

On 4 January 1951 one platoon of the 3rd Transportation Amphibian Truck Company helped withdraw friendly troops across the Han River, while the rest of the Company was pulled out of Korea. During the departure, six DUKWs condemned by Ordnance were stripped of usable parts and their hulks sank in Inchon harbor. Upon return to Yokohama on 9 January the unit was issued 50 rebuilt DUKWs, turning in their veteran vehicles.

Later, six DUKWs of the 558th Amphibious Truck Company were used to assist the 1st Cavalry Division in the Hwacheon Reservoir Operation 9-11 April 1951. The 532nd was also used to lighter in supplies from the Incheon harbor after 85 USMC DUKWs had been sent forward with the 1st Marines to support river crossings.

Civilians and a few officers are being treated to a ride on DUKWs with markings for the U.S. Army Transportation Corps around 1950. The bows in the cargo compartments provide hand-holds for the passengers. The city is not identified, but, judging by the Cities Service gas-station sign, it was in the United States. (U.S. Army Transportation Museum)

Republic of Korea Marines are boarding DUKWs of the 5th Marine Regiment before advancing to the Han River area for an offensive against North Korean forces on 18 September 1950. Clear details are visible of features on the stern of the DUKW in the foreground. (U.S. Army Quartermaster Museum)

Army personnel look on as a DUKW lays down wire-mesh matting on a riverbank in Korea. The matt-laying apparatus, developed in May 1943 by Tri State Engineering of Washington, Pennsylvania, had a new lease on life during the Korean War. (U.S. Army Engineer School History Office)

On 20 September 1950, a DUKW of the 5th Marine Regiment lays down matting on the approach to the Han River to prepare the bank for use by other DUKWs during a coming offensive. The steel-wire matting was stowed in folded, accordion fashion on the rear of the DUKW, and the frame supported the mesh as the movement of the DUKW laid it down. (U.S. Army Engineer School History Office)

271

An empty DUKW enters the harbor at Inchon, Republic of Korea, to retrieve supplies from a ship on 12 June 1951. A noncommissioned officer of the 558th Amphibian Truck Company was directing DUKW operations from a dispatch shed along the shore that date. (U.S. Army Engineer School History Office)

DUKW registration number 7024047-S of the 558th Amphibian Truck Company, attached to the 2nd Engineer Special Brigade, which controlled the Port of Inchon, is taking on cargo from a Victory ship at Inchon on 12 June 1951. Built during the last two years of World War II, Victory ships were similar to Liberty Ships. (U.S. Army Engineer School History Office)

At an ammunition dump at Inchon on 12 June 1951, a crawler crane hoists a net full of 105mm ammunition from a DUKW and will deposit it in the railroad car in the background for transportation to the front. (U.S. Army Engineer School History Office)

Right: Korean laborers assist in unloading DUKWs of the 558th Amphibian Truck Company and moving supply crates at Inchon, 12 June 1951. Unloading of ships' cargos at Inchon was under the supervision of the 532nd Engineer Boat and Shore Regiment. (U.S. Army Engineer School History Office)

Below: DUKWs of the 3rd Amphibian Truck Company of the 2nd Logistical Command ferry supplies from ship to shore at Pusan Harbor, Republic of Korea, on 15 June 1951. To the right is the Victory ship *Blue Island Victory*. (National Archives)

A flotilla of DUKWs crosses Pusan Harbor on 15 June 1951. DUKWs were custom-made for moving supplies at Pusan Harbor because, although congestion at the docks made it impossible for all arriving ships to discharge their cargoes there, DUKWs could receive the cargoes and deliver them to depots on land. (National Archives)

At the Hwacheon Reservoir in the Republic of Korea on 18 October 1951, a DUKW A-frame boom has hoisted a 105mm howitzer preparatory to loading it on a DUKW of the 1st Amphibious Truck Company, 1st Marine Division. Subsequently, the DUKW will transport the piece to a new position. (National Archives)

After arriving at a supply dump with cargo received from a ship in Pusan Harbor, a DUKW of the 3rd Amphibian Truck Company is being unloaded by a crawler crane on 15 June 1951. Korean laborers in the cargo compartment assist with the unloading. (National Archives)

DUKWs clear ice from the way adjacent to a cargo ship off Thule, Greenland, on 20 July 1951. On the closer vehicle, two bumpers have been installed on the bow for this purpose. This was in connection with Project Blue Jay, a secret project to build a U.S. Air Force base at Thule. (U.S. Army Engineer School History Office)

In an aerial view taken during Operation Supply Over the Beaches, at the harbor of Le Verdon, France, on 4 June 1952, the freighter SS Nevadan unloads supplies onto DUKWs and landing craft, mechanized (LCMs). The DUKWs are the smaller craft operating around the ship. (U.S. Army Transportation Museum)

A DUKW with U.S. Navy markings and the name "Seabees" on the hull comes ashore with a load marines near St. Paul's Bay, Malta, during Exercise Beehive II in June 1952. Attached to the aft deck is what appears to be a frame for holding a cable reel. (Imperial War Museum)

A DUKW assigned to the 8541st Labor Service Engineer Amphibious Truck Company ferries a Jeep across the Main River in Germany on 5 February 1953. (National Archives)

Above: Soldiers of Company A, 5th Engineer Battalion, Seventh Army, inflate pontoons during training maneuvers in Germany on 5 February 1953. Resting partially ashore in the background is a DUKW with crewmen in the driver's and assistant driver's positions. (National Archives)

Left: In April 1953, members of Detachment C, 497th Signal Company, scramble over the rail of a ship and down the nets to an awaiting DUKW at La Pallice, the industrial harbor of La Rochelle, France. The DUKW will take these troops to shore. Another DUKW with personnel aboard is departing. (National Archives)

Below: A DUKW filled with passengers crosses La Pallice on 15 April 1953. Extra heavy rope fenders are on the bow of this vehicle. The bridge in the background is part of the Mole d'Escale (Long Pier), which extends far out into the harbor. (National Archives)

A DUKW bearing personnel of Detachment C, 497th Signal Company, comes ashore at La Pallice, La Rochelle, France, on 15 April 1953. The "AECZ" stenciled on the front of the cowl appears to have stood for the U.S. Army in Europe Communications Zone, which administered various European ports, including La Rochelle. (National Archives)

General Data

Model	DUKW-353
Net weight	14,880 pounds
Gross weight	20,055 pounds
Maximum towed load	7,500 pounds
Length	372 inches
Width	98⅞ inches
Height	106 inches
Track	63⅞ inches
Tire size	11.00-18
Maximum land speed	50 m.p.h.
Maximum water speed	6 m.p.h.
Fuel capacity	40 gallons
Range on land	325 miles
Range on water	50 miles
Electrical	6 volt negative ground
Transmission speeds	5
Transfer speeds	2
Turning radius on land	35 feet (right) 36 feet (left)
Turning radius on water	20 feet (right) 22½ feet (left)

Two DUKWs come ashore carrying cargo from a ship in an unidentified harbor in the Republic of Korea around the mid-1950s. The small flags on poles in the water evidently mark the location of the vehicle ramp. (U.S. Army Transportation Museum)

Above: Several DUKWs sit at a vehicle park at an unidentified base in the Republic of Korea around the mid-1950s. The engine-access doors of two of the vehicles are secured in the open position. (U.S. Army Transportation Museum)

Right: A group of DUKWs undergo maintenance at a base in the Republic of Korea. To the right sits a crawler crane. Routine vehicular maintenance of DUKWs was much easier to accomplish during peacetime than during active combat operations. (U.S. Army Transportation Museum)

At an unidentified location in the Republic of Korea, U.S. Army DUKWs are parked near a battle-damaged building. There is variety in the size and locations of the white recognition stars on the sides of the hulls. (U.S. Army Transportation Museum)

Chapter 23

Peace Again

With a cease-fire declared in Korea, the military use of the DUKW declined. Fort Story remained home to the amphibians, which gradually began to be replaced with larger, but not necessarily better, amphibians. As we shall see, General Motors produced two larger amphibians, the Superduck and the Drake, both of which met expectations, however, the Army preferred to purchase vehicles developed by the US Army Research Command, the family of vehicles known as LARCs (Lighter, Amphibious Resupply, Cargo) in 5, 15 and 60-ton capacities, none of which ultimately lived up to expectations and all of which suffered from poor handling.

With their replacements on the way in, the Army continued to rebuild DUKWs, with a rebuild center for the DUKW operating at Toole Army Depot (Utah) until at least 1963. DUKW use by the army centered primarily on training during this period. The 458th Transportation Company (Amphibious Truck) at Camp Leroy Johnson, New Orleans, was responsible for the safe evacuation of 1,550 civilians in the aftermath of flooding caused by Hurricane Flossy in September 1956.

This performance was repeated three years later, May 1959, during the flooding of Kenner, Louisiana. Near Fort Story, historic flooding caused by the Ash Wednesday Storm of 1962 once again brought DUKWs to the rescue of civilians, this time in the hands of the 10th Transportation Battalion.

Although the DUKW continued to be listed in army supply catalogs through 1969, when the amphibian truck companies went to Vietnam, the venerable vehicles were left at home, the newer LARC, despite their flaws, going to Southeast Asia. The Coast Guard, which as Rod Stephens had predicted in 1942 would be interested in DUKWs, continued to use the vehicles at east and west coast lifeboat stations into 1970.

In the 1950s, a display of U.S. amphibian-vehicle and landing-craft might is assembled on a beach. To the side of the crawler crane is a row of DUKWs, aft of which are three BARCs (barge, amphibious resupply, cargo), a vehicle that easily could hold a DUKW in its cargo compartment. Also on the shore are several landing craft. (U.S. Army Transportation Museum)

A DUKW assigned to the 458th Amphibian Truck Company based at Camp Leroy Johnson, New Orleans, assists in rescue efforts during flooding at Bissonette Plaza, Jefferson Parish, Louisiana, on 1 June 1959. The flooding was caused by Tropical Storm Arlene. (U.S. Army Transportation Museum)

Above: The U.S. Coast Guard acquired a quantity of DUKWs from the U.S. Army. This example from the T-5000 series was acquired in 1944. It has the early, vertical windshield, a reinforced bow surfboard, and the windshield surfboard in the deployed position.

Left: U.S. Coast Guard DUKW T-13067 comes ashore with a cargo of undoubtedly very excited boys. This vehicle was radio equipped: a whip antenna is mounted on the starboard side of the driver's compartment. (USCG Historian's Office)

Below: Coast Guard DUKW T-13510, seen in a preceding photograph, rescues flood victims. The vehicle's number is on the side of the hull as well as on a U.S. Government license plate on the front of the starboard side of the cowl. (USCG Historian's Office)

The USCG crew of DUKW T-13068 assists civilians with their luggage during a flood evacuation. A clear view is provided of the U.S. Government license plate with the DUKW's USCG number, on the front of the driver's compartment cowl. (USCG Historian's Office)

Right: A USCG DUKW, number T-13068, pauses on a bridge recently ravaged by flood waters. Mounted on the top center of the windshield frame is a flashing light. The front edges of the two steps on the side of the hull have been picked out in a dark color for visibility. (USCG Historian's Office)

Below: The Coast Guard obtained the T-13000-series in 1948, and these vehicles were stationed on both U.S. coasts. Although some USCG DUKWs were stationed at lifeboat stations, they provided their most useful service as rescue craft in flooded areas. (USCG Historian's Office)

Chapter 24

Flying DUKW

The relatively low water speed of the DUKW had been a concern since the earliest days of its development. In the 1950s a radically faster DUKW was produced, known as the "Flying DUKW." The application of hydrofoils to a DUKW was not a radically new idea, having been suggested by the Stevens Institute during World War II, but it would not be until full decade later that this was actually done.

In the early 1950s hydrofoils were of increasing interest to the US military. Vannevar Bush had advocated the use of such by the Navy, even constructing a prototype. The Korean war had driven further interest – specifically for hydrofoil-equipped landing craft. A request for bids was sent out, asking for proposals to make a LCVP capable of making 35 knots vs. the standard 8. Miami Shipbuilding Corporation was the successful bidder, and by 1957 had successfully constructed and demonstrated such a LCVP, which they named Halobates.

By that time, however, the Navy's attention had begun to shift to air-cushioned vehicles. But, before the Navy completely lost interest in the hydrofoil program, it did issue a contract modification that called for for the installation of a gas turbine powerplant in Halobates. This powerplant, a Lycoming T53, was installed and operated successfully.

As the navy's interest in hydrofoils began to wane, the army's interest was piqued. Col. Frank Speir, who in October 1943 had authored the definitive report on DUKW operations in Italy and Sicily, was now Project Engineer for the army amphibious warfare program, and was intrigued with the possibility of using hydrofoils to increase the speed of the vehicle. The army contracted with the Lycoming Division of AVCO to create such a vehicle, with Lycoming turning to Miami Shipbuilding to execute the concept. Speir and Rod Stephens visited Miami Shipbuilding and participated in one of the Halobates trials. Speir was killed in the crash of his private plane on 8 July 1956, and Julius Grigore succeeded him as Project Engineer.

The Stevens Institute conducted tank tests on a model DUKW hull with hydrofoils under Grigore's supervision in 1957. Full-size tow tests of a conventional DUKW followed. Chesapeake Bay was the site for these tests, with the Navy lending the use of a high speed transport as a towing vessel, and the army providing a DUKW. The navy crew was able to get the DUKW up to about 20 knots, satisfying the Miami Shipbuilding engineers of the practicality of the concept.

The firm installed hydrofoil and autopilot equipment similar to that on Halobates on DUKW at their Florida shipyard, with a Lycoming T53 furnishing the power for hydrofoil operations. During subsequent trials the modified vehicle, dubbed the Flying DUKW, was successfully operated at speeds in excess of 30 knots. The powerplant fully occupied the cargo compartment of the DUKW, making this impractical as a specific vehicle, but proving the concept of hydrofoil amphibian trucks.

The Flying DUKW, tested in the late 1950s and early 1960s, mated two forward and one aft hydrofoils to a DUKW powered by a Lycoming T53 gas turbine engine, in an effort to field an amphibian vehicle capable of making a high-speed run from a ship to a beach. The vehicle achieved speeds six times that of the stock DUKW. (USMC Museum)

The Flying DUKW's aft foil was mounted on a retractable strut, and the marine propeller was mounted on the front of a gear case at the bottom of that strut. Atop the cargo compartment was a shed-shaped housing with outward-opening access doors. (USMC Museum)

Above: For operating at low speeds, the Flying DUKW advanced with foils submerged, as seen here. The exhaust of the gas-powered turbine protrudes above the enclosure over the cargo compartment. (USMC Museum)

Right: The Flying DUKW employed two forward foils with spans of nine feet, mounted on retractable struts by means of a hinge pin, which allowed the attitude of the foil to be adjusted. The attitude of the foils was controlled manually or by the vehicle's autopilot. The redesigned bow is also evident. (USMC Museum)

283

During low-speed cruising with the foils submerged, the Flying DUKW produced a significant wake. The craft could go from slow speed to high speed very rapidly, and when running at high speed, it produced very little wake and was very stable. (USMC Museum)

The Flying DUKW makes a high-speed run. The marine propeller on the lower front of the aft foil strut churned up some spray, but the vehicle produced much less wake than when operating at low speeds. The Flying DUKW did not go into production but formed the basis for later hydrofoil designs. (U.S. Army Transportation Museum)

To convert from low speed to high speed, the Flying DUKW required about a 200-foot taxi run at 415 horsepower, after which the hull lifted out of the water. This "takeoff" could be shortened in an emergency, and the attitude of the foils influenced the rate of rise. (USMC Museum)

Chapter 25
Superduck

Even before World War II had drawn to a close, the Army began laying the groundwork for a new generation of wheeled vehicles. These vehicles would have vastly interchangeable parts across all sizes as well as all-around increased performance. One of the Boards set up for studying the future needs of army transport was the War Department Equipment Review Board, popularly known as the Cook Board.

Their report, tendered on 13 December 1945, noted concerning the DUKW that "This is an excellent vehicle in its present form, but should be improved in accordance with the general principles listed in paragraphs 4 and 5 above." Those paragraphs referred to an overall improvement in rust resistance, paint, lighting and other details desired for all military vehicles. Regarding the specifics of wheeled amphibians, the Board suggested 5-, 8-, and 12-ton amphibians similar to the DUKW be developed.

Not surprisingly, as GM developed a new series of 2½ ton 6x6 trucks (the M135/M211 family), work also got underway on a new generation of amphibians. Designated the XM147, the key men in

this project were Project Manager Frank Speir, Rod Stephens, GM engineers E.T. Todd (incidentally, one of the pioneers in automotive air conditioning) and Cory Smith; and Mr. Charles D. Roach, director of marine transportation for the Army Transportation Corps, and Samuel Hickson, also with the Transportation Corps. The XM147 was designated a 4-ton vehicle, as opposed to the WWII DUKW's rating of 2½ tons.

The initial version of the Superduck, XM147, was badly damaged by swamping in heavy 22-25-foot surf at Monterey California. The limited testing that had been conducted prior to this had indicated that the Superduck had better land mobility than did the WWII Duck, but the WWII vehicle had superior performance in the surf. Based on this, the design was modified, becoming the XM147E2, which had strengthened hull sides and a redesigned, and taller, bow. Ten of the experimental amphibians were constructed.

During 1956 the USMC borrowed a Superduck and conducted numerous tests. The Marines liked the vehicle, and favored its adoption, but lacked the funds for such procurement.

The XM147 Superduck was an small series of experimental vehicles built by GMC for the U.S. Army Ordnance Department in the 1950s. It had a hull similar to that of the DUKW but with many improvements and changes, such as recessed headlights, a cab over engine, and a hard top for the driver's compartment. (General Motors)

Top: Several Superducks were produced for evaluation, with slightly different hull styles. The hull on this example undergoing construction is the early type, with two rub rails on the side. A later type of hull would have four rub rails on each side. The redesigned front deck had one hatch. (General Motors)

Center: The same vehicle is viewed from an angle more to the front. The coaming around the cargo compartment did not slope up toward the rear, as on late-production DUKWs, but had a uniform height. The driver's compartment had yet to be installed. (General Motors)

Left: The cab-over-engine driver's compartment of the Superduck featured a slanted windshield, side windows, and a hard top. The driver's seat was adjustable fore and aft. A removable cover was provided to the starboard of the seat for access to the engine compartment. Above the cover under the dashboard is the central tire inflation system control panel. (General Motors)

Above: A Superduck with the early-style hull with two rub rails is viewed from the port side. Because of the cab-over-engine design, which allowed the driver's compartment to be positioned much farther forward on the DUKW, the Superduck had more cargo space than the DUKW. (General Motors)

Right: Although the shape of the sides of the hull of the Superduck were similar to that of the DUKW, the stern had a much different appearance, since the Superduck lacked the recess in the upper center of the stern of the DUKW to accommodate the winch. (General Motors)

Below: Power for the Superduck was provided by a GMC Model 302 engine, a larger version of the GMC 270 that powered the DUKW. The 302 developed 145 horsepower at 3,600 rpm. The transmission was a Hydramatic. Visible on the side of the engine are the AC oil filter, the distributor, and the generator. (General Motors)

The winch on the Superduck, a Braden with a 20,000-pound capacity, was hidden below the aft deck; a 360-degree-rotating head on the aft deck served the winch cable, and the cable could be routed to the rear or forward. The driver operated the winch with controls to his left. The floor panels of the cargo compartment were removable, with oblong hand holes. (General Motors)

Right: This early Superduck displays U.S. Army registration number 7042378. Two other early Superducks were assigned registration numbers 7042379 and 7042380. The spare tire was stored vertically behind the port side of the driver's compartment. (General Motors)

Below: Early-model Superduck registration number 7042379 also bore the identification number 347-50 on its hull. Banded loads of boxes are in the cargo compartment. Three round reflectors were mounted on the upper part of the hull side. Bumpers were fastened to the bow. (U.S. Army Transportation Museum)

Superduck 7042379 is on display with a placard on the bow noting that it represents the U.S. Army Transportation Corps, Fort Story, Virginia. The service headlights gained some protection from brush and floating debris from two vertical guards in the recess. (U.S. Army Transportation Museum)

Right: Superduck 7042378 is parked along a harbor. The design of the forward deck and the driver's compartment top are particularly visible from this angle. On each side of the cowl is a blackout marker lamp. (U.S. Army Transportation Museum)

Below: During speed tests in moderate surf in the Pacific Ocean at Fort Ord, California, on 20 July 1953, an early Superduck comes ashore moments before a DUKW. The Superduck had a speed of about 6.2 miles per hour on calm water, propelled by its 31-inch-diameter, three-bladed propeller. (U.S. Army Transportation Museum)

Left: An improved Superduck was produced under the designation XM147E2. This example is U.S. Army registration number 4A2308, also marked 347-34. It had several noticeable differences from the XM147 Superduck, such as four rub rails on the hull instead of two, and a different bow design that included two tiers of rubber bumpers. (General Motors)

Below: A feature the XM147E2 had that the XM147 lacked was two large, recessed steps in the side of the hull. Above and aft of the top step are two small, square openings covered with wire mesh, which may have been bilge-pump outlets. The spare tire was stored to the front of the cargo compartment. (General Motors)

Details of the front of the Superduck are available in this view taken on a beach during trials, including the forward tow shackles and the rubber bumper. The bumper is interrupted to accommodate an opening for feeding out the winch cable when that cable was deployed to the front of the vehicle. (General Motors)

Superduck 7042378 is parked on a beach. While a preceding, overhead photo of this vehicle showed it with blackout marker lights mounted on the face of the cowl, by the time this photo was taken, these composite lights were mounted atop the cowl, and the front deck and cowl had been redesigned. (General Motors)

Above: Superduck registration number 7042378 was swamped and sank during surf tests in Monterey, California during July 1953. The vehicle was recovered, damage assessed, and ultimately repaired and continued with the test program. The winch drum is visible through the open hatch on the aft deck, and the rotating head of the winch is still in place on that deck. (General Motors)

Right: The same Superduck that appears in the preceding photo is now making its way along a very rough stretch of test track, the 12.50-20 12-ply tires thus far able to navigate the ground. When negotiating surfaces such as this, the driver had to keep in mind that the vehicle had a ground clearance of 12 inches. (USMC Museum)

Left: The recessed service headlights lacked guards. Marked next to the port headlight is "Exp. 362." To the starboard of the center hat-channel stiffener on the bow is a tall, rectangular opening, within which is a grille. A boat hook and composite blackout marker lights are on top of the cowl. (General Motors)

Below: The aft corners of the XM147E2 were protected by wrap-around rubber bumpers. This example has four recesses in the stern for tail-light assemblies, two per side. Above the aft deck, the rotating head for the winch cable is visible, along with the cable and hook. (General Motors)

XM147E2 Superduck registration number 4A2308 appears as it did following a major redesign project. The bow was changed from a sloping design to a non-sloping one, and the formerly straight top of the hull alongside the coaming of the cargo compartment now had a pronounced dip from the driver's compartment nearly to the stern. (General Motors)

Above: The redesign work on the XM147E2 also raised the stern and aft deck. A third recessed step was added to the side of the hull. A pole that seems to have been a permanently mounted A-frame leg is visible along the top of the cargo compartment coaming. It is secured with a pin to a bracket at the stern, and a similar pole was on the opposite side. (General Motors)

Right: With the revamping, the four recessed tail lights were reduced to two, and the winch was moved from below the aft deck to on top of that deck. The structures attached to the deck aft of the winch appear to have been cable guides. The propeller and the rudder are visible in the propeller tunnel. (General Motors)

In a photo taken at the GMC Truck & Coach Division, the nearest four vehicles are XM147E2s, with registration numbers 4A2313, 4A2306, and 4A208 being visible. Next come the three XM157 Drakes, a huge, eight-wheeled DUKW derivative, and finally there are four more XM147E2s. (General Motors)

Chapter 26
Drake

From the earliest days of the DUKW development, it was recognized that a larger version was needed. Concurrently with the initial DUKW design renderings had been created detailing the construction of a similar vehicle based on the 6-ton 6x6. Combat use of the DUKW during WWII reinforced the need for a larger amphibian, as well as the advantages of a stern loading ramp. Concurrently with the design and construction of the XM147 Superduck, work began on a larger amphibian, the XM157 Drake.

Rather than being a 6x6, the Drake was an 8x8, and featured an 8-ton capacity. Power was provided by two GMC 302 cubic-inch straight-six engines driving through automatic transmissions. While on road, the right-hand engine drove the fourth axle, while the left-hand engine drove the third axle.

On soft terrain, the right engine would drive both the even-numbered axles, and the left the odd-numbered axles. In water, each drove its own propeller. Both propellers were retractable, another concept originally tried very early in army amphibian development.

The hull of the Drake was aluminum. Not only did the Drake feature Central Tire Inflation, the vehicle's air system also was used through the vehicle's air suspension to retract and extend the wheels during water operation – a drag-reducing technique that Rod Stephens had suggested during the initial hydrodynamic testing of the DUKW hull at Stevens Institute a decade earlier.

The three Drake prototypes tested in Michigan, California and Yuma, Arizona. Ultimately, rather than to move forward with the Drake, the Army opted to proceed with the development of the LARC V over the protestations of many involved in the Drake program. Project Manager Julius Grigore notes that the Drake was ready for production, that the evaluation team had recommended no changes from the configuration of the three trial vehicles. Ironically, the LARC V had a somewhat protracted and painful development. Ultimately, the three Drakes were declared surplus and presumably scrapped, with one having been spotted at Silverstein's Surplus in Detroit in the 1970s.

The XM157 Drake was a small series of 8-ton, 8x8 experimental amphibian vehicles that GMC Truck & Coach Division produced in the 1950s. Although it owed its ancestry to the DUKW, it was much larger, more powerful, and more technologically sophisticated. Here, XM157 U.S. Army registration number 7042382 comes ashore. (General Motors)

Powering the XM157 were twin GMC 302-55 engines with Allison CTP-4 Powermatic transmissions below the cab, each routed to a two-speed transfer case, driving two marine propellers and the axles. The rig depicted here appears to have been an experiment using DUKW 7030278 to test the concept of two dedicated rear-mounted engines for the propellers and an engine to drive the axles in the front. (General Motors)

Left: Rather than the conventional ladder-type frame utilized on the DUKW, the Drake utilized a space frame. Here the aluminum space frame of an XM157 can be seen under construction at GMC Truck & Coach Division on 25 May 1955, illustrating a much different appearance than the DUKW hulls produced at that plant a decade earlier. In the background is a frame lying on its side, bow to the right, and in the foreground is one lying upside down, with openings for the aft axles in view. (General Motors)

Below: The evolutionary links between the DUKW, right, the XM147 Superduck, center, and the XM157 Drake are clearly discernible in this posed group portrait. Their relative sizes are apparent, too, with the Drake dwarfing both of its ancestors. (General Motors)

The XM157 Drakes suspension relied on two sets of air suspensions: one using air bellows to act as shock absorbers, and the other to retract the suspension when the vehicle was in the water, to reduce the drag created by the wheels. The plate with the hole in it to the right is an engine exhaust port. (General Motors)

Superduck and Drake General Data

MODEL	XM147E2	XM157
Net weight	18,000 pounds	32,000 pounds
Gross weight	23,000 pounds	48,000 pounds
Engine	302 cid, 6-cylinder, gas	2 x 302 cid, 6-cylinder, gas
Transmission	GM Hydramatic	CTP-4 Powermatic
Length	384 inches	504 inches
Width	105 inches	120¼ inches
Height	108½ inches	130 inches
Tire size	12.50-20	14.75-20
Max. land speed	55 m.p.h	45 m.p.h.
Max. water speed	7 m.p.h	9 m.p.h.
Fuel capacity	120 gallons	240 gallons
Electrical	24 volt negative ground	24 volt negative ground
Turning radius on land	35 feet	50 feet
Suspension	Leaf spring	Air
Ground clearance at axle center	13 inches	15¾ inches
Ground clearance under hull	17½ inches	18¾ inches
Angle of approach	40½ degrees	34 degrees
Angle of departure	24 degrees	23 degrees

Like the XM147 Superduck, the XM157 Drake had a cab-over-engine design. With the access cover in the driver's compartment removed, the twin GMC 302-55 engines are visible. The air cleaners were tilted to provide clearance for them. In the foreground are the Allison CTP-4 Powermatic transmissions. At the top are the footboard and the dashboard. (General Motors)

The XM147 was equipped with two marine propellers, as seen in a 12 June 1956 photo. They were equipped with a mechanism that tilted them up and out of the way for operation on land. The propeller shafts were fitted with protective skids. For extra steering maneuverability, one propeller could be driven in forward and the other in reverse. (General Motors)

Above: The driver's compartment of a Drake is viewed with the seats removed. Aft of the engine cover are the shift levers; the long ones were gear-shift levers for land or water operation, and the short ones controlled the bilge pumps and the winch. At the center of the dashboard is the rather extensive control panel for the central tire inflation system. On the wall to the left are the marine propeller up/down controls and the surfboard control. (General Motors)

Right: GMC XM157 USA number 7042383 is parked in the factory parking lot around the mid-1950s, sand on its tires from a recent test run. The surfboard is visible on the forward deck. Three recessed steps were located on the hull. A rubber bumper was affixed to perimeter of the top of the hull. (General Motors)

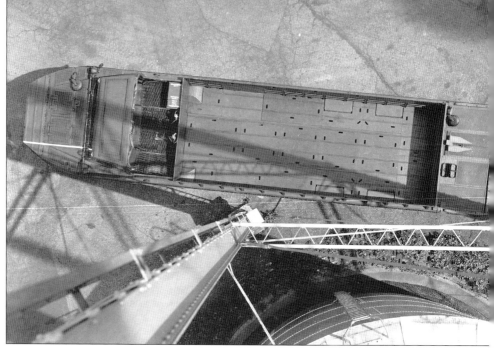

An XM157 Drake is observed from overhead. A small wheel on a caster mount is stored on the forward deck and the aft deck. The floor between the driver's compartment and the cargo compartment was grille panels. The floor of the cargo compartment comprised removable panels with oblong hand holes. On the aft deck were an anchor and two holders for five-gallon liquid containers. (General Motors)

Left: GMC XM157 registration number 7042381 makes a turn during a transit through a town, probably in California. On this example, oblong holes were cut at intervals in the rub rails as a measure to let out water that infiltrated between the spot-welds. (General Motors)

Below: During surf tests, XM157 7042381 is entering the water, surfboard extended on the bow. Rolled up at the rear of the top of the driver's compartment is a closure. The tires, which were 14.75-20 nylon 10-ply with desert treads, appear to be negotiating the sand very well. (General Motors)

An XM157 Drake tied to a dock is loaded with several large crates in the cargo department, probably just deposited there by the crane on the truck, or about to be hoisted from the compartment. The Drake had a cargo capacity of eight tons. The white stripe on the forward deck and surfboard appears to have been a standard marking on the Drake. (General Motors)

During vehicular tests at the ocean, an XM157 Drake pauses on the beach. Like the DUKW, the Drake had a central tire-inflation system, but the external portion of the Drake's CTIS was much less visible than that of the DUKW. (Robert McDowell collection)

During surf trials, probably on the California coast, XM157 registration number 7042381 comes ashore, surfboard still extended. For operation on water, both engines drove both propellers, but when driving on land, various combinations of one or two engines driving one or more axles were possible, depending on the conditions. (General Motors)

Above: GMC XM157 registration number 7042381 is parked on a beach during an exercise, next to an army truck with a cargo of 55-gallon drums. The central tire-inflation system fittings on the wheels, visible here, were much more subtle and compact than the CTIS devices on the DUKW. (General Motors)

Right: Unlike its predecessors, the DUKW and the Superduck, the XM157 Drake had the capability of loading and unloading cargo through the rear of the hull. Here, the men have raised the aft-deck panels and are preparing to lower the tailgate. (General Motors)

The tailgate is now lowered, revealing details of the construction of the stern compartment. The floor comprises grille panels. To the left is a DUKW. The propellers have not been raised, and they are digging into the sand. (General Motors)

Chapter 27
Contemporary Use

At the conclusion of WWII, like most U.S. war material, much of the Army's DUKW fleet became surplus. While some were made available to municipalities for use by fire departments and law enforcement agencies, others were sold to the public as surplus. Wartime restrictions on the production of new vehicles combined with heavy wartime traffic had resulted in many of the nation's trucking firms being in desperate need of new vehicles. One such firm was located in Milwaukee, and owned by Melvin H. Flath. Responding to an announcement of an upcoming sale of surplus trucks in California, Flath journeyed to the west coast in hopes of acquiring some low-mileage trucks for his cartage company. Upon arriving he learned that the trucks being offered were in fact the amphibian DUKWs.

Disappointed but undeterred, he purchased one of the cumbersome vehicles and began the two-week drive back to Milwaukee. At last arriving in Milwaukee, Flath was still unsure what the future of his DUKW would be. But, on a weekend soon after his arrival, he took his wife Ida, their children and some friends to nearby Pewaukee Lake for a water ride. The unique properties of the amphibian delighted the passengers and caught the attention of weekend beach goers, who clamored for a ride. Flath mounted used bus seats in the cargo area, and returned the next weekend, offering rides for 50 cents per passenger.

After only a few weeks, someone suggested that Flath take his DUKW to Wisconsin Dells, a resort area 120 miles northwest of Milwaukee. The area, with the sandstone gorges of the Wisconsin River, had been a tourist destination since the mid-1800s. Flath quickly secured land leases and established his "Amphibian Line" and began offering 90-minute land and water tours of the area. The business was a success, and the fleet of DUKWs expanded. Seeing Flath's success, others quickly mimicked his operation in the area, and tourists spread the news of this tourist experience, resulting in similar operations springing up over the following decades not only in the Wisconsin Dells area, but across the United States and around the world.

Most DUKWs used in tourist operations today have been heavily modified with automatic transmissions and commercial Diesel engines replacing the original GMC 270 and five-speed manual transmission. As these vehicles operate from prepared boat ramps rather than crossing sandy beaches, the central tire inflation system is often removed as well, along with the winch and most other military hardware.

Other DUKWs repowerd by Diesel engines are used by the Royal Marines. The Royal Marines of 11 Amphibious (Trials and Training) Squadron Instow, maintain a small group of the vintage vehicles in active service. The DUKWs are used as safety cover for Royal Marines learning to ford vehicles and operate rigid inflatable boats.

Today seeing a DUKW preserved in military configuration often requires a trip to a military museum, several of which house examples. As an alternative, a number of the vehicles have been restored by enthusiasts and can be seen at vintage military shows such as those hosted by the Military Vehicle Preservation Association.

The first commercial user of the DUKW was in all likelihood Melvin Flath, who beginning with a single DUKW purchased in 1946, started operating land and water tours in the Wisconsin Dells area. Flath did not maintain a monopoly for long as others followed his lead. (Suzanne Field collection)

Today, the daughter of Melvin Flath, Suzanne Field, continue her father's legacy of operating tour DUKWs. Their company, Dells Army Ducks, is but one of dozens globally that use these vehicles in ways far removed from their original intent. (Photo by Author)

Above: Not surprisingly, some DUKWs have found a second life retelling the tales of the combat exploits of the DUKW and its crews. This DUKW is taking part in the filming of *Flags of our Fathers* on a beach in Iceland. (Jim Gilmore)

Left: The final active military use of the DUKW is likely that of the Royal Marines, who still use a handful of the vintage vehicles as this book goes to press. The DUKWs have been repowered – modern Diesels replacing the vintage GMC 270 – but otherwise the vehicles retain most of their 70-year-old equipment. (David Walker)

Below: The producers of *Flags of Our Fathers,* went to considerable effort to faithfully recreate the markings and operations of wartime DUKWs. This DUKW, however, lacks its central tire inflation system. (Jim Gilmore)

So useful are these antiques that the Royal Marines in the 21st century actively rebuilt the vehicles, and have even acquired an additional vehicle. Here one of the veteran DUKWs gives a lift to a group of veterans of another type. (David Walker)

In the United States, DUKWs can be seen in many cities providing tours of city streets as well as waterways, providing a unique vantage point for sightseeing. Age and carrying capacity are catching up with the vehicles, and genuine DUKWs such as this one are in many cases being phased out in favor of modern replicas. (Boston Duck Tours)

Of the 21,147 DUKWs produced by General Motors during World War II, today only a handful of these vehicles survive in original configuration. Many of these are static displays in various museums, but a few – like this example – have been fully restored by dedicated enthusiasts. At various military vehicle events around the world the DUKW can still be seen in original form – a display of arguably the most successful amphibian design in history. (John Adams-Graf)